RISC System/6000
PowerPC™ System Architecture

First Edition (July 1994)

This edition notice applies to the *RISC System/6000 PowerPC System Architecture Manual.*

The following paragraph does not apply to the United Kingdom or any country where such provisions are inconsistent with local law:

> **Notice**
>
> This publication is printed "as is" without warranty of any kind, either express or implied, including, but not limited to, the implied warranties of merchantability or fitness for a particular purpose. Some states do not allow disclaimer of express or implied warranties in certain transactions; therefore, this statement may not apply to you.

This publication could include technical inaccuracies or typographical errors. Changes are periodically made to the information herein; these changes will be incorporated in new editions of the publication.

It is possible that this publication may contain reference to, or information about, products (machines and programs), programming, or services that are not announced in your country. Such references or information must not be construed to mean that such products, programming, or services will be offered in your country. Any reference to a licensed program in this publication is not intended to state or imply that you can use only the licensed program indicated. You can use any functionally equivalent program instead.

The following are trademarks of the International Business Machines Corporation in the United States and/or other countries:

AIX	IBM System/370	Micro Channel
OS/2	Personal System/2	POWER
PowerPC	PowerPC System Architecture	PowerPC Architecture
PowerPC 601	PowerPC 603	PowerPC 604
PowerPC 620	Powerstation	RISC System/6000

IBM is a registered trademark of International Business machines Corporation.

The following are trademarks of other companies:

Motorola 680x0 is a trademark of Motorola

Micro Channel is a trademark of International Business Machine Corporation in certain countries

NT is a trademark of Microsoft Corporation

PowerOpen is a trademark of PowerOpen Association

IBM®

PowerPC™

INTERNATIONAL BUSINESS MACHINES, INC.

RISC System/6000
PowerPC™ System Architecture

Edited by Frank Levine & Steve Thurber

MORGAN KAUFMANN PUBLISHERS, INC.   SAN FRANCISCO, CALIFORNIA

To order copies of this book, please contact the publisher at (800)745-7323 or your IBM Marketing Representative.

Morgan Kaufmann Publishers, Inc.
Editorial Office:
340 Pine Street, Sixth Floor
San Francisco, CA 94104

Executive Editor: Bruce M. Spatz
Production Manager: Yonie Overton
Assistant Editor: Douglas Sery
Production Coordinator: Julie Pabst
Cover Design: Carron Design
Printer: Courier Companies, Inc.

This book was typset by the authors, using Interleaf.

Printed in the United States of America

98   97   96   95   94   5   4   3   2   1

Library of Congress Cataloging-in-Publication Data is available for this book.

ISBN 1-55860-344-1

Table of Contents

Chapter 4 Bring-Up and Configuration Architecture

Chapter 5 NVRAM Contents and Mapping

Chapter 6 Bus Unit Controller (BUC) Architecture

Chapter 13 Vital Product Data (VPD)

Chapter 14 AIX Based Diagnostics Requirements

Appendix A Processor Dependencies

Appendix B Standard I/O Interface

Appendix C Target Market Categories

Appendix D Memory Controller Example

Appendix E System Exception Implementation Examples

Figures

Tables

Preface

About this Book

This book is intended to provide for the support of a wide range of products, including both Uni-Processor (UP) and Symmetric Multiple Processor (SMP) systems. It allows for the building of many system features, such as, memory with caches. Its primary objective is to define an architecture, which allows each Operating System (OS), in particular, the AIX Operating System, to run unchanged on all systems that comply with this architecture. This objective is met by providing a consistent interface to software across a broad range of system implementations.

The RISC System/6000 model 250 follows the architecture in this book. Other future RISC System/6000 models will follow this architecture. Those products that follow the architecture in this book are referred to in this book as "RISC System/6000 PowerPC systems."

This book identifies at a high level the state of the system when the Operating System receives control. This book identifies those items which must be initialized by the hardware (which includes Initial Program Load (IPL) Read Only Memory (ROM)) prior to passing control to the Operating System. In addition, this book documents those items which must be initialized by the Operating System, i.e., that are architecturally not yet handled or not accomplished via the hardware, but are needed to have an operational system. Although this book does not provide specifications for AIX configuration, it does provide all hardware/software dependencies necessary for a successful system configuration process. This book also defines the memory architecture as it relates to defining the interface between the hardware and software.

Referenced documents' details take precedence over this book in case of ambiguities or conflicts. If an item is identified as "optional architectural support," then this support is not required, but if done should be done in the specified manner.

Who Should Use this Book

This book provides an overview of the operation of the system. It is intended for programmers and engineers who understand computer architecture and programming concepts and who develop hardware and software products for the system family. This includes adapter design and the software device driver required to access the adapter. In addition this book may be used by System Programmers, involved in Operating System Design as well as the System Integrators building products and part producers for these products.

How to Use this Book

Prerequisite Documentation

■ *PowerPC Architecture* (books I, II, III)

Related Documents

■ *PowerPC 601 User's Manual* and other Processor specific books as they become available

■ *IBM Personal System/2 Hardware Interface Technical Reference – Architectures* (S84F-9808)

■ POWERstation and POWERserver Hardware Technical Information General Architectures (SA23-2643)

■ POWERstation and POWERserver Common Diagnostics and Service Guide (SA23–2687)

Overview of Contents

This book contains the following:

■ Edition notice, which includes referenced trademarks.

■ Table of Contents.

■ Preface, which describes the general system objectives (the class of products which follow or are expected to follow this architecture), the audience for this book, how to use this book, an overview of the contents, and acknowledgements.

■ Chapter 1, "Introduction," describes at a high level an overview of the architecture, some important terms, and the addressing notation.

■ Chapter 2, "PowerPC Processor Architecture," provides a high level description of the prerequisite book and related documents and how some of the instructions are to be interpreted from a system point of view.

■ Chapter 3, "Architected System Memory Map," details the placement in the real address space of the architected system facilities. A brief description of many of the system facilities is defined in this chapter.

■ Chapter 4, "Bring-Up and Configuration Architecture," defines the interface between hardware and software that allows software to identify and set up (configure) each variable component of the system.

■ Chapter 5, "NVRAM Contents and Mapping," details the usage and architected mappings of the Non-Volatile Random Access Memory which contains information that persists across Initial Program Loads (IPLs) and power cycling.

■ Chapter 6, "Bus Unit Controller (BUC) Architecture," describes some of the system and processor addressing interfaces for BUCs including both T=0 and T=1 addressing, address protection, data consistency and ordering requirements, and error reporting. In addition, BUC Interrupt handling requirements are discussed.

■ Chapter 7, "IOCC [Input/Output Channel Controller] Architecture," is a special case of the BUC architecture as it relates to the Micro Channel bus support functions for Load and Store instructions, interrupt, and channel control. Familiarity with the *IBM Personal System/2 Hardware Interface Technical Reference – Architectures* (S84F-9808) is helpful for understanding this chapter. This chapter describes bit and byte numbering conventions, I/O bus protocols, the programming model, load and store instructions, the translation, protection, commands, I/O interrupts, special facilities, the system I/O and standard I/O, exception reporting and handling, and implementation details.

■ Chapter 8, "System Resources," describes the facilities which are present on all RISC System/6000 PowerPC systems. It includes the operator interface facilities such as the display Light Emitting Diode (LED) interface, the Initial Program Load (IPL)/Operation modes (keylock switch positions), and operator reset support. In addition, this chapter briefly identifies some other system facilities such as the timer facilities.

■ Chapter 9, "External Interrupt Architecture," describes the interfaces external to the processor to handle interrupts, that is, the signalling of a processor than an "interrupt condition" exists at a given "source." This chapter describes the system level interrupt registers which are defined for a Symmetric Multi-Processor (SMP) system. This chapter defines the facilities required to identify which processors are available for handling interrupt support, which processors are available for handling interrupts that can go to any processor (the global queue) and the software interface to tell the hardware its current priority and that it has completed processing an interrupt.

- Chapter 10, "System Exception Processing," describes the architecture related to the system requirements for processing (error detection, error recording, and recovery) of system exception conditions, including items such as parity errors, address range errors and time-outs.

- Chapter 11, "System Bus Architecture," gives a brief overview of some example system busses.

- Chapter 12, "Bring-Up Function and IPLCB," describes the Power-On hardware requirements to bring up an SMP system without a Service Processor. It also describes the IPLCB, which contains information needed by the OS to understand the machine characteristics, similar to the PRePs residual data area.

- Chapter 13, "Vital Product Data (VPD)," defines the format of the electronically sensed data which uniquely describes each hardware, software, and microcode configurable element of the system.

- Chapter 14, "AIX Based Diagnostic Requirements," defines the dependencies that the AIX based diagnostics has on the system resources (Chapter 8), the IPL ROM, and the VPD. This chapter also includes the Operator Panel Display interface message format, including the codes that are displayed on the LEDs during bring up. The information in this chapter is required by maintenance package developers.

- Chapter 15, "Feature ROM Scan (FRS) Architecture," gives the highlights of a specific aspect of the configuration architecture.

- Appendix A, "Processor Dependencies," identifies some of the system dependencies on PowerPC processor implementation details that are not part of the PowerPC processor architecture.

- Appendix B, "Standard I/O Interface," defines the addresses typically allocated to each of the standard I/O devices as they are addressed in T=1 space.

- Appendix C, "Target Market Categories," defines a range of machine classes which is intended to be used in conjunction with the System

Exception Architecture (Chapter 10) to assist in understanding the applicability of the system exception architecture to a particular implementation.

■ Appendix D, "Memory Controller Example," documents some of the configuration and exception support in the memory controller used in the RISC/System 6000 model 250.

■ Appendix E, "System Exception Implementation Examples," documents the exception support in the RISC/System 6000 model 250. and provides additional approaches for other types of systems, including SMPs.

■ Appendix F, "IPLCB Example," provides detailed descriptions of individual sections in the IPLCB.

■ Appendix G, "AIX Dependencies on the IPLCB," identifies AIX restrictions on changes to the IPLCB.

■ Appendix H, "AIX Command and Event Indicators," lists the message indicators representing AIX command and events which are displayed by AIX on LEDs when the normal AIX Operating System is not operational, that is, typically during initialization.

■ Appendix I, "Power IOCC Architecture versus PowerPC IOCC Architecture," identifies the changes made to the Power IOCC Architecture to get to the PowerPC IOCC Architecture.

■ Appendix J, "32-Bit/64-Bit BUC Architecture Differences and Considerations," summarizes the differences between 32-bit and 64-bit BUC implementations.

■ Appendix K, "Big-Endian and Little-Endian Tutorial," describes the big-endian and little-endian numbering conventions.

■ Glossary contains the acronyms and many of the phrases used in this book, along with a brief definition or where to find additional information.

■ Index typically contains the first and some of the more important references of many of the phrases and acronyms used in this book.

Acknowledgements

The IBM technical owners and editor/authors responsible for this document are Frank Levine and Steve Thurber. We give special acknowledgement to Richard Arndt and John O'Quin for their diligence in reviewing and providing input to this book as requested. Many other people participated in providing input and participated in creating this book. These people included Ravi Arimilli, Doug Benignus, Dr. William Brantley, Pat Buckland, John Cook, George Dawkins, Dennis Gregoire, Jim Hanna, John Kaiser, John Kingman, Dr. Luan Nguyen, Eliseo Pena, and Scott Wagert. We appreciate the efforts of these people and all the others at IBM that reviewed this document and provided input.

Introduction

This book identifies at a high level the state of the system when the Operating System receives control. It defines the hardware/software interfaces at the system level, that is, outside of the PowerPC processors.

1.1 Memory Architecture

This book defines the memory architecture as it relates to defining the interface between the hardware and software. Memory access is often used as a means of communication between the hardware and software and "architected addresses" are used to facilitate this communication, refer to Section 3.1 on page 7 for these addresses. See the NVRAM chapter starting on page 35 for the layout of the Non-Volatile Random Access Memory.

There should be no software dependency on any particular characteristic of the memory subsystem structure, such as, the location of caches. In fact, the PowerPC architecture does not require any particular cache organization and is intended to allow many different implementations. Software may however, do system performance tuning, by using the cache management instructions which are provided.

Figure 2 (System Block Diagram on page 60) contains a logical view of a system, where memory is directly attached to the system bus to allow transfers of data among the various components of the system. The interface between the physical memory and the system bus is part of the memory controller. In order to get consistency among all RISC System/6000 PowerPC systems, the bus controller interface of the memory controller must be designed according to the "Bus Unit Controller (BUC) Architecture" starting on page 59.

The *PowerPC Architecture* (book I) defines storage as a linear array of bytes indexed from 0 to a maximum of 2**64–1 on a 64-bit machine (a machine that implement the 64-bit architecture) and 2**32–1 on a 32-bit machine (a machine that implements the 32-bit subset architecture). Each byte is identified by its index, called its address. The *PowerPC Architecture* (book II) and *PowerPC Architecture* (book III) expand this simple storage model to include virtual storage, caches and shared storage multiprocessors. Refer to the "PowerPC Processor Architecture" chapter staring on page 5 for more information on what can be found in the *PowerPC Architecture* (books I–III).

The RISC System/6000 PowerPC systems implement a virtual storage model for applications. This means that a combination of hardware and software can present a storage model which allows an application to exist within a "virtual" address space larger than either the effective address space or the real address space. Each program can access 2**64 bytes on a 64-bit machine and 2**32 bytes on a 32-bit machine of "effective address" space (see *PowerPC Architecture* (book I) for effective address calculation), subject to limitations imposed by the Operating System. In a typical RISC System/6000 PowerPC system, each program's effective address space is a subset of a larger virtual address space managed by the Operating System. The Operating System is responsible for managing the real (physical storage) resources of the system by means of a "storage mapping" mechanism. Storage is always allocated and managed in units of "pages" which have a fixed, 4096 byte size. The storage mapping process translates accesses to pages in the Effective address space to real pages in main storage *PowerPC Architecture* (book III).

The PowerPC architecture specifies a weakly consistent storage model, this model provides an opportunity for significantly improved performance over the strongly consistent model. For SMP enabled programs or for programs which perform I/O on UPs, the weakly consistent storage model places the responsibility on the program to ensure that ordering or synchronization instructions are properly placed when necessary for the correct execution of the program.

1.2   Definition of Terms

The terms and notation identified in this section are used throughout this book. Use the glossary to find the usage of acronyms and the index to find the definition of terms defined elsewhere in this book.

1.2.1   Reserved

The term "reserved" is used within this document to refer to memory areas, words, bit fields or values of bit fields reserved for future architecture use or for bits that are implementation dependent and not available for architecture use. These bits may or may not be implementation dependent and may or may not be "reserved/unimplemented" see Section 1.2.2. In either case, software shall write these bits as 0 (unless indicated otherwise in the text of this document). Unless noted elsewhere, hardware shall return either 0 or the value last written by software. Software should assume that the reserved bits may be used some day and therefore may not be returned as 0's in the future. Software should therefore ignore the reserved bits before using the data returned from a Load instruction in order to assure future compatibility.

1.2.2 Reserved/Unimplemented

The term "reserved/unimplemented" is used within this document to refer to memory areas, words, or bits that have not been assigned an architectural use. Unimplemented bits are a special case of reserved bits. Often, these bits are "reserved" for future architecture use. These bits may become implementation dependent or they may be assigned an architected use. In any case, software shall write these bits as 0 (unless indicated otherwise in the text of this document). Hardware shall return either 0 or the value last written by software. If these bits are truly "unimplemented" and not in main memory, then for a memory mapped (T=0) access, hardware shall ignore the write and shall return 0's when the bits are read back. In some Bus Unit Controller (BUC) implementations, with T=1 access, the results may be different, see Section 6.1.3.1 on page 66 for more details. Software should assume that the unimplemented bits may be used some day and therefore may not be returned as 0's in the future. Software should therefore ignore the unimplemented bits before using the data returned from a Load instruction in order to assure future compatibility.

Architecture Note

Reserved bits within RAM resident control block structures, such as, TCEs (see Section 6.1.4 on page 68) shall typically return to software the last value written by software.

1.2.3 Addressing Notation

Bit and byte numbering in this book is assumed to be in the "Big Endian" format, where bit 0 is the high order bit, unless specified otherwise. The Big Endian format is defined as the byte ordering with the most significant byte first (e.g., Big End first) and located at the referenced address. Refer to the Appendix "Big-Endian and Little-Endiant Tutorial" starting on page 293 and the *PowerPC Architecture* (book I) for additional details. Addresses and displacements in this book use the C programming conventions, with 0x1bc2 representing a hexadecimal number, 0b10101011 representing a binary number, and 25 representing a decimal number. In addition, leading or trailing zeroes are used to unambiguously represent the value of the number.

The addressing notation of 0xf...ff as a prefix to a hexadecimal number represents a hexadecimal number with the high order sign bit extended as necessary to indicate the highest allowable address on the machine. That is, 0xf...ff123456 represents the address 0xff123456 on a 32-bit machine, and 0xfffffffff123456 on a 64-bit machine. For example, on a 64-bit machine that only supports 48 bits of real address, the actual implementation shall map the 0xf...ff123456 to the real address of 0xffffff123456.

Architected Addresses, such as, those that are defined in the Memory Map section, Section 3.1, starting on page 7, are restricted to the upper four (4) gigabytes because on a 64-bit word machine, software shall assume that the upper 32-bits are all ones. This is true for those items that are allowed to be at machine dependent locations.

1.2.4 Symbolic Notation

C symbolic notations are used throughout this book, for example, "if (a==b)" is used to represent "if a is equal to b."

1.3 Reliability, Availability, and Serviceability (RAS)

Product owners are expected to identify the Reliability, Availability, and Serviceability (RAS) requirements for their products and to meet their own product objectives.

PowerPC Processor Architecture

The PowerPC Processor Architecture consists of the instructions and facilities described in *PowerPC Architecture* (books I, II, and III).

Book I defines the User Instruction Set Architecture. This Book describes the registers, instructions, storage model, and execution model that are available to all application programs.

Book II defines the Virtual Environment Architecture. This Book describes features of the architecture that permit application programs to create or modify code, to share data among programs in a multiprocessors system, and to optimize the performance of storage accesses.

Book III defines the Operating Environment Architecture. This Book describes features of the architecture that permit Operating Systems to allocate and manage storage, to handle errors encountered by application programs, to support I/O devices, and to provide the other services expected of secure, modern, multiprocessor Operating Systems.

2.1 PowerPC Implementation Specific User's Manual

There are a number of books that cover the details of the implementation of specific microprocessors which are beyond the scope of the PowerPC Architecture Books I, II, and III. For example, for 601 PowerPC processor, there is a corresponding book with the title *PowerPC 601 User's Manual*. This book provides a technical overview of the specified microprocessor implementation. As other processors are released, other chip specific User Manuals will be released.

Engineering Note

Different processor implementations may cause substantial difference in system design consideration, for example, because the 603 processor orders bus accesses, it does not broadcast either *eieio* or *sync* instructions. System designers using the 603, for example, must use this strong ordering feature of the 603 to guarantee ordering across I/O space.

BUCs may allow software to force or to guarantee completion of I/O by a variety of means: For example, software may be allowed to read back the data written when the data is returned from the end target. Another approach would be to have the BUC provide a status word which can be polled via the software to indicate that the I/O is complete. Also, the BUC may issue an interrupt upon the completion of the I/O.

BUCs that are designed to work in all system structures should have those registers that can be cached in the processor's cache placed in system memory, or shadowed in system memory. The reason for this is that not all system structure will allow processor cacheable memory locations to be located on the I/O.

2.1.1 Processor Requirements

See Appendix A,"Processor Dependencies," starting on page 233 for the Processor requirements used by the RISC System/6000 Architecture.

2.1.2 Hardware I/O Design Instruction Support Requirements

In order to provide for a consistent hardware software interface, System Designers are responsible for ensuring that *eieio* and *sync* guarantee ordering across I/O space.

In addition, BUCs must provide an implementation dependent mechanism to the software that allows software to know or to guarantee that a previously issued I/O is complete. An I/O operation is defined to be complete when all side effects of the I/O have occurred, including any error status reporting or interrupts. For additional information related the hardware I/O design requirements, see Chapter "BUC Common Architecture" starting on page 59.

Architected System Memory Map

The System Memory Map in the PowerPC (32-bit/64-bit) system architecture consists of n gigabytes (GB) of real memory and is shown on the left of Figure 1.

The Architected System Memory Space, which is located in the upper 16 megabytes (MB) of the overall System Memory Map, is expanded on the right of Figure 1. Note that, for simplicity, the resolution of this figure is 1 MB.

3.1 Memory Map Layout

Table 1 contains more details regarding the layout, the descriptions, and the specific ranges of addresses in the 16 MB of Architected System Memory Space. All RISC System/6000 PowerPC products comply with the RISC System/6000 PowerPC Architecture and support each facility in this architecture, unless the facility is specifically identified as optional under the details regarding the specific facility. (It is possible for an IBM product to follow the architecture but be allowed to deviate from the architecture due to business reasons. When this occurs, the deviation is expected to be documented in the product specific documentation.)

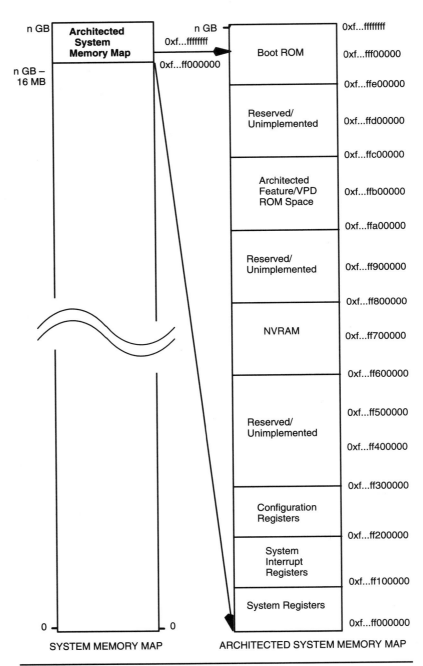

Figure 1. **System Memory Map**

Start Address	End Address	Fixed Address Required	Description
0xf...ff000000	0xf...ff000fff	Partial	Architected System Registers
0xf...ff001000	0xf...ff001fff	Yes	System Specific System Registers
0xf...ff002000	0xf...ff0fffff	Yes	Reserved/Unimplemented, see Section 1.2.2 on page 3.
0xf...ff100000	0xf...ff17ffff	Yes	Architected System Interrupt Registers
0xf...ff180000	0xf...ff181fff	No	SMP Global Queue Interrupt Routing Masks (GQ_IRMs)
0xf...ff182000	0xf...ff182003	Yes	SMP Early Power Off Warning (EPOW) External Interrupt Vector Register (XIVR)
0xf...ff182004	0xf...ff1fffff	Yes	Reserved/Unimplemented, see Section 1.2.2 on page 3.
0xf...ff200000	0xf...ff200fff	Yes	Architected Configuration Registers
0xf...ff201000	0xf...ff201fff	Yes	Device Specific Configuration Registers
0xf...ff202000	0xf...ff5fffff	Yes	Reserved/Unimplemented, see Section 1.2.2 on page 3.
0xf...ff600000	0xf...ff7fffff	Yes	NVRAM
0xf...ff800000	0xf...ff9fffff	Yes	Reserved/Unimplemented, see Section 1.2.2 on page 3.
0xf...ffa00000	0xf...ffbfffff	Yes	Architected Feature/VPD ROM Space
0xf...ffc00000	0xf...ffdfffff	Yes	Reserved/Unimplemented, see Section 1.2.2 on page 3.
0xf...ffe00000	0xf...ffffffff	Yes	IPL ROM

Table 1. **Architected System Memory Map**

Currently the only item in Table 1 with a "Fixed Address Required" field value of "No" is the SMP Global Queue Interrupt Routing Mask (GQ_IRM) field. The IPLCB software interface allows the SMP Global Queue Interrupt Routing Mask (GQ_IRM) register to be placed at different physical locations than the actual address in the table. The "Architected System Registers" item in Table 1 with an "Fixed Address Required" field value of "Partial" has some facilities which are allowed to be placed in different machine dependent locations, see Table 3 for additional details. The placement of these facilities is restricted to the upper four (4) gigabytes because on a 64-bit word machine, software shall assume that the upper 32-bits are all ones. The IPLCB software interface must allow for the different machine dependent placements to be in NVRAM. Because NVRAM may not have parity in some implementations, a CRC is often used when updates are made. The "access_id" interface is provided in the

Engineering Note

For those items, whose addresses are allowed to float, Table 1 identifies the "recommended placement of the facility," which should help facilitate hardware component reuse. If the attached addresses are "fixed" in the hardware, different hardware components should not have conflicting addresses, that is, one address used for two different purposes. Conflicting addresses can also be avoided by allow the facilities to be placed at configurable locations.

Engineering Note

For those items, whose addresses are allowed to float, Table 3 identifies the "recommended placement of the facility," which should help facilitate hardware component reuse. By fixing the attached addresses in the hardware, different hardware components should not have conflicting addresses, that is, one address used for two different purposes. Conflicting addresses can also be avoided by allow the facilities to be placed at configurable locations.

Architecture Note

The PIDI register is not intended to be used as an interface between hardware and software to allow software to know its current processor ID. The usage of the PIDI register may be implemented by strictly controlling the bring up of the individual processors. The initialization firmware may use other mechanisms to load the individual processor's PIRs. The PIR may be read by software and is used to put out bus tags which are used for DSIER responses and Programmed I/Os (PIOs).

There is no required relationship between the value of the PIR and the Interrupt Server Number, refer to Table 8 on page 15. It is highly recommended, however, that the numbers be the same for ease of system debug.

IPLCB to distinguish between normal memory mapped accesses and NVRAM, refer to Section "IPLCB/Implementation Dependent Placements" starting on page 271 for more information related to the "access_id." In AIX, if "access_id" == 1, then the OS routine "machine Device Driver" (machine DD) is used to isolate the special processing required). Refer to Chapter "NVRAM Contents and Mapping" starting on page 35 for more information related to the usage of NVRAM for the placement of the architected facilities that are implementation dependent.

The sections that follow expand on each of the major address space ranges in Table 1.

3.2 Architected System Registers

All systems may not provide all the functions defined by this set of registers. Functions that are provided in a system must be compatible with this architecture. The IPLCB software interface allows some of the architected system registers to be placed at different physical locations than the actual address in the table. Items in Table 3 with a "Fixed Address Required" field value of "No" are allowed to be placed in different machine dependent locations. The bit definitions within each of these facilities is not allowed to change when the location is changed.

3.2.1 Physical Identifier Initialization (PIDI) Register

The Physical Identifier Initialization register (PIDI) is an optional facility that may be used by SMP systems. The primary purpose of the Physical Identifier Initialization register is to provide an architected mechanism for IPL ROM to load the internal Processor ID Register (PIR) for each processor in the system. The PowerPC processor architecture requires that the processor load the internal Processor ID Register (PIR) [refer to *PowerPC Architecture* (book III) in the implementation specific Special Purpose Register (SPR) appendix] in the processor SPR before it can generate any identification tags.

Bit	Description
0–23	Reserved/Unimplemented, see Section 1.2.2 on page 3.
24–31	Physical Identifier This field provides a unique number for each processor reading this location. It is used by processors to differentiate themselves in multiprocessor configurations. Processor identifiers are assigned starting with 0 and incrementing upward.

Table 2.   **Physical Identifier Initialization Register 0xf...ff000008**

Start Address	End Address	Fixed Address Required	Description
0xf...ff000000	0xf...ff000007	Yes	Reserved/Unimplemented, see Section 1.2.2 on page 3.
0xf...ff000008	0xf...ff00000b	Yes	Physical IDentifier Initialization (PIDI) Register
0xf...ff00000c	0xf...ff00000f	Yes	Connectivity Configuration Register
0xf...ff000010	0xf...ff00004f	Yes	Connectivity Reset Registers
0xf...ff000050	0xf...ff0000bf	Yes	Reserved/Unimplemented, see Section 1.2.2 on page 3.
0xf...ff0000c0	0xf...ff0000dc	Yes	Time of Day Registers
0xf...ff0000dd	0xf...ff0000df	Yes	Reserved/Unimplemented, see Section 1.2.2 on page 3.
0xf...ff0000e0	0xf...ff0000e3	No	System Reset Count Register
0xf...ff0000e4	0xf...ff0000e7	No	Power Status/Keylock Register
0xf...ff0000e8	0xf...ff0000eb	No	Software Power On Reset Control Register
0xf...ff0000ec	0xf...ff0000ef	No	Software Power Off Control Register
0xf...ff0000f0	0xf...ff0000ff	Yes	Reserved/Unimplemented, see Section 1.2.2 on page 3.

Table 3. **Architected System Register Address Map**

3.2.2 Connectivity Configuration Register

For more information regarding the Configuration Architecture, see Chapter "Bring-Up and Configuration Architecture" starting on page 19 and Section 4.2.1, "Configuration Sequence," on page 22 for the detailed usage of this register. The bit description is in Table 4.

Bit	Description	Init
0	Enable Configuration This signal enables slot selection for Configuration cycles. 0b1 = enable configuration	0b0
1–22	Reserved/Unimplemented, see Section 1.2.2 on page 3.	
23–31	Connectivity Configuration Select This binary encoded number selects a physical Connectivity node location as the target for configuration cycles	don't care value

Table 4. **Connectivity Configuration Registers 0xf...ff000000 –> 0xf...ff00000c**

3.2.3 Connectivity Reset Register

The hardware system designer is responsible for making sure that each configurable entity has a unique bit assigned in the Connectivity reset register.

For more information regarding the Configuration Architecture, see Chapter "Bring-Up and Configuration Architecture" starting on page 19 and Section 4.2.1, "Configuration Sequence," on page 22 for the detailed usage of this register. The bit description is in Table 5.

Bit	Description	Init
0–31	Connectivity Enable This register is bit significant. Writing a 0 into a bit position resets the physical Connectivity node location represented by that bit position. Writing a 1 removes the reset.	0x00000000

Table 5.   **Connectivity Reset Registers 0xf...ff000010 –> 0xf...ff00004f**

3.2.4 Time of Day Registers

The Time of Day clock function is accessed via the locations 0xff0000c0–> 0xff0000dc. The definition of these registers is implementation specific.

3.2.5 System Reset Count Register

During system initialization, the firmware initializes the reset count register as per Table 6.

Bit	Description	Init
0–30	Reserved/Unimplemented, see Section 1.2.2 on page 3.	
31	System Reset Count 0b0 Warm Boot 0b1 Cold Boot Power-On Reset (POR) or Software POR (write to 0xf...ff0000e8) forces this bit to a 1.	0b1

Table 6.   **System Reset Count Register (recommended address: 0xf...ff0000e0)**

3.2.6 Power/Keylock Status Register (PKSR)

During system initialization, the firmware initializes the Power/Keylock Status Register as per Table 7. The system shall initiate an Early Power Off Warning (EPOW) interrupt after the system has been initialized whenever any power related status changes, that is, any change to the Power/Keylock Status Register other than bits 28–31, the keylock position. Refer to Table 60 on page 168 regarding the EPOW interrupt and the XISR special value that indicates the power status change.

0–32	Power Interrupt Decode
	0b0000 No Interrupt
	0b0001 Running on Battery
	0b0010 Programmed Power off
	0b0011 Manual Switch off
	0b0100 Remote Power off
	0b0101 Thermal High Limit
	0b0110 Internal Power Supply Failure
	0b0111 Power Supply Overload
	0b1000 Loss of Primary Power
	0b1001 Fan 1 Fault
	0b1010 Fan 2 Fault
	0b1011 Fan 3 Fault
	0b1100 Fan 4 Fault
	0b1101 Fan 5 Fault
	0b1110 Fan 6 Fault
4–6	Power Up Decode
	0b000 Manual On Button Pushed
	0b001 Remote On Signal from external
	0b010 Timed Power On from TOD Clock
	0b011 Remote On Signal from Power Control I/F
	0b100 Automatic Restart
7	0b1 Thermal Warning: Indicates that the operating temperature of the System is above a normal safe level.
	0b0 No Thermal Warning
8	0b1 Backup Battery Installed
	0b0 Backup Battery not Installed
9	0b1 Low Battery: Indicates a discharged or faulty Backup Battery
	0b0 Backup battery OK (if installed)
10–27	Reserved/Unimplemented, see Section 1.2.2 on page 3.
28–31	Keylock position – refer to Table 56 on page 155.
	The Keylock Decode may be invalid for up to 25 milliseconds following Power On.

Table 7.   **Power/Keylock Status Register (recommended address: 0xf...ff0000e4)**

Architecture Note

The Software Power On
Reset Control register is
intended to be written to
when the system is
mainly powered down. If
the system is not
powered down, then it
should force the system
into a graceful reset,
where operations are
completed or cleared
from the system prior to
actually initiating the cold
restart.

The Software Power Off
Control register is
intended to force the
system into a graceful
power off, where
operations in process
are completed or cleared
from the system prior to
actually forcing the
power to being off.

3.2.7 Software Power On Reset Control Register

Any write to the Power On Reset Control register (recommended address 0xf...ff0000e8) shall generate a reset to all processors.

3.2.8 Software Power Off Control Register

Any write to the Power Off Control register (recommended address 0xf...ff0000ec) shall create a software power off. This register is optional and is not required in all implementations.

3.2.9 System Specific System Registers

This space is allocated for general system support type functions that may be unique for each System Product. It is available to each Device to allow whatever specific system-wide registers are necessary. This address space, if implemented, shall always be available. The operation of these System Specific System Registers are independent of the operation of the Architected System Registers.

3.3 Architected System Interrupt Registers

See Chapter "External Interrupt Architecture" starting on page 157 for the explanation of the Architected System Interrupt registers. Table 8 contains the mapping for the Architected System Interrupt registers.

3.3.1 Data Storage Interrupt Error Register (DSIER)

**Architecture and
Programming Note**

In some
implementation(s), a
Store instruction issued
to the DSIER may cause
loss of state information.

The value of the data in
the DSIER at startup
time is indeterminate.
This register shall get set
to meaningful data the
first time a DSI is taken.

This register is a 4-byte register which traps the value of the last I/O Load or Store instruction exception as well as various other exception conditions. The DSIER logic shall trap the error status information on the bus which is returned with an I/O Load or Store instruction reply or error packet when that reply or error packet indicates a DSI has occurred. Each processor in the system has its own DSIER. As an example of DSIER usage for Micro Channel errors, refer to Section 7.4.8.1, "Recoverable Load and Store Error Conditions," on page 144. The bits in the DSIER are defined in Table 9.

The DSIER is in real memory space at address BA+8. Refer to Section 9.1.3 on page 163 for the definition of BA. A Store instruction issued to the DSIER shall either be performed or it shall be a NOP. This register is never reset, the value in the register is just overlaid each time a DSI occurs.

Address Bits	Description
0–12	Interrupt Register Region – refer to Chapter "External Interrupt Architecture" starting on page 157 for the description of this facility at the address indicated. This region begins at 0xfe200000 and these address bits contains the value 0b1111111100010.
13–16	Reserved for additional Optional MFRRs (non-zero values).
17–24	Interrupt Server Number Servers are either Processor Servers, which start at server number 0x00 and increment upward, or Global Servers, which start at server number 0xff and decrement downward.

25–31	Interrupt Registers
	
	Address of Processor Server Registers
	
	0x00 External Interrupt Request Register (XIRR)
	
	    XIRR = CPPR + (XIRR)
	
	    No Side Effects
	
	0x04 External Interrupt Request Register (XIRR)
	
	    XIRR = CPPR + XISR
	
	    With Load/Store Side Effects
	
	0x08 Data Storage Interrupt Error Register (DSIER)
	
	0x0c Most Favored Request Register (MFRR)
	
	0x10–>0x7c Optional MFRRs
	
	Address of Global Server Most Favored Requested Registers
	
	0x00 First Global Server MFRR for Global Server 0xff
	
	Global Server MFRR Registers start at 0x0 and incrementing upward.

Table 8. **Architected System Interrupt Address Map**

Bits	Description
0–1	Reserved: These bits are reserved, see Section 1.2.1 on page 2.
2	Reserved: This bit is reserved. This bit corresponds to the completion bit (the bit indicating the error) in the reply packet. On a Load instruction, the value of this bit shall be 0.
3–11	Source: These bits designate the source (BUID) of the error.
12–27	BUC specific: These bits are defined differently depending on the BUC which had the error (as indicated by the source field of this register). On a Load instruction, the value of the unused bits shall be 0.
28–31	Reserved: These bits are reserved, see Section 1.2.1 on page 2.

Table 9. *DSIER* Definition

3.3.2 SMP Early Power Off Warning (EPOW) External Interrupt Vector Register (XIVR)

Refer to Section 6.2.2 on page 72 for the XIVR definition.

3.3.3 IPLCB/Global Queue Interrupt Routing Mask Location Interface

The following interface allows all the GQ_IRM support for a single global queue for an SMP system with up to 32 processors to be kept in a single 32-bit register by using the same Real Address (both read and write) of each processor and different bit masks. It also allows the support to be separated such that multiple registers are supported and each register supports one or more processors with different write and read/verify addresses. Systems capable of more than 32 processors must use multiple registers or registers larger than 32 bits.

It is recommended that these GQ_IRMs be compacted and be found in the architected system memory map with the recommended addresses from 0xf...ff180000 to 0xf...ff181fff. This recommendation allows for a variable number of GQ_IRMs with the queues starting from 0xff and working downward. It also allows up to 256 processors. The recommended placement of the GQ_IRM for global server 0xff is 32 bytes starting at 0xf...ff180000 through 0xf...ff18001f and the GQ_IRM for the next global server 0xfe is also 32 bytes starting at 0xf...ff180020 through 0xf...ff18003f .

The Software interface to the GQ_IRMs is defined in Table 10, where:

(IF (access_id_pn_waddr == 0) then normal memory map for
                                   loc_pn_waddr)

(IF (access_id_pn_waddr == 1) then machine DD for
                                   loc_pn_waddr)

(IF (access_id_pn_raddr == 0) then normal memory map for
                                   loc_pn_raddr)

(IF (access_id_pn_raddr == 1) then machine DD for
                                   loc_pn_raddr)

Byte	Length (in bytes)	Identifier	Description
0	4	num_processors	Number of Processors (N)
4	4	access_id_p1_waddr	Access Identification of type of Access for loc_p1_waddr
8	4	loc_p1_waddr	Real Address of First Processor 32-bit (software write address) word
12	4	access_id_p1_raddr	Access Identification of type of Access for loc_p1_raddr
16	4	loc_p1_raddr	Real Address of First Processor Verification (software read address) 32-bit word
20	4	p1_mask	32-bit word Mask for First Processor
24	4	access_id_p2_waddr	Access Identification of type of Access for loc_p2_waddr
28	4	loc_p2_waddr	Real Address of Second Processor 32-bit (software write address) word
32	4	access_id_p2_raddr	Access Identification of type of Access for loc_p2_raddr
36	4	loc_p2_raddr	Real Address of Second Processor Verification (software read address) 32-bit word
40	4	p2_mask	32-bit word Mask for Second Processor
.	.	.	.
.	.	.	.
.	.	.	.
$4+20(n-1)$	4	access_id_pn_waddr	Access Identification of type of Access for loc_pn_waddr
$8+20(n-1)$	4	loc_pn_waddr	Real Address of nth Processor 32-bit (software write address) word
$12+20(n-1)$	4	access_id_pn_raddr	Access Identification of type of Access for loc_pn_raddr
$16+20(n-1)$	4	loc_pn_raddr	Real Address of nth Processor Verification (software read address) 32-bit word
$20+20(n-1)$	4	pn_mask	32-bit word Mask for nth Processor

Table 10. **IPLCB/Global Queue Interrupt Routing Mask Interface**

Bring-Up and Configuration Architecture

The PowerPC system design defines the architected interfaces among the set of processors, memory cards, I/O adapters, and other components during the system configuration. System configuration is an integral part of the IPL Process, and may be re-run after IPL in response to new conditions.

The primary purpose of the Bring-Up and Configuration Architecture is to define the interface between hardware and software that allows software to identify and set up (configure) each variable component of the system. The configuration software uses the component identification to allocate system resources (e.g., address space, interrupt levels, etc...) to the component and communicates these allocations to the component and/or its controlling software. The Bring-Up and Configuration Architecture defines the elements that are common to components, the method of identifying each component, and the methods of communicating with it. Due to a legacy of system components, the architecture allows for components which do not implement the optimal configuration functionality. Those component designs that do not incorporate the required features specified in this document require approval as architectural deviations and risk additional development expense as well as extended time to market.

All I/O adapters shall have adapter specific functionality defined in ROM on the adapter. There are many reasons for this. Among them are the following:

- The system IPL ROM will not need to keep adapter specific contents.

- Boot device and display device supported by IPL ROM are simplified.

- AIX display and bosboot diskettes will not need to keep adapter specific contents.

- Very Large Scale Integration (VLSI) and Application Specific Integrated Circuits (ASIC) parts should not have to have adapter level personality hardwired and/or built into them (such as adapter ID values); but instead, should extract these values from a ROM.

Features and adapters which are not I/O devices must follow a common configuration architecture along with the I/O devices. The architecture permits ample flexibility for implementation details.

4.1   Device Configuration Architecture

Engineering Note

Care should be taken when designing an I/O device, to consider which of the device specific configuration registers should be in the Architected System Memory address space and which should be in the normal address space. Because the configuration synchronization requirements, the performance of the on-line system may be degraded.

Because of this potential degradation, registers which shall be used often during run-time should NOT be placed in the address space of the Architected Configuration Registers.

The Connectivity Reset register provides a unique setup signal for each logical system bus slot and/or system interconnect port (refer to Section 3.2.3 on page 12). Note that if the setup signal is asserted, then the configuration address space shall be decoded; otherwise, the normal address space shall be decoded (refer to the "Architected System Memory Map," Section 3.1, on page 7 for the architected configuration address range to be decoded by BUCs).

The configuration address space is contained within the last 16 megabytes of physical address space of the system. On a 64-bit system, software addresses these real addresses by assuring that the upper 32 bits of address are all one's. Included in this 16 Megabyte address space are the registers for system control (e.g., the Connectivity Reset registers, the Connectivity Configuration register,...), the architected registers for device configuration, the architected System Interrupt registers, the SMP Available Processors registers, the SMP Early Power Off Warning (EPOW) External Interrupt Vector Register (XIVR), the System IPL ROM, and the device Feature ROM Scan address space.

The Architected System Memory address locations 0xf...ff000000 through 0xf...ffffffff are reserved for system support and configuration functions.

Configuration system bus cycles are basic protocol (T=0) cycles.

System bus I/O devices shall contain VPD for self identification (refer to Chapter "Vital Product Data (VPD)" starting on page 191). The system itself shall have VPD, which shall be used for device independent and standards items.

Each device that is attached to the PowerPC System Interconnect (e.g., 60X system bus, 6XX system bus,...) and many other features of each system shall have device IDentifications (IDs). The device IDs are 32-bit quantities. Each new device shall be assigned unique values (refer to Section 4.2.3.2 on page 27).

For any other adapters (e.g., Micro Channel adapters) that are attached to the PowerPC system via IOCC, please refer to Chapter "IOCC Architecture" starting on page 75.

4.1.1 Hardware Architecture Assumptions and Requirements

1. RISC System/6000 PowerPC systems are expected to provide flexible configurability.

2. RISC System/6000 PowerPC system bus attached features must be able to be configured, enabled, and used as a console or boot device without requiring an AIX device driver. IPL ROM meets this requirement by executing the Feature ROM Scan functions for boot and display devices.

3. Different systems may have different structures requiring configuration support ranging from the simple and low cost to the large and high cost multiprocessor systems. In simple and low cost systems, system failure due to base processor failure is acceptable and it may not require additional diagnostic processor such as OCS. In large multiprocessor systems, a diagnostic processor may be required.

4. Required functions for configuration architecture include:

   – identify items attached to the system bus

   – support device "self identification"

   – assign address spaces to system bus attached items

   – ROM scan procedure for boot and display device support

5. PowerPC processor architecture accesses only memory (T=0) space when operating in real mode.

6. Gaps (non-contiguous allocations) are acceptable in real memory space

   – between Single In-line Memory Module (SIMMS) on a single memory controller

   – between memory controllers

   – inside the address space decoded by a PowerPC adapter

7. PowerPC processor architecture requires that the processor load the internal Processor ID Register (PIR) [refer to *PowerPC Architecture* (book III) in the implementation specific SPR appendix] in the processor Special Purpose Register (SPR) before it can generate any identification tags. External devices cannot access this register. The value of the internal Processor ID Register (PIR) is loaded via Physical Identifier Initialization register defined in the "Architected System Memory Map," Section 3.2.1,

Note

The real memory space address assignment granularity must be greater than or equal to 2 megabytes.

Any processor speed data (if required) shall be contained in VPD.

Device Feature ROM must be able to be enabled and/or disabled independently of the bus device enable/disable state.

Feature ROM Scan contents are copied to RAM prior to execution.

System logic must prevent system hang during configuration cycles.

on page 10. The initialization firmware is responsible for setting up the latter Physical Identifier Initialization register.

8. Only one process(or) at a time can own, via software locking mechanisms, a specific common system resources such as the configuration address space, boot ROM, NVRAM areas, and the operator panel.

9. During configuration, the BUC must report an error condition via some means that preferably allows system operations to continue, but may involve a machine check or even a checkstop.

10. Hardware shall implement fixed addresses. However, AIX locates most of the resources via pointers passed from the System Boot ROM in the IPL Control Block (IPLCB).

4.2 Configuration Registers

Each System Bus Unit responds to accesses in these address ranges only when its configuration signal is active (see Connectivity Configuration register). System Bus Unit must fully decode the first 20 bits of the address to guarantee that the memory access is to Configuration Space. Configuration Space is split into two areas: The first is the address space of the Architected Configuration Registers. The second is the address space of the Device Specific Configuration Registers.

4.2.1 Configuration Sequence

Initially, software may receive control from the initialization firmware with some number of devices already configured. Devices that have been configured from the initialization firmware shall have their reset removed, that is, a one shall be in the appropriate bit position of the Connectivity Reset register. The information as to whether a device can be reconfigured by the software is passed to software in the IPLCB. There also may be some number of devices which cannot be reset by the software. The information as to whether a device can be reset by the software is passed to software in the IPLCB.

Devices that have not been configured shall be left in the reset state (bit positions in the Connectivity Reset registers that represent devices that have not been configured shall be zero). If the device supports dynamic reconfiguration, then software may configure each of the configurable entities by inactivating the "Reset" or by writing a one into the bit position for the device. Software can determine if a bit position is supported by reading back the Connectivity Reset register and verifying that a one is in the bit position, that is, that the reset is removed. The number of bits implemented is optional but shall be contiguous starting with bit 0 through bit 31 of consecutive address starting from 0xf...ff000010 moving upward in 32-bit word increments. Also there has to be at least one unimplemented bit left in the architected address space so that software can algorithmically determine the maximum number of supported bits without being dependent on the last architected address to determine that no more devices can be selected.

The Connectivity Reset register allows software to reconfigure the hardware. It consists of 64 bytes of system address space. Software is allowed to access any 32-bit word on a 32-bit word boundary within the architected facility range. The number of bits implemented within the facility is system specific. Bits shall be implemented contiguously starting at bit 0 of the lowest address.

When software has written a one into an implemented bit of any position in the Connectivity Reset registers and the reset for the selected hardware has been removed, software can configure specific devices under the control of the hardware whose reset has been removed by writing to the Connectivity Configuration register. There is a one-to-one correspondence between the bit number of the Connectivity Reset register and the Connectivity Configuration Select value of the Connectivity Configuration register. Software sets bit zero on and uses bits 23–31 as a binary value to select the specific bit position of the Connectivity Configuration register.

After software writes to the Connectivity register, it must issue a completion barrier (e.g., *sync* instruction in most of the cases) to make sure that the hardware has asserted the configuration signal.

Following the completion barrier, software may read the Device Characteristics Register (DCR), (see Table 13 on page 25 for an example), to determine if a device is actually present and if so, what type of device is present (bits 0–3 return this information). Further information about the device can be determined by reading the Device ID register (see Table 14 on page 27 for an example). Once the type of device is determined, software can configure the device by writing to the Device Bus Unit ID n (n=1, 2, 3, or 4) register (see Table 16 on page 28) and to the Device Base Real Address n (n=1 or 2) register (see Table 17 on page 28 for an example). After configuring the device, the software must disable the configuration of the device by issuing a write to the Connectivity Configuration register by either selecting another device or setting bit 0 to one to disable configuration and issuing a completion barrier.

Programming Note

Software may turn on bits within the facility one at a time; thereby, activating the facilities one at a time. Reading the facility shall allow software to determine if the bit was implemented. Software shall have activated all facilities when it reaches the first unimplemented bit.

Engineering Note

In the RISC System/6000 model 250, the bit for resetting its I/O controller is bit number 3. The corresponding Connectivity Configuration Select value is 0b00000011.

4.2.2 Architected Configuration Registers

The Architected Configuration Registers are intended to provide a consistent interface to software regardless of the system interconnect topologies (e.g., system bus, cross bar switch, ring, star...) and types within each topology (e.g., 60X, 6XX, PCI,... within system bus). There are, however, a few differences related to the size of the real addresses supported on the system.

4.2.3 Architected Configuration Register Address Map

Engineering Note

Because of the diversity of system bus connections possible on the PowerPC system, the spacing of the architected configuration registers is not constant for all devices or on all hardware reference platforms. The construct of a device configuration word address increment value, called i, is used to compute the offsets. For a given device on a given reference platform, the value of i is provided by the three bit field (bits 27–29) in the first architected configuration register, named Device Characteristics Register. The spacing of other configuration registers is defined by delta where delta = 2**(2+i). Typically, i=0, and these registers are spaced on 4 byte boundaries (delta=4.) As another example, if i=1, then these registers are spaced on 8 byte boundaries (delta=8).

Table 11 contains the Architected Configuration Register Address Map used for machines using the 60X bus (32-bit word bus) as a system bus. Table 12 contains the Architected Configuration Register Address Map used for machines using the 6XX bus (64-bit word bus) as a system bus. Delta, used in these tables, is computed using the device configuration word address increment field, i, bits 27–29 in Table 13, where delta = $2**(2+i)$.

For the 6XX bus, the value of i that defines the word increment field should always have the value 0b000 and in this case, delta has the value of 4.

4.2.3.1   Device Characteristics Register

This is a one word read only register found at fixed address 0xf...ff200000. It has the bit definitions shown in Table 13. It is composed of several fields.

All I/O devices shall use the same value of 0b0011 in the Device Class field of the Device Characteristics Register, bits 0–3 in Table 13. I/O Devices shall use this value, whether or not they are addressed in Memory Space or I/O space. Distinction between I/O Devices shall be from the Device ID Type fields of the Device ID register, bits 8–23 and 24–31 in Table 14.

There are particular considerations to the mapping of Device ROM into the Memory Space. The device feature/VPD ROM indicator mask field (j), bits 25–26 in Table 13 indicates whether word access may be used. Byte access shall be permitted, in all cases. The device configuration word address Increment field, bits 27–29 in Table 13 indicates the mapping of bytes of the Device ROM into the System Feature/VPD ROM address space. When the word address increment field has the value 0b000, then there is a one to one mapping of bytes of the Device ROM into the address space. When the word address increment field has the value 0b001, then each four-byte of the Device ROM are mapped into an eight-byte range of the address space, and specifically into the addresses in which bit 29 is 0.

Address	Description
0xf...ff200000	Device Characteristics Register
0xf...ff200000+delta	Device ID Register
0xf...ff200000+2*delta	Device Bus Unit ID 1 Register
0xf...ff200000+3*delta	Device Bus Unit ID 2 Register
0xf...ff200000+4*delta	Device Bus Unit ID 3 Register
0xf...ff200000+5*delta	Device Bus Unit ID 4 Register
0xf...ff200000+6*delta	Device Base Real Address 1 Register
0xf...ff200000+7*delta	Device Base Real Address 2 Register

Table 11. **Architected Configuration Register Address Map for 60X Bus**

Address	Description
0xf...ff200000	Device Characteristics Register
0xf...ff200000+delta	Device ID Register
0xf...ff200000+2*delta	Device Bus Unit ID 1 Register
0xf...ff200000+3*delta	Device Bus Unit ID 2 Register
0xf...ff200000+4*delta	Device Bus Unit ID 3 Register
0xf...ff200000+5*delta	Device Bus Unit ID 4 Register
0xf...ff200000+6*delta	Device Base Real Address 1 Register
0xf...ff200000+8*delta	Device Base Real Address 2 Register

Table 12. **Architected Configuration Register Address Map for 6XX Bus**

Bit	Description	
0–3	Device Class	Description
	0b0000	Device present but not ready
	0b0001	Executable Memory
	0b0010	Processor
	0b0011	I/O Device
	0b0100	Cache Controller Device
	0b0101	Bus Bridge
	0b1111	Device not present
	other	Reserved

Table 13. **Device Characteristics Register 0xf...ff200000**

Bit	Description
4–5	**BUID Allocation Indicator**
	0b00 No BUID required
	0b01 1 BUID
	0b10 2 BUIDs
	0b11 4 BUIDs
6–7	Reserved
8–11	Memory Allocation Indicator 1
	0b0000 No allocation required
	0b0001 1 MB (Minimum Allocation)
	0b0010 2 MB
	0b0011 4 MB
	0b0100 8 MB
	0b0101 16 MB
	0b0110 32 MB
	0b0111 64 MB
	0b1000 128 MB
	0b1001 256 MB
	0b1010 512 MB
	0b1011 1 GB
	0b1100 2 GB
	0b1110 Reserved
	0b1111 Reserved
12–15	Memory Allocation Indicator 2
	Same encodings as bits 8–11.
16–24	Reserved
25–26	Device Feature/VPD ROM Indicator (j)
	0b00 No Feature/VPD ROM Present
	0b01 Reserved
	0b10 Byte-Wide ROM (8 bits)
	0b11 Word-Wide ROM (32 bits)
27–29	Device Configuration Word Address Increment (i)
	0b000 4 Byte Increment, value of delta is 4
	0b001 8 Byte Increment, value of delta is 8
30–31	Reserved

Table 13. **Continued**

4.2.3.2 Device ID Register

The Device ID register is a one word read-only register found at address increment delta. It has the bit definitions shown in Table 14. The 32-bit value must be unique for a given device. No device shall have more than one unique value. No two devices shall have the same value.

Assigning the value 0bxxxxxxxx000000000000000000000000 to the Device ID register shall mean that the Device ID register of the Feature/VPD ROM holds the actual value. There shall be strong, device-specific requirements on programmability and similarity between all devices that have the same value of bits 8–23, except for the case where bits 8–23 have the value 0x0000.

Bit	Description
0	IBM Device 0b0 Adapter is an IBM logo adapter 0b1 Adapter is an OEM adapter (non-IBM)
1–7	Reserved Must be set to 0b0000000
8–23	Device ID Type Field Used to identify the type of a device. The set of unique types is defined in the table shown below of Device ID Types Registry.
24–31	Specific Device ID of a particular type The following bit assignment applies for devices that don't have VPD: Bit 28–31: Specific Device Engineering Level ID

Table 14. **Device ID Register**

Hex Value	Description
0x0000	Base Devices
0x0040	Display Adapter
0x1000	Memory Controller
0x3000	IOCC

Table 15. **Device ID Types Registry**

4.2.3.3 Device Bus Unit ID n (n=1, 2, 3, or 4) Register

Device Bus Unit IDs are required if Devices reside in I/O space or generate interrupts. Bus Unit IDs are assigned as required by configuration software.

The Device Bus Unit ID n register is a one word register found at address increments 2*delta, 3*delta, 4*delta, and 5*delta. It has the bit definitions shown in Table 16. This register is present only if the Bus Unit IDentification (BUID) Allocation indicator field, bits 4–5 of the Device Characteristics Register in Table 13 indicates that BUID assignments are required. The system configuration software uses this register to set the Bus Unit ID needed by the device.

Bit	Description
0–6	Unimplemented/reserved, see Section 1.2.2 on page 3
7–15	Bus Unit ID
16–31	Unimplemented/reserved, see Section 1.2.2 on page 3

Table 16. **Device Bus Unit ID Register n (n=1, 2, 3, or 4)**

4.2.3.4   Device Base Real Address n (n=1 or 2) Register with 60X as a System Bus

Device Base Real Addresses are required if the devices resides in Memory Space. Up to 2 regions in memory space may be allocated to a single Device. The minimum memory space allocation is 1 MB. Memory spaces are assigned on boundaries equal to the allocation (e.g., a 256 MB space is allocated on an even 256 MB boundary).

Because the allocation of Memory Space shall always be aligned, devices may implement the register(s) as left-justified registers which hold only enough bits necessary to define the proper size and alignment. All other bits must be ignored on write and must return 0 on read.

Each register shall be a one word register found at address increments 6*delta and 7*delta, respectively. Each shall have the bit definitions shown in Table 17. This register is present only if the Memory Allocation Indicators in the Device Characteristics Register are non-zero. System configuration software shall use this register to set the base real memory address that is recognized by the device.

Bit	Description
0–11	Device Base Real Address
12–31	Unimplemented/reserved, see Section 1.2.2 on page 3

Table 17. **Device Base Real Address Register n (n=1 or 2) for 60X Bus**

4.2.3.5 Device Base Real Address n (n=1 or 2) Register with 6XX as System Bus

Device Base Real Addresses are required if the devices resides in Memory Space. Up to 2 regions in memory space may be allocated to a single Device. The minimum memory space allocation is 1 MB. Memory spaces are assigned on boundaries equal to the allocation (e.g., a 256 MB space is allocated on an even 256 MB boundary).

Because the allocation of Memory Space shall always be aligned, devices may implement the register(s) as left-justified registers which hold only enough bits necessary to define the proper size and alignment. All other bits must be ignored on write and must return 0 on read.

Each register shall be a 64-bit word register found at address increments 6*delta and 8*delta, respectively. Each shall have the bit definitions shown in Table 18. This register is present only if the Memory Allocation Indicators in the Device Characteristics Register are non-zero. System configuration software shall use this register to set the base real memory address that is recognized by the device.

Bit	Description
0–43	Device Base Real Address

Table 18. **Device Base Real Address Register n (n=1 or 2) for 6XX Bus**

4.2.4 Device Specific Configuration Registers

This space is available to each Device to allow whatever configuration or Device setup features it requires. There are no system requirements on the implementations of registers or devices which decode this address space.

4.3 Feature ROM Scan (FRS) Architecture

4.3.1 Address Range

The Feature/VPD ROM Space occupies the region from 0xf...ffa00000 to 0xf...ffbfffff. This space is defined in the Architected System Memory Space definitions in Section 3.1 on page 7.

Access to the Feature/VPD ROM Space shall only be meaningful when the Architected System Register that controls enablement of bus slots has been written to enable a particular slot. The Feature/VPD ROM of at most one device at a time shall be mapped into the Architected Feature/VPD ROM address space.

4.3.2   Criteria for Required ROM

The definitions in this section present the architected interface that shall be supported on each device in a PowerPC system that meets the following criteria:

■ The device sets the Class field, bits 0–3 of the architected Device Characteristics Register (refer to Table 13 on page 25 to the value 0b0011, and

■ The device sets the ROM Indicator field, bits 25–26 in Table 13 on page 25 of the architected Device Characteristics Register to a non-zero value.

4.3.3   ROM Type Attributes

The architecture anticipates several types of ROM. The three main variations are:

■ A basic, byte device which only holds a limited amount of VPD, or

■ A byte device which holds VPD, feature ROM, and potentially other objects in the ROM, or

■ A word device which holds VPD, feature ROM, and potentially other objects in the ROM.

4.3.3.1   Specifying Device ID and Type

An I/O device may choose to put its device ID into the Feature/VPD ROM Space by placing the value 0bxxxxxxxx 00000000 00000000 00000000 into the Device ID register, refer to Section 4.2.3.2 on page 27.

4.3.3.2   Feature ROM Addressability

Access to the contents of the Feature/VPD ROM space are governed by the same rules as found in the Architected Configuration Registers space. Recall that the Device Characteristics Register defines the device feature/VPD ROM indicator bits 25–26 in Table 13 on page 25. In this section, the value j represents the ROM indicator field value, where the value of bits 25–26 is 0b10 means j is one byte and the value of 0b11 means j is 4-bytes or a 32-bit word. The Device Characteristics Register also defines the device configuration word address increment field (i), where bits 27–29 having a value of 0b000 defines a 4-byte increment value of delta and a value of 0b001 defines an 8-byte increment value of delta.

4.3.3.3   Computation of Lengths and Offsets

All lengths in this section are independent of the value of delta. The lengths apply to contents only. For example, in the case of a device configuration word address increment value of 0b001, where delta is 8 bytes, the total content length of the ROM shall be 1/2 of the address space consumed by the ROM, due to the skipping of each word in which address bit 29 is 0b1.

All offsets in this section, however, do include the value of delta. The offsets are used to generated addresses relative to BASE, which is 0xf..ffa00000. Addressing schemes for the ROM shall be able to compute addresses much easier in this fashion. Offsets within the objects themselves are almost always relative to the start of the object.

4.3.3.4   The ROM Has Two Distinct Forms

Tables 20 and 21 show the layout of the Feature/VPD ROM. Table 20 on page 33 shows the layout of the Feature/VPD ROM Space for the basic byte device which only holds limited VPD. Only devices which are extremely constrained by space or cost considerations shall use this minimal layout.

All other devices shall use the layout specified in Table 21 on page 33.

Differentiation between the two forms is based on the contents of the word at offset delta from the BASE of the Feature/VPD ROM space.

4.3.3.5   The Standard Form Supports Objects of Several Kinds

The Feature/VPD ROM is composed of several kinds of objects. Table 19 describes the Architected Objects. They fall into three categories, shown below. They are differentiated by three bit flags set in the ID of the object.

■ Architected Objects, some of which are required for all devices.

■ Objects that are defined for all devices that share the same value of the Device Type field of the Device ID register.

■ Objects that are uniquely defined for only the unique Device ID.

4.3.3.6   External Requirements on the Organization of the Feature ROM

The Feature/VPD ROM is composed of a set of nested blocks of ROM. For compatibility with previously released software, some redundancy exists between the inner and outer blocks.

ID Value	Description
0x8000 0001	Title: Architected VPD Object
	This object holds the VPD data for the device. It is a required object. All devices shall provide VPD.
0x8000 0002	Title: Architected Feature ROM Scan Object
	This object holds the Feature ROM Scan data for the device. It is a required object for devices which are boot or base display devices.

Table 19. **Architected Feature / VPD ROM Object IDs**

4.3.3.7   Considerations for the Architected Feature ROM Scan Object

There are some important data structures to consider when discussing adapter configuration. The data structures all apply to the Feature ROM Scan (FRS) Architecture. The data structures describe how the processor reads the contents of the FRS contents of the adapter and interprets them.

The FRS architecture utilizes a set of software structures that are linked together by pointers or by offset values. The ROM contents of a given adapter contain the set of all of these structures completed and linked together.

The root structure of this set is called the FRS header. It has certain properties that make it easily located in a search of bus memory address space. It has offset variables that point to the other structures. In non-Micro-Channel adapters, none of the members of the structure would need to be changed.

The FRS header contains the total length of the ROM and an offset to the beginning of a linked list of other data structures. The data structures that form the linked list are called FRS blocks. The header and the blocks are assumed to be contiguous and are protected by a summation checksum residue calculation.

Each FRS block holds the offset of the next block. It also holds two special fields. If the proper values are found in the special fields, then the FRS block is assumed to contain pointers to the desired data.

One member of the FRS block structure is the block ID. Another is the ID string field. For example, all FRS block IDs for RISC System/6000 adapters are set to the value of 1. Similarly, the ID string field for RISC System/6000 boot devices is "RISC6000", while the ID string field for video devices is "RISC6002".

4.3.3.8   Considerations for the Architected Feature ROM Scan Object

The full details of creation of a Feature ROM are outside the scope of this document.

Address	Description
0xf..ffa00000 (BASE)	Field Name: Feature/VPD Device ID This is a 32-bit quantity. The device ID has exactly the same form as that of the Device ID Register described in "Device ID Register," Section 4.2.3.2, on page 27.
BASE+1*delta	Field Name: Feature/VPD ROM Characteristics Word For the case of "simple VPD only," this word is set to 0xrrrr rr00 Where r is a reserved nibble and is presently required to be the value 0x0.
BASE+2*delta to BASE+63*delta	Field Name: Simple VPD Data For the case of simple VPD data, there are 248 bytes of VPD character data that follow the Device ID and Characteristics Word. The full 248 bytes must be addressable. Note that the spacing of the bytes is dependent on the addressing scheme set forth by the Device Characteristics Register.

Table 20. **Architected Feature / VPD ROM Space for the Case "Simple VPD Only"**

Address	Description
0xf..ffa00000 (BASE)	Field Name: Feature/VPD Device ID This is a 32-bit quantity. The device ID has exactly the same form as that of the Device ID Register described in "Device ID Register," Section 4.2.3.2, on page 27.

BASE+1*delta	Field Name: Feature/VPD ROM Characteristics Word
	Composed of two fields:
	
	0brrrrrrrr rrrrrrrr rrrrrrr NNNNNNNN
	
	The "r" field is reserved and is presently required to be the value "0", thus
	
	0b00000000 00000000 00000000 NNNNNNNN
	
	The "N" field is the number of ROM objects that follow. N must satisfy the following constraint:
	      N = NA + NT + ND
	      N != 0
	
	Where NA is the number of architected objects, and
	            1 <= NA <= 2, and
	            NT is the number of device-type objects
	            required for all objects of this device type, and
	            ND is the number of device-ID specific objects
	            for this unique device.

Table 21. **Architected Feature / VPD ROM Space**

Address	Description
BASE+2*delta	**Field Name:** Feature/VPD Length and CRC This is a 32-bit quantity. It is divided into two fields. 0bssssssss sssssss cccccccc cccccccc The field "s" is the size of the total ROM in units of 512 byte blocks, from the BASE until the last byte. The ROM shall be padded with "0" to complete the last block. The length shall be less than the quotient of the architected length of the Feature/VPD ROM address space divided by the word increment value. The field "c" is the CRC residue calculated on the contents of the ROM from BASE+3*delta until the last byte of ROM, inclusive.
BASE+3*delta to BASE+3*delta+ 3N*delta	**Field Name:** Feature/VPD Block Array This is an array of dimension "N", where N is the number of objects named in the Feature/VPD ROM Characteristics Word. Each item in the array is the same size, which is 3 words. The array items are used to locate the ROM objects. The array items are organized as follows: WORD 0: Holds the ID of the ROM object. The word has the following format: 0bCTDrrrrr rrrrrrr IIIIIIII IIIIIIII "C" is a flag that says the object is common to all Feature/VPD ROM I/O devices "T" is a flag that says the object is defined for any device that has a device type of the same value as this device "D" is a flag that says the object is only defined for objects with the unique 32 bit device ID value. "I" The 16 bit I field is the unique block ID WORD 1: Holds the offset in bytes from BASE to the start of the block of ROM WORD 2: Holds the length in bytes of the block of ROM.
BASE+3N*delta+ 4*delta	**Field Name:** Start of ROM Blocks From this word on, the ROM blocks defined in the Block Array begin. Each block shall begin on a double-word aligned address. There are particular requirements on the internal contents of each ROM block.

Table 21. **Continued**

NVRAM Contents and Mapping

Non-Volatile Random Access Memory (NVRAM) is the primary interface used to communicate between the hardware and the Operating System for those items which are needed to tailor the initialization of the Operating System.

All NVRAM addresses are offsets from the NVRAM base address, refer to Section 3.1, "Architected System Memory Map" on page 7 for the architected starting address.

The current architecture allows for the effective implementation of some hardware facilities in NVRAM space, for example, the Light Emitting Diode (LED) display interface and the Available Processor Mask (APM). These facilities may be monitored by a Service Processor which may use unarchitected hardware support to perform the desired function. Although it is preferable that NVRAM be protected via hardware parity bits, this is not a hardware requirement at this time. For this reason, the burden of providing the appropriate RAS characteristics may require a coordinated effort between the hardware and the software.

5.1 NVRAM Usage

There is a battery backed up RAM, Non-Volatile Random Access Memory (NVRAM). This NVRAM is utilized by software to store information that must persist across IPLs and power cycling. The NVRAM size is at least 64 kilobytes (KB) and can grow bigger to include additional functions for a particular product. The NVRAM is primarily intended for:

■ Fast Path Boot

Engineering Note

There are platform dependent NVRAM areas that are not defined in this document. Consult the appropriate platform specification for details.

Architecture and Programming Note

If the "access_id" field is set to one, then AIX will use the machine DD to access the NVRAM area and the range will be used to determine the type of checking. If real-time validation is required, not just at initialization, it may be appropriate to have another value assigned to the "access_id."

■ A persistent save area (with a simple access) path for fatal error information

■ An alternative to requiring OEM IPL device ROMs for extending planar IPL ROM

■ Customer tailoring of IPL source and search order (both Normal and Service Modes)

The detailed NVRAM utilization by AIX and IPL ROM on the RISC/6000 platform is as follows:

■ LED Access and LED String Output

■ IPL device list for Normal and Service modes

■ Last device IPLed from

■ SCSI adapter initiator addresses for slots 0–15

■ On-Card Sequencer (OCS) communications, logout areas, and work area

■ Network Boot Support (and ROM Diagnostics)

■ Dynamically managed software area

■ Up to two alternate IPL device – device drivers loaded and executed by IPL ROM

■ Last Error Log Entry

■ Manufacturing Use (during manufacturing test)

Systems can contain a micro-processor that is used to provide initialization of the CEC (Central Electronics Complex). These micros also allow scanning of the VLSI scanable storage chains (latches). The original version of this micro-processor capability in the RISC System/6000 has been named OCS (On-Card Sequencer). Future systems can contain other versions of such a micro-processor and we will hereby define the term "SP" (for "scanning processor" or "service processor") to indicate any OCS-like micro-processor that has similar capabilities. The OCS or SP cannot write NVRAM at offsets 0–0x2ff (768 bytes) but is able to read all of NVRAM and write any location from 0x300. The following information details each field in the NVRAM, when and who initializes it, updates it and reads it.

5.1.1 ROM Specific Areas and Their Management

5.1.1.1 NVRAM Area from 0x00 to 0x2ff

The area from 0x00 – 0x2ff is an area that is maintained by a CRC check and is accessed by IPL ROM and system software for boot control. On systems with network boot IPL ROM support, this area of NVRAM is initialized by the system IPL ROM whenever the CRC is not valid. Systems with this level of IPL ROM will also support two NVRAM status bits in the IPL Control Block. This field is defined as NVRAM_section_1_valid, resides in the ipl_info structure within the IPL Control Block, and has the following definition:

bits 0 thru 28 are reserved and contain 0s
bit 29 = 0 if NVRAM battery test okay
bit 29 = 1 if NVRAM battery test failed (machine dd will log failure)
bit 30 = 0 IPL ROM did not initialize NVRAM
bit 30 = 1 IPL ROM did initialize NVRAM (machine dd will log)
bit 31 = 0 NVRAM CRC miscompare
bit 31 = 1 NVRAM CRC is okay

The area of NVRAM from offset 0 to offset 0x2ff is initialized by IPL ROM if the CRC for this area is determined to be invalid. The Machine Device Driver (DD) code also has the ability to initialize this area if the CRC is found bad. However, if the IPL ROM was unsuccessful in initializing the area, the Machine DD will most probably fail as well. Such a failure will not prevent the IPL ROM from starting the system, and it is up to AIX to report an unsuccessful attempt to correct the CRC of the area.

5.1.1.2 NVRAM Address 0x0000–0x0003, Intentionally Unused

5.1.1.3 NVRAM Address 0x0004–0x0007, NVRAM Size

Contains the number of contiguous good bytes starting from offset zero

■ Read by: Machine DD to determine NVRAM size, if NVRAM CRC is valid

5.1.1.4 NVRAM Address 0x0008–0x000b, NVRAM Contents Version Number

Contains NVRAM Contents Version number for distinguishing NVRAM layout changes

■ Read by: Machine DD, IPL ROM

■ Current Value: integer 0x0001

5.1.1.5   NVRAM Address 0x000c–0x000f, Pointer to Dynamic Software Area

Pointer to dynamic software area start

■ Read by: Machine DD

5.1.1.6   NVRAM Address 0x0010–0x001f, Slots 1–16 SCSI Initiator Addresses

Read by: IPL ROM, SCSI adapter configuration methods (default set to **SCSI Initiator** Address 7 by IPL ROM if CRC is bad)

Updated by: SCSI adapter configuration methods

Format:

Offset	**Definition**
0x0010–0x001f	SCSI Initiator Address for BUID 0x20 and BUID 0x21
	0x0010 – slot 0, ..,0x001f – slot 15
	low nibble – BUID 0x20
	high nibble – BUID 0x21
	nibble definition
	SCSI address 0 – 7

5.1.1.7   NVRAM Address 0x0020–0x00ff, BUID 0 Address 0x1000–0x10d0

Memory Bit Steering Regs

Read by: IPL ROM

Written by: IPL ROM to provide bit steering if the IPL ROM test indicates steering is required. This allows software to set up bit steering due to memory problems when warm IPL takes place.

5.1.1.8   NVRAM Address 0x0100–0x01fb, Remote Boot Information

Maintained by: IPL ROM

Read by: IPL ROM

Written by: IPL ROM

Format:

Offset	**Definition**
0x0100–0x0101	Two byte validity ID (ASCII "rs," 0x7273)
0x0102–0x0111	Token Ring Speed Area and 3COM Ethernet Port Selection
	0x0102 – slot 0, .., 0x0111 – slot 15
	low nibble – BUID 0x20
	high nibble – BUID 0x21
	nibble bit definition
	0bxx00 – Token ring speed not set
	0bxx01 – 4 MB
	0bxx10 – 16 MB
	0b00xx – Ethernet port not set
	0b01xx – BNC port
	0b10xx – DIX port
	0b11xx – Twisted Pair port
0x0112	Console Type Code
	0 – None set
	1 – RS232 tty
	2 – RS422 tty
	3 – Graphics display
0x0113–0x011a	ASCII String for Console
	location
	bus_eu
	slot – two characters
	unit – two characters
	port – two characters
	ser port 1– 0000S100
0x011b	Language Code

0 – not set	1 – English
2 – German	3 – Spanish
4 – French	5 – Swedish
6 – Norwegian	7 – Belgium
8 – Italian	

0x011c–0x011d	Reserved
0x011e–0x0121	Reserved
0x0122–0x0125	Reserved
0x0126–0x0129	Reserved
0x012a	Integrated Ethernet Transceiver Configuration
	bit definition
	0b1xxx xxxx – SQE expected
	0bxxxx x1xx – IBM transceiver
	0bxxxx xx00 – None or unknown
	0bxxxx xx01 – 10 Base 2 transceiver
	0bxxxx xx10 – 10 Base T transceiver
0x012b–0x013a	3 COM 15 Pin D Connector Transceiver Ethernet Configuration
	0x012b – slot 0, .., 0x013a – slot 15
	low nibble – BUID 0x20
	high nibble – BUID 0x21
	nibble bit definition: –0b1xxx – SQE expected –0bx1xx – IBM transceiver –0bxx00 – None or unknown –0bxx01 – 10 Base 2 transceiver –0bxx10 – 10 Base T transceiver
0x013b–0x01fb	Reserved (ex: FCS, FDDI, ...)

5.1.1.9   NVRAM Address 0x01fc–0x01ff, IPL ROM Boot State Information Save

Maintained by: IPL ROM

Read by: IPL ROM

Written by: IPL ROM

Format:

Offset	**Definition**
0x01fc	Reserved for IPL ROM usage
0x01fd	Rampost Flag Used to control memory testing by rampost code

0x01fe   NVRAM boot device list current entry count

0x01ff   bit usage

    0x01 – resume bootlist if ROM Scan device returns

    0x02 – keyswitch state (normal vs service)

    0x04 – controls entering the menus

    0xf8 – these bits are undefined

5.1.1.10 NVRAM Address 0x0200–0x0223, Normal Mode Previous Boot Device

Descriptor for normal mode previous boot device

Maintained by: IPL ROM, Sys Method, bootlist utility

Read by: IPL ROM

Format: Same descriptor format as for a device list but only a single specific device list entry is allowed (refer to Section 5.1.1.11, "NVRAM Address 0x0224–0x0277, Normal Mode BOOT Device List" for a description of a device list entry). Unlike a normal or service mode device, the previous boot device is only processed once (refer to Section 5.1.1.11.1, "Device List Format").

5.1.1.11 NVRAM Address 0x0224–0x0277, Normal Mode BOOT Device List

A device list contains one or more entries defining a device which is a potential candidate for containing IPL code. Each entry may describe a general type of device that is independent of its logical address in the system (e.g. any type drive that may exist on the SCSI bus). Or, it may describe a very specific device, including the necessary addressing information which IPL ROM needs to directly access it. IPL ROM will process the list of devices in sequential order, attempting to IPL from each. The list processing will terminate only if an IPL attempt is successful. In other words, if all the devices in a list fails to produce a successful IPL, the list will be retried from the beginning.

A few noteworthy comments:

1. A list is present if its 2 byte validity header is present.

2. IPL ROM does its best to validate each entry. If it detects an invalid entry, that entry will be skipped and it will proceed to the next.

3. On systems that support network boot, service mode device list processing may be interrupted in service mode by a call to a menus display if the

service mode list fails to produce a successful IPL before the list is exhausted.

4. Current RISC/6000 systems do not have the capability to detect a SCSI device as being internal or external. Hence, any references to internal SCSI devices and any references to external SCSI devices should be interpreted as "internal OR external."

Maintained by: bootlist utility

Read by: IPL ROM

Contents: 2 byte validity header (ASCII "JM", 0x4a4d), 82 bytes for descriptors, terminated by 0.

5.1.1.11.1 Device List Format

The following list of "type codes" is for completeness, only, since they must be unique. Details of their meanings are to be obtained from the device list entries described below. The type values identify an IPL device.

A	Global memory device. This represents an area of global memory that may contain an executable image of the Operating System.
C	A SCSI CDROM device.
D	An ethernet device.
E	A SCSI external DASD device.
F	A diskette device.
G	A "general" device. This code is modified by one of the other type codes. Refer to the description below for more details.
I	An SCSI internal DASD device.
K	OBSOLETE placeholder (was SJL device).
M	A ROM scan device.
N	A diskette device.
O	A token ring device.
P	A FDDI device.
R	OBSOLETE placeholder (was expansion code device).
S	A SCSI specific device.
V	A "volume ID" device.

A device list entry begins with a descriptor length value, n.

The next n bytes of any device entry is the descriptor itself.

The IPL ROM will process each device entry in turn, attempting to IPL from each device, until a 0 descriptor length is encountered or the end of the list is encountered.

The n bytes of descriptor information is made up of one or more sequences of a device type code followed by device specific information and is described below (unless otherwise noted, numerics are pure numbers and characters are ASCII)

General Device List Entry (if there is more than one of the general devices on a system, IPL ROM will search for them in an internally defined order)

length	type	specifics	comments
2	G	A	Global memory
2	G	C	SCSI CDROM
2	G	D	Ethernet
2	G	E	SCSI external DASD
2	G	F	Diskette
2	G	I	SCSI internal DASD
2	G	M	Feature ROM
2	G	O	Token ring
2	G	P	FDDI
2	G	T	SCSI tape

NVRAM Expansion Code Device List Entry

length	type	specifics	comments
2	R	1 or 2	Expansion code area 1 or 2

Diskette Device List Entry

length	type	specifics	comments
2	N	0 or 1	Diskette unit 0 or 1

Feature ROM, Ethernet or Token Ring Device List Entry

length	type	specifics	comments
3	M		ROM Scan type
	D		Ethernet type
	O		Token Ring type
		0x20–0x21/0–15	BUID/slot for device

8 Byte SCSI Device List Entry

length	type	specifics	comments
8	S		1byte type followed by 7 bytes SCSI id information:
		0x20–0x21	byte 1 (BUID value)
		I or E	byte 2 (internal or external)
		0 – 15	byte 3 (slot value)
		0 – 7	byte 4 (initiator SCSI id, not used by IPL ROM)
		1, 3, or 4	byte 5 (DASD, CDROM, or TAPE)
		0 – 7	byte 6 (device SCSI ID)
		0 – 7	byte 7 (device LUN ID)

8 Byte Ethernet or Token Ring Device List Entry

length	type	specifics	comments
8	D		Ethernet type
	O		Token Ring type (1-byte type, followed by 7 bytes specific data)
		0x20–0x21	byte 1 (BUID value)
		0 – 15	byte 2 (slot value)
		B	byte 3 (indicates a BOOTP server IP address follows)
		pppp	bytes 4 thru 7 (IP address)

15 Byte Ethernet or Token Ring Device List Entry

length	type	specifics	comments
15	D		Ethernet type
	O		Token Ring type (1-byte type, followed by 14 bytes specific data)
		0x20–0x21	byte 1 (BUID value)

0 – 15	byte 2 (slot value)
B	byte 3 (indicates a BOOTP server IP address follows)
pppp	bytes 4 thru 7 (IP address)
H	byte 8 (indicates a Hardware address follows)
hhhhhh	bytes 9 thru 14 ("burned-in" adapter address)

17 Byte SCSI Device List Entry

length	type	specifics	comments
17	V		1 byte type followed by:
			8 bytes of ignored data followed by:
			8 Byte SCSI Device List Entry

18 Byte Ethernet or Token Ring Device List Entry

length	type	specifics	comments
18	D O		Ethernet type Token Ring type (1-byte type, followed by 17 bytes specific data)
		0x20–0x21	byte 1 (BUID value)
		0 – 15	byte 2 (slot value)
		W	byte 3 (indicates a Gateway IP address follows)
		pppp	bytes 4 thru 7 (Gateway IP address)
		B	byte 8 (indicates a BOOTP server IP address follows)

pppp	bytes 9 thru 12 (IP address)
L	byte 13 (indicates local or client IP address)
pppp	bytes 14 thru 17 (IP address)

25 Byte SCSI Device List Entry

length	type	specifics	comments
25	V		1 byte type followed by: 16 byte PVID (Physical Volume ID) followed by:
			8 Byte SCSI Device List Entry

25 Byte Ethernet or Token Ring Device List Entry

length	type	specifics	comments
25	D O		Ethernet type Token Ring type (1-byte type, followed by 24 bytes specific data)
		0x20–0x21	byte 1 (BUID value)
		0 – 15	byte 2 (slot value)
		W	byte 3 (indicates a Gateway IP address follows)
		pppp	bytes 4 thru 7 (Gateway IP address)
		H	byte 8 (indicates a Hardware address follows)
		hhhhhh	bytes 9 thru 14 ("burned-in" adapter address)
		B	byte 15 (indicates a BOOTP server IP address follows)

PPPP	bytes 16 thru 19 (IP address)
L	byte 20 (indicates local or client IP address)
PPPP	bytes 21 thru 24 (IP address)

5.1.1.12 NVRAM Address 0x0278–0x02cb, Service Mode BOOT Device List

Maintained by: BOS Install, bootlist utility

Contents: 2 byte validity header (ASCII "WR", 0x5752), 82 bytes for descriptors, terminated by 0

Device List Format: Same as 5.1.1.11, "NVRAM Address 0x0224–0x0277, Normal Mode BOOT Device Lit."

5.1.1.13 NVRAM Address 0x02cc–0x02f7, NVRAM Dev. Driver #1 & #2 Header Blocks

Maintained by: nvload utility (This function, NVRAM Device Driver, is no longer supported)

Read by: IPL ROM

Format:

Offset	**Definition**
0x02cc–0x02cd	Driver #1 two byte validity ID (0xa5a5)
0x02ce–0x02cf	Driver #1 byte length (16 bit unsigned int)
0x02d0–0x02d3	Driver #1 starting offset location in NVRAM
0x02d4–0x02d7	Driver #1 code CRC value
0x02d8–0x02e3	Reserved for expansion (twelve bytes)
0x02e4–0x02e5	Driver #2 two byte validity ID (0xa5a5)
0x02e6–0x02e7	Driver #2 byte length (16 bit unsigned int)
0x02e8–0x02eb	Driver #2 starting offset location in NVRAM
0x02ec–0x02ef	Driver #2 code CRC value
0x02f0–0x02f7	Reserved for expansion (8 bytes)

5.1.1.14   NVRAM Address 0x02f8, TCW/TCE Table Size

Maintained by: IPL ROM and AIX busconfig when DMA limit attribute is set (special bail out for non-standard adapters). IPL ROM verifies that the value meets system requirements for each machine type

Read by: IPL ROM when NVRAM CRC is good. If the size is larger than the default determined by IPL ROM, the size is used. If not (or if the NVRAM CRC is bad), IPL ROM uses a machine based internal algorithm to determine table size.

Note

Only used on systems using system RAM for TCW/TAG/TCE table space (as opposed to IOCC space for example). This includes all future systems such as PowerPC.

The TCW/TCE size value is the same as the value that is stored in the IOCC configuration register.

Offset	Definition
0x2f8	TCW/TCE space size
	– low nibble – BUID 20
	– high nibble – BUID 21

5.1.1.15   NVRAM Address 0x02f9–0x02fb

Reserved for future use.

5.1.1.16   NVRAM Address 0x02fc–0x02ff, CRC for SEQ/OCS Read Only Area

Maintained by: Any write to 0x0004–0x02fc by IPL ROM or Machine DD.

Read by: IPL ROM. If the value is determined to be incorrect, IPL ROM will initialize the area and recheck this value. The results of the initialization and checking procedure will be reported in the IPL Control Block (refer to Section 5.1.1.1, "NVRAM area from 0x00 to 0x2ff").

5.1.2   OCS/SP Implementations

The areas described below are read/write addressable by the OCS, however only designated areas are indeed written by the OCS. The only area that is CRC checked when read is in the software dynamic allocation area.

5.1.2.1   NVRAM Address 0x0300–0x0307, LED Data Mirrored

Written by: OCS/SP, IPL ROM, Machine DD (LEDs support)

Read by: Machine DD

5.1.2.2 NVRAM Address 0x0308–0x030b, Checkstop Count

Written by: OCS/SP – Set to zero on Power-on, incremented on checkstops. Also set to zero by diagnostics or OS SYS method.

Read by: OCS/SP, If count >= 3 then stop with LED Error Displayed, Error Log Daemon Init – reads and clears count. If it was non-zero, reads checkstop log and saves in error log and associated file.

5.1.2.3 NVRAM Address 0x030c–0x030f, Pointer to OCS/SP Checkstop Logout Area

Maintained by: OCS/SP

Read by: Error Log Daemon Init – If Checkstop count is not equal to 0 then this pointer is used to locate the checkstop logout area, which must be on at least a word (4 byte) boundary.

The high order byte of this pointer, SP_TYPE, is used to indicate the type of SP that is present. The next three bytes, LOG_PTR, define the location of the logout area in NVRAM.

If SP_TYPE and LOG_PTR is equal to 0, there is no SP (or OCS).

If SP_TYPE is equal to 0, the SP is an OCS type processor in a uni-processor environment.

> LOG_PTR defines a hybrid form of offset to the NVRAM logout area. This form of offset is understood by extant versions of AIX and will remain unchanged to maintain compatiblity. The logout area is of fixed size.

If SP_TYPE is equal to 1, the processor is a SP in an SMP environment.

> LOG_PTR defines the offset, from the base NVRAM address, to the beginning of a partitioned logout area. The logout area is partitioned as follows:

■   The first word of each section contains a size field, LOG_SIZE, and an offset field NEXT_LOG_OFFSET. LOG_SIZE is the high order byte of the word and defines the number of contiguous 1 K (1024) byte blocks in the current logout section. The minimum value of LOG_SIZE is 1. The remaining three bytes are NEXT_LOG_OFFSET, which defines the offset, from the base NVRAM address, to the next logout area. If NEXT_LOG_OFFSET is equal to 0, the current section is the last.

If SP_TYPE is greater than 1, reserved.

5.1.2.4   NVRAM Address 0x0310–0x0313, OCS Code E/C Level

Maintained by: OCS

Read by: Sys Method and stored in System Customized object class (system VPD)

5.1.2.5   NVRAM Address 0x0314–0x0317, OCS "Seed" EPROM E/C Level

Maintained by: OCS

Read by: Sys Method and stored in System Customized object class (system VPD)

5.1.2.6   NVRAM Address 0x0318–0x031b, Manufacturing Control

Maintained by: OCS and useable by SP for manufacturing purpose.

Read by: IPL ROM, OCS/SP, Manufacturing (through VRAM DD)

5.1.2.7   NVRAM Address 0x031c–0x031f, Pointer to Manufacturing Data Area

Maintained by: Manufacturing Test using NVRAM DD and SP usage

Read by: Manufacturing test

5.1.2.8   NVRAM Address 0x0320–0x035f, LED String Output Area

Maintained by: Machine DD (LEDs Access)

Read by: OCS/SP/Boot ROM

Usage: Output string is sequenced through LEDs when Reset button pushed

5.1.2.9   NVRAM Address 0x0360–0x0363, Pointer to OCS Code Execution Area

Maintained by: OCS

Read by: OCS, IPL ROM (execution area used as temporary scratchpad by IPL ROM)

5.1.2.10 NVRAM Address 0x0364–0x0367, Pointer to OCS Work Area

Maintained by: OCS

Read by: Future use to indicate OCS area that must not be modified by system

Also assigned to Salmon for LED string output pointer used by sequencer hardware

5.1.2.11 NVRAM Address 0x0368–0x037b, Machine Check Save Area – 20 Bytes

Maintained by: Machine DD

Written by: Machine Check Handler

Read by: Error Log Daemon

5.1.2.12 NVRAM Address 0x037c–0x037f, OCS/RS Command Interface

Written by: OCS/SP, Machine DD

Read by: OCS/SP, Machine DD
    Bit 1 = 0 indicates a POR reset
    Bit 1 = 1 indicates a push button reset
    Bit 7 = 0 indicates step mode inactive
    Bit 7 = 1 indicates step mode active

5.1.2.13 NVRAM Address 0x0380–0x03ff, OCS Information Area

Written by: OCS/SP

Read by: IPL ROM, Sys Method (system VPD)

Content: System Vital Product Data

5.1.2.14 NVRAM Address 0x0400–0x43ff, OCS Transient Work/Code Area (16 KB)

Written by: OCS, IPL ROM

Read by: OCS, IPL ROM

Content: Data Area for OCS, Transient Code execution area for OCS

OCS Checksums 0x0400–0x2000 internal code/work area

OCS Checkstop Logout area 0x2000–0x43ff

IPL ROM Temporary Data Area 0x1000–0x1fff

■ 0x1000–0x17ff Temporary tables, statistics, memory error info for bit steering

■ 0x1800–0x187f Bad memory extent information (found during memory configuration)

■ 0x1880–0x18C7 Memory Card VPD temporary save area

■ 0x1C00–0x1fff IPL ROM Work Area (1KB)

    – 0x1C00–0x1C03   4 byte validity ID (ASCII "IPLR", 0x49504c52)
    – 0x1D00–0x1eff   Reserved
    – 0x1f00–0x1f23   Service Mode Previous Boot Device
    – 0x1ff8–0x1ffB   Reserved
    – 0x1ffC–0x1fff   CRC value for IPL ROM Work Area

OCS/SP Checkstop Logout area 0x2000–0x43ff

■ This area may be partitioned. If so, it will be partitioned as defined by NVRAM Addresses 0x30c – 0x30f. In any event, the remaining format, other than the partition definition, is defined by the extant service processor.

5.1.2.15   NVRAM Address 0x4400–0x47ff, Medialess IPL ROM Diag./Boot Info Save

1 KB medialess IPL ROM only

Written by: IPL ROM

Read by: IPL ROM

Contains: Diagnostic and system boot information that must be saved across power sequences, but is not accessed by system software.

5.1.2.16   NVRAM Address 0x4400–0x7fff, Dynamically Controlled Software Area

15 KB non-medialess IPL ROM

5.1.2.17   NVRAM Address 0x4800–0x7fff, Dynamically Controlled Software Area

14 KB medialess IPL ROM

Written by: NVRAM DD

Read by: IPL ROM and NVRAM DD

Current Utilization

- NVRAM Device Driver (DD) Allocation Structures

- Up to two alternate IPL device – device drivers

- Fatal Error Log Information

- Manufacturing Test Area (during mfg test only)

5.1.3 Non-OCS Implementations

5.1.3.1 NVRAM Address 0x0300–0x0303, LED Data Mirrored

- Written by: Sequencer, IPL ROM, Machine DD (LEDs support)

- Read by: Machine DD

5.1.3.2 NVRAM Address 0x0304–0x0317, Reserved

5.1.3.3 NVRAM Address 0x0318–0x31b, Manufacturing Control

- Read by: IPL ROM and Manufacturing (through NVRAM DD)

5.1.3.4 NVRAM Address 0x031c–0x031f, Pointer to Manufacturing Data Area

- Maintained by: Manufacturing Test using NVRAM DD

- Read by: Manufacturing Test

5.1.3.5 NVRAM Address 0x0320–0x035f, LED String Output Area

- Maintained by: Machine DD (LEDs Access)

- Read by: Boot ROM for LED Step.

- Usage: Output string is sequenced through LED when Reset button is pushed

5.1.3.6   NVRAM Address 0x0360–0x0363, MFG Information

■ Maintained by: IPL ROM

■ Written by: IPL ROM

■ Read by: IPL ROM (mfg mode)

5.1.3.7   NVRAM Address 0x0364–0x0367, IPL ROM supported LED String Output Ptr

■ Maintained by: IPL ROM

■ Read by: IPL ROM

5.1.3.8   NVRAM Address 0x0368–0x037b, Machine Check Save Area (20 bytes)

■ Maintained by: Machine DD

■ Written by: Machine Check Handler

■ Read by: Error Log Daemon

5.1.3.9   NVRAM Address 0x037c–0x037f, LED Step Interface

■ Maintained by: Boot ROM set to 0 at POR, Machine DD for LED step

■ Written by: Boot ROM, Machine DD

■ Read by: System Reset Count, LED Step Mode Enable

   – Bit 1 = 0 indicates a POR reset
   – Bit 1 = 1 indicates a push button reset
   – Bit 7 = 0 indicates step mode inactive
   – Bit 7 = 1 indicates step mode active

5.1.3.10 NVRAM Address 0x0380–0x03ff, Reserved

5.1.3.11 NVRAM Address 0x0400–0x07ff, IPL ROM Diag, & Scratch pad area (1kb)

■ Written by: IPL ROM

■ Read by: IPL ROM

■ 0x0400–0x07ff IPL ROM Work Area (1 KB)

 – 0x0400–0x0403   4 byte validity ID (ASCII "IPLR", 0x49504c52)
 – 0x0404–0x04ff   Reserved
 – 0x0500–0x06ff   Diagnostics config table
 – 0x0700–0x0723   Service Mode Previous Boot Device
 – 0x0724–0x07f5   Reserved
 – 0x07f6–0x07fb   Ethernet Randomized Network Address
 – 0x07fc–0x07ff   CRC value for IPL ROM Work Area

5.1.3.12 NVRAM Address 0x0800–0x1fff, Dynamically Controlled Software Area (6 KB)

■ Written by: NVRAM DD

■ Read by: IPL ROM, NVRAM DD

■ Current Utilization:

 – NVRAM DD allocation structures
 – Fatal error log information (512 bytes)
 – Dump status area (64 bytes)
 – 0x0800–0x13ff Manufacturing run-in test posr return codes
 – 0x1400–0x17ff IPL ROM Work Area 2 (1 KB) Written/Read by IPL ROM

   ■ 0x1400 – 0x1403   4 byte validity ID (ASCII "IPLR", 0x49504c52)

   ■ 0x1404 – 0x17fb   reserved for IPL ROM

   ■ 0x17fc– 0x17ff CRC   value for IPL ROM Work Area 2

5.1.3.13 NVRAM Usage Summary

The common NVRAM area usage is summarized in Table 22 on page 56. The OCS/SP usage is summarized in Table 23 on page 57. The non-OCS/SP usage is summarized in Table 24 on page 58.

Offset	Size	Description
0x0000–0x0003	4 bytes	Reserved
0x0004–0x0007	4 bytes	NVRAM size
0x0008–0x000b	4 bytes	NVRAM initialization data
0x000c–0x000f	4 bytes	Pointer to dynamic software area
0x0010–0x001f	16 bytes	SCSI initiator address for slots 1 – 16
0x0020–0x00ff	224 bytes	Memory control and error registers, BUID 0, address 0x1000 – 0x10D0
0x0100–0x01fb	252 bytes	Remote BOOT information
0x01fc–0x01ff	4 bytes	IPL ROM BOOT state information save area
0x0200–0x0223	36 bytes	Normal mode previous boot device
0x4800–0x7fff	14 KB	Dynamically controlled software area (medialess)
0x4400–0x7fff	15 KB	Dynamically controlled software area (non-medials)
0x0224–0x0277	84 bytes	Normal mode BOOT device list
0x0278–0x02cb	84 bytes	Service mode BOOT device list
0x02cc–0x02f7	44 bytes	NVRAM device driver headers (no longer supported)
0x02f8–0x02f8	1 byte	TCW/TCE table size
0x02f9–0x02fb	3 bytes	Reserved
0x02fc–0x02ff	4 bytes	CRC for NVRAM area 0x0000 thru 0x02fb

Table 22. **NVRAM Usage (Common Area) Summary**

Offset	Size	Description
0x0300–0x0307	4 bytes	LED data mirrored
0x0308–0x030b	4 bytes	Checkstop count
0x030c–0x030f	4 bytes	Pointer to OCS/SP checkstop logout area
0x0310–0x0313	4 bytes	OCS code E/C level
0x0314–0x0317	4 bytes	OCS "seed" EPROM E/C level
0x0318–0x031b	4 bytes	Manufacturing control
0x031c–0x031f	4 bytes	Point to manufacturing data area
0x0320–0x035f	64 bytes	LED string output area
0x0360–0x0363	4 bytes	Pointer to OCS code execution area
0x0364–0x0367	4 bytes	Pointer to OCS work area
0x0368–0x037b	20 bytes	Machine check save area
0x037c–0x037f	4 bytes	OCS/RS command interface
0x0380–0x03ff	128 bytes	OCS information area
0x0400–0x43ff	16 KB	OCS transient work/code area
0x4400–0x47ff	1 KB	IPL ROM diagnostic BOOT save area (medialess)
0x4800–0x7fff	14 KB	Dynamically controlled software area (medialess)
0x4400–0x7fff	15 KB	Dynamically controlled software area (non-medialess)

Table 23. **NVRAM Usage (OCS/SP Implementations)**

Offset	Size	Description
0x0300–0x0303	4 bytes	LED data mirrored
0x0304–0x0317	20 bytes	Reserved
0x0318–0x031b	4 bytes	Manufacturing control
0x031c–0x031f	4 bytes	Point to manufacturing data area
0x0320–0x035f	64 bytes	LED string output area
0x0360–0x0363	4 bytes	Manufacturing information
0x0364–0x0367	4 bytes	IPL ROM supported LED string output pointer
0x0368–0x037b	20 bytes	Machine check save area
0x037c–0x037f	4 bytes	LED step interface
0x0380–0x03ff	128 bytes	Reserved
0x0400–0x07ff	1 KB	IPL ROM diagnostic and scratch pad area
0x0800–0x1fff	6 KB	Dynamically controlled software area

Table 24. **NVRAM Usage (NON-OCS/SP Implementations)**

Bus Unit Controller (BUC) Architecture

Figure 2 on page 60 illustrates the logical view of RISC System/6000 PowerPC systems. The system interconnect allows for the transfer of data among the various components of the system: the processor, memory, I/O attached via a Bus Unit Controller (BUC) which is directly attached to the system interconnect, and the Micro Channel Input/Output (I/O) bus via the I/O Channel Controller (IOCC). For information on the architecture of the IOCC, see the Section "IOCC Architecture," beginning on page 75. There may also be System Bus(es) generated from the processor chip set or memory controller to which BUCs are attached. The system interconnect may be one of several different constructs (for example, a System Bus, a switch, etc.) and is system dependent. Any given system may or may not have an IOCC and may or may not have a BUC, but shall have at least one of these. The IOCC can be thought of as an implementation of a BUC for a specific application, namely that of providing a Micro Channel bus on a system.

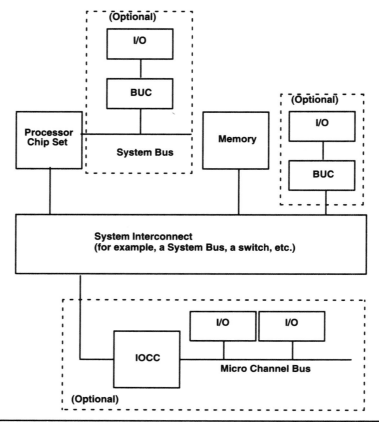

Figure 2. **System block diagram**

6.1 BUC Addressing

A BUC can be designed such that a program can gain access to its address space by one of several approaches:

■ A BUC design can allow access only for addresses with the T bit set to a 1 (the T bit is in the Segment Register (SR), for 32-bit machines, or in the Segment Table Entry (STE), for 64-bit machines). This is sometimes called addressing by direct-store segments. See *PowerPC Architecture* (book III), "Storage Segments" for additional information. The device address space for T=1 is partitioned into 16 segments of 256 megabytes (MB) each for a total of 4 gigabytes (GB) of address space per BUID (see Figure 6 on page 67).

■ A BUC design can allow access only for addresses with the T bit set to a 0. This is sometimes called addressing by ordinary segments or sometimes referred to as memory mapped addressing. For T=0 access, the "System Memory Map" is described in Section 3.1 on page 7.

■ A BUC design can allow access for addresses with both T=0 and T=1.

There are a number of differences in the designs for the T=0 and T=1 cases. This book does not go into details on all of the differences, instead, it only describe the architectural differences (there are implementation differences also).

SRs (32-bit machines) or STEs (64-bit machines) provide access authority to the BUC address spaces for I/O Load and Store instructions. They are protected resources within the system and generally cannot be changed except by the Operating System.

The architectural differences for BUCs which get addressed with T=0 versus T=1 fall into several categories:

■ SR or STE definition

■ Protection mechanisms

■ Error reporting

In addition, a BUC can be designed to operate in a 32-bit machine or a 64-bit machine. Architectural differences between 32-bit and 64-bit machines include:

■ Use of SRs (32-bit machines) versus STEs (64-bit machines)

■ Use of 32-bit TCEs (32-bit machines) versus 64-bit TCEs (64-bit machines) because a longer Real Page Number (RPN) is needed in 64-bit machines

These items are discussed in following sections.

6.1.1 Addressing with T=0 (Memory Mapped or Ordinary Segments)

BUCs which are addressed with T=0 have their address spaces mapped into the physical memory address space. These devices are addressed like any other piece of memory. For an example of a memory controller implementation, refer to the Appendix on page 243.

Engineering Note

Some *systems* may not allow for both T=0 and T=1 I/O, and so BUC designs should take into consideration the architecture of the *systems* in which they may be used.

Engineering Note

Most T=0 I/O shall be set up such that the pages to which the Load or Store operations are done are marked as cache inhibited. However, for the case where the I/O is performed to cached pages, care must be taken in design of the BUC to take the coherency scheme into account, and to not use Store data before it is guaranteed to be good.

6.1.1.1   SR (32-Bit Machines) and STE (64-Bit Machines) Definitions for T=0

The SR and STE definition for T=0 addressing is described in the *PowerPC Architecture* (book III).

6.1.1.2   BUC Protection Mechanism for T=0

The processor's storage protection scheme which protects accesses to memory applies for T=0 memory access. Refer to the *PowerPC Architecture* (book III) "Storage Protection" for more information regarding storage protection.

6.1.1.3   BUC Error Reporting for T=0

Some systems and BUCs may not have a way of recovering from a T=0 error. See the appropriate BUC Architectures for more information.   BUC Architectures must be defined to assure that errors which might cause data integrity problems are not allowed to propagate, and this may mean producing an unrecoverable error like a checkstop. "Unrecoverable errors" are those that can not be recovered without taking down the Operating System and rebooting the machine.

Note

T=1 Load and Store operations are inherently non-cached.

On a Load instruction, SR bits 3 to 31 or STE Dword 1 bits 0 to 63 shall be returned by the hardware as the same value that software previously stored into them with a Store instruction.

6.1.2   Addressing with T=1 (Direct-Store Segments)

BUCs which are addressed with T=1 have their address spaces disjoint from the physical memory address space. These devices use a Bus Unit ID (BUID) in the SR or STE for addressing of the BUC in order to get this disjoint address space.

6.1.2.1   SR (32-Bit Machines) and STE (64-Bit Machines) Definitions for T=1

The SR and STE definition for T=1 addressing is shown in Figure 3 on page 63.

For more details on the processor-specific fields, see the *PowerPC Architecture* (book III). Table 25 on page 64 details the usage of the SR and STE bits.

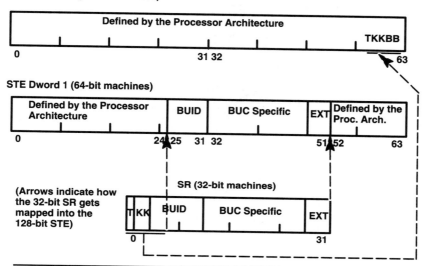

Figure 3.   SR and STE definition for T=1

6.1.2.2   BUC Protection Mechanism for T=1

It is recommended that all BUC implementations make BUC facilities
(registers, commands, and other addressing spaces) accessible to Load and
Store instructions from the system processor only when the applicable K bit in
the SR or STE is set to a value of 0. There are actually two K bits in the SR or
STE; these are the supervisory state storage key bit and the problem state
storage key bit. Throughout this document the phrase "applicable K bit" is used
to mean the K bit which is being used by the processor at the time it is executing
the Load or Store instruction. In BUCs which use the applicable K bit in this
way for protection, if the BUC facilities are accessed with the K bit set to a value
of 1, a Data Storage Interrupt (DSI) with invalid operation error status shall be
sent to the processor which issued the I/O Load or Store instruction for logging
into that processor's Data Storage Interrupt Error Register (DSIER). BUCs
may also choose to implement other protection mechanisms in addition to, or
instead of, the K bit protection mechanism.

SR Bit	STE Bit Dword 0	Dword 1	Description
–	0–35	–	Effective Segment ID
–	36–55	–	Defined by the Processor Architecture
–	56	–	Valid bit
0	57	–	T bit: Direct-store segment bit. Set equal to a value of 1 for this definition of the SR and STE.
1	58	–	K_s bit: Supervisory state storage key (see note). This bit is sent to the BUC if the processor is in the supervisory state when the Load or Store instruction takes place. The usage of this bit by the BUC is implementation dependent.
2	59	–	K_p bit: Problem state storage key. This bit is sent to the BUC if the processor is in the problem state when the Load or Store instruction takes place. The usage of this bit by the BUC is implementation dependent.
3–4	60–61	–	BUID (bits 0–1): These are the first 2 bits of the Bus Unit ID. These bits are placed on the bus during a T=1 Load or Store instruction, and are used by the BUCs to determine whether or not the Load or Store operation is directed towards them.
–	62–63	–	Defined by the Processor Architecture
–	–	0–24	Defined by the Processor Architecture
5–11	–	25–31	BUID (bits 2–8): These are the least significant 7 bits of the Bus Unit ID. These bits are placed on the bus during a T=1 Load or Store instruction, and used by the BUCs to determine whether or not the Load or Store operation is directed towards them.
12–27	–	32–47	BUC specific: These bits can be used by individual BUCs for their own purposes. Note that some of these bits may not be passed from the processor to the BUC, depending on the processor and system implementations (see Appendix beginning on page 233 for information on processor dependencies). The BUC specific fields should be defined by the documents defining the individual BUCs. For the IOCC, see Section 7.4.1.2, "IOCC SR (32-bit machines) and STE (64-bit machines) Definitions," on page 106.
28–31	–	48–51	EXT: Address extent field. These bits are appended to the low order 28 bits of the processor effective address to form the 32-bit I/O address. They are appended as the most significant bits of the 32-bit address.
–	–	52–63	Defined by the Processor Architecture

Table 25. **SR and STE Definition for T=1**

6.1.2.3 BUC Error Reporting for T=1

Errors which occur synchronously with the I/O Load or Store instruction being executed (that is, before a positive completion message is sent to the processor) shall result in a DSI with an appropriate error status which is sent to the processor which issued the I/O Load or Store instruction for logging into that processor's Data Storage Interrupt Error Register (DSIER). The DSIER has the following basic definition (see Section 3.3.1 on page 14 for additional information):

- One per processor

- In T=0 address space

- Holds the status of failing I/O Load and Store instructions

Some systems may not be able to recover from errors which occur asynchronously with the instruction execution (that is, which are not reported as a DSI for the Load or Store instruction which causes the error). This is implementation dependent. See the appropriate BUC Architectures for more information. System and BUC Architectures must be defined to assure that errors which might cause data integrity problems are not allowed to propagate, and this may mean producing an unrecoverable error, such as, a checkstop.

6.1.3 Load and Store Addressing Model

For T=0 accesses, the real address is generated the same way that it would be for any other memory access, and will not be discussed further in this section. For T=1 accesses, the 32-bit I/O address is formed by concatenating the least significant 28 bits of the effective address (bits 4 to 31 for 32-bit machines, or bits 36 to 63 for 64-bit machines) with the 4 extent (EXT) bits from the SR or STE. Figure 4 on page 66 illustrates this concatenation process for 32-bit machines and Figure 5 on page 66 illustrates this process for 64-bit machines.

By appending the four EXT bits to the 28 low order bits of the address, the device address space for T=1 is partitioned into 16 segments of 256 megabytes (MB) each for a total of 4 gigabytes (GB) of address space per BUID (see Figure 6 on page 67). Separate SRs or STEs must be used to address adjacent segments. Results of crossing a T=1 segment boundary with a single Load or Store operation is implementation dependent, and may be dependent on the implementation of both the processor and the BUC.

Engineering Note

BUCs should be designed to take into account that PowerPC processors expect BUCs to provide data for an entire Load instruction operation, even if an exception occurs on the load operation. Failure to provide data can result in stale data being clocked into the processor registers, and present a data security problem. The data provided can be all-1's, all-0's, or other data (as long as there is not security exposure with the data being provided), and should have good parity.

Note

Some BUCs may use one or more of the BUC specific bits in the SR or STE to create additional address spaces.

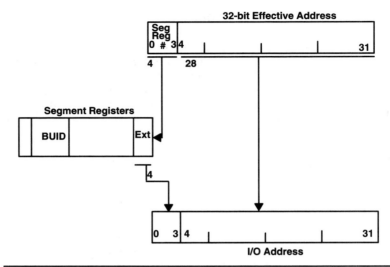

Figure 4.   Creation of the I/O address for 32-bit machines (T=1)

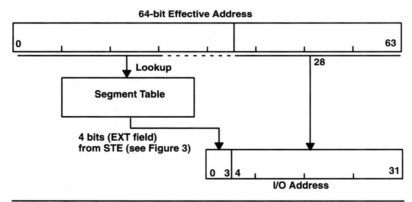

Figure 5.   Creation of the I/O address for 64-bit machines (T=1)

6.1.3.1   BUC Control Address Spaces

Most of the BUC address spaces shall have some of their address space designated for control purposes. Results of attempts to access control address spaces in the BUCs which are "reserved," see Section 1.2.1 on page 2, will depend on the architecture of the BUC. For T=0 BUCs, the result shall be the data being ignored on a Store instruction and returned as a 0 on a Load instruction. For T=1 BUCs, the result will either be a DSI or the data being

ignored on a Store instruction and returned as a 0 on a Load instruction. A Load
or Store instruction which starts in an unimplemented address space and spills
over into an implemented address space will be treated as if all of the operation
had accessed unimplemented addresses. A Load or Store instruction which
starts in an implemented address space and spills over into an unimplemented
address space will have implementation dependent results.

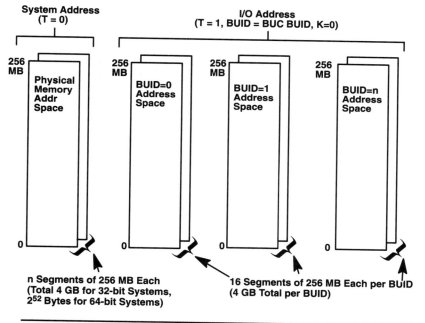

Figure 6.   **Addressing model for Load and Store instructions**

6.1.3.2   Load with Reservation and Store Conditional Instructions

BUCs are not required to support atomic reservation type operations like those
provided by the following processor instructions:

■ Load Word and Reserve Indexed (*lwarx*)

■ Load Doubleword and Reserve Indexed (*ldarx*)

■ Store Word Conditional Indexed (*stwcx*)

■ Store Doubleword Conditional Indexed (*stdcx*)

6.1.4 BUC Translation Control Entry (TCE)

TCEs are kept in system memory and are used by the BUC for Direct Memory Address (DMA) real memory access.

The TCE mechanism in a BUC provides a facility to translate accesses from the BUC's address space into the real system memory address space. This allows data to be scattered throughout the real memory pages, but to have a contiguous virtual memory address space mapped to a continuous BUC address space (that is, the TCE provides a scatter and gather type of operation). In addition, the TCE provides for some BUC specific bits which can be used by the BUC for various purposes (for example, the IOCC uses some of the bits to provide Load and Store access protection, and some for bus master page mapping control). TCEs are optional and not all BUCs need to implement TCEs, but those BUCs which do implement TCEs should define them as shown in Figure 7 and Table 26 on page 69.

TCEs are located in system memory. For performance reasons, most BUC implementations will also contain a local copy of the TCE in the BUC. The BUC shall keep its local TCE copy or copies (its cached copies) coherent with the copy in system memory. The BUC shall use the TCE in effect at the time a request was issued.

A BUC is not required to maintain consistency with its own internal TCE cache (if any) when DMAing into its own TCE table area.

Figure 7 on page 68 shows the TCE layout for both 32-bit and 64-bit machines. For 32-bit TCEs, the TCEs will be adjacent to one another in the table with no gaps in between (that is, there will be two TCEs per doubleword of storage).

Engineering Note

Data coherency and TCE coherency are related. If software issues a Store instruction to a TCE such that the BUC must invalidate any copy of that TCE in a BUC cache or buffer, then if any data associated with the page represented by that TCE is in a BUC cache or buffer, it must be written to system memory, if modified, and invalidated if modified or not. Only after any associated data in the cache is flushed and/or invalidated can the TCE be invalidated.

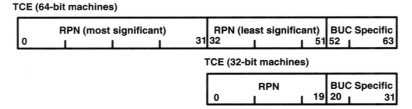

TCE (64-bit machines)

| RPN (most significant) 0 ... 31 | RPN (least significant) 32 ... 51 | BUC Specific 52 ... 63 |

TCE (32-bit machines)

| RPN 0 ... 19 | BUC Specific 20 ... 31 |

Figure 7.   **TCE layout**

32-Bit TCE	64-Bit TCE	Description
–	0–31	RPN: The most significant bits of the Real Page Number (RPN) when operating with a 64-bit TCE. In certain BUC implementations, all of these bits may not be required.
0–19	32–51	RPN: The least significant bits of the RPN when operating with 64-bit TCEs, or the entire RPN when operating with 32-bit TCEs.
20–31	52–63	BUC specific: can be used by individual BUCs for their own purposes. If these bits are not used by a particular BUC implementation, then they shall be treated as reserved bits, see Section 1.2.1 on page 2.

Table 26. **TCE Bit Definitions**

6.1.5 BUC TCE Address Register

This register specifies the starting address and size of the TCE table in system memory. This register is set up by the IPL ROM code or the device configuration code before enabling the BUC to DMA, and should not be changed thereafter. This register will only exist in the BUC if the BUC implements TCEs. If the BUC implements TCEs, then it must also implement this register.

Figure 8 on page 70 illustrates the BUC TCE Address register, Tables 27 on page 70 and 28 on page 70 define the fields within this register. This register is a 2-word register. Word 0 will only exist in 64-bit implementations. In 32-bit implementations, word 0 will not exist and attempts to access word 0 will have the same results as accessing any other "reserved" address (see Section 6.1.3.1, "BUC Control Address Space," on page 66). In 64-bit implementations, the register will always have two words, even if the implementation has a 32-bit mode of operation and is switched to the 32-bit mode.

The BUC specific fields in the TCE should be defined by the documents defining the individual BUCs.

The BUC TCE Address register resides in the BUC address space, and the address of the register is defined by the architecture of the BUC.

The value of the data in the BUC TCE Address register at startup time is indeterminate. The IPL ROM code or the device configuration code should initialize this register before enabling the BUC to start DMA.

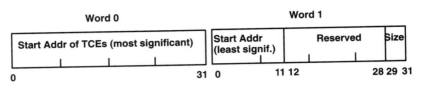

Figure 8. **BUC TCE Address register**

Bit Definitions	Description
0–31	TCE Table Starting Address: These bits compose the most significant bits of the real page number in system memory of the starting address of the TCE table when operating with 64-bit TCEs. In certain BUC implementations, all of these bits may not be required.

Table 27. **TCE Address Register Bit Definitions for Word 0**

Bit Definitions	Description
0–11	TCE Table Starting Address: These bits compose the least significant bits of the real page number in system memory of the starting address of the TCE table when operating with 64-bit TCEs, or the complete address for 32-bit tables. Software must guarantee that the table starting address is aligned on an appropriate byte boundary, as defined in the table, below.
12–28	Reserved, see Section 1.2.1 on page 2.
29–31	Number of TCE Table Entries: These bits allow specification of the amount of system memory to be used for TCEs. Different applications require different amounts of TCE table, and the architecture allows this size to be varied. This provides the flexibility to optimize cost and function across a wide range of system applications. These bits are defined as follows:

Bit			Number of	Table Alignment
29	30	31	TCE Entries	Boundary
0	0	0	8 K	1 MB
0	0	1	16 K	1 MB
0	1	0	32 K	1 MB
0	1	1	64 K	1 MB
1	0	0	128 K	1 MB
1	0	1	256 K	2 MB
1	1	0	512 K	4 MB
1	1	1	1024 K	8 MB

The maximum number of TCEs supported by an implementation is implementation dependent and is presented to the software by the BUC in a software accessible register. In the IOCC hardware, this is in the IOCC Configuration register (see Section 7.4.5.2, "IOCC Configuration Register," on page 132).

Table 28. **TCE Address Register Bit Definitions for Word 1**

6.2 BUC Interrupt Structure

The mechanism used to manage BUC external interrupts consists of several registers. One of these is common to all BUCs, some are specific to the individual BUC architectures, and some are system level registers. The register which must be common to all BUCs is described in this section. The registers which are unique to the IOCC architecture is described in Section 7.4.6, "IOCC Interrupt Structure," on page 137. The registers which are system level are documented in Section 3.2, "Architected System Registers" on page 10. The BUC structure is shown in Figure 9 on page 71. The system level interrupt structure is described in Section "External Interrupt Architecture," beginning on page 157.

The eXternal Interrupt Vector Registers (XIVRs) that are common to all BUCs have the following basic functions:

■ One per interrupt source in each BUC.

■ Up to a maximum of 16 per BUID (a BUC which has more than 16 sources requires the use of more than one BUID for the BUC, and the multiple BUIDs must be consecutive).

■ In T=0 or T=1 address space, depending on the BUC implementation.

■ Provides a table lookup of the interrupt priority for each external interrupt.

■ Provides a interrupt server affinity field for each external interrupt.

The XIVR is described in more detail in Section 6.2.2 on page 72.

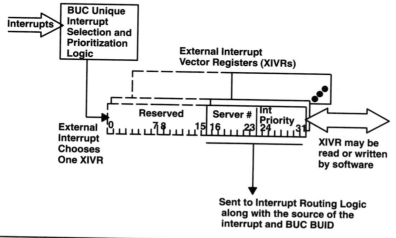

Figure 9.   **BUC interrupt structure**

6.2.1 BUC Interrupt Scenario

When an interrupt comes in to a BUC (or when a BUC generates an interrupt internally), the following happens:

■ The BUC unique logic selects and prioritizes the external interrupt(s) for that BUC. When an external interrupt is selected, this interrupt is used to select one of the External Interrupt Vector Register(s) (for a BUC which supports only one interrupt, only one XIVR will be implemented).

■ The XIVR information is sent to the system interrupt routing logic, along with information about the interrupt source and BUC Bus Unit IDentification (BUID).

■ The interrupt may be rejected by the interrupt routing logic for various reasons. If the interrupt is rejected and the condition which generated the interrupt has not been reset, then the hardware must try to re-present that interrupt at a later time.

■ Even after the interrupt is accepted by the system, it may be rejected by the interrupt routing layer at a later time. This could happen, for example, if the software issues a Store instruction to the Current Processor Priority Register (CPPR) with a priority which is more favored than the previously accepted interrupt priority. If this rejection happens, then the BUC must re-present that interrupt to the system if the external interrupt is still active (that is, has not been reset by the software or has been reset but the device has raised the interrupt again).

6.2.2 External Interrupt Vector Register (XIVR)

Each BUC contains one External Interrupt Vector Register for each external interrupt that it will support. The bits in each of these registers are defined in Table 29.

These registers reside in the BUC address space, and the addresses of these registers are defined by the architecture of the BUC.

The value of the data in these registers at startup time is indeterminate. The IPL ROM code shall initialize these registers before enabling interrupts for the BUC.

Bits	Description
0–15	Reserved, see Section 1.2.1 on page 2.
16–23	Interrupt Server Number: This determines to which interrupt service queue in the system that the interrupt should be vectored.
24–31	Interrupt Priority: This field specifies what priority should be assigned to the incoming interrupt.

Table 29. **XIVR Register Description**

6.2.3 End Of Interrupt (EOI) Command

Following the presentation of an I/O interrupt to the system, the BUC must automatically mask off that particular interrupt signal so the presentation is made only once. An "End Of Interrupt" (EOI) command unmasks a particular interrupt signal so that it can interrupt again, when it is active. An EOI command is issued to the BUC by software issuing either a load instruction or a store instruction to the BUC. On a Store instruction, the data is ignored. On a load instruction, the data is indeterminate. This command may be issued following the interrupt service, once the interrupt has been reset at the source. This command performs exactly the same function as the interrupt rejection mechanism (see also the information on the system level interrupt registers, Section 9.1.1 starting on page 159), and if the interrupt has not been reset at its source, then interrupt will be re-presented to the system.

The interrupt number field in the address of this command indicates the level of interrupt to be unmasked.

This command is implementation dependent. BUCs which don't present interrupts to the system do not need to implement this command. BUCs which do present interrupts to the system must implement an EOI command.

6.3 BUC Data Consistency and Ordering Requirements

Different BUCs can have varying needs for data coherency (coherency not necessarily implying any ordering requirement) or consistency (consistency implying an ordering requirement) due to differing expressed or implied architectural assumptions of the entities (devices, buses, etc.) that they are controlling. Individual BUC architectures should specify the level of coherency or consistency support that they require from the hardware. When the processor is accessing the same page as an I/O Direct Memory Access (DMA) operation or when it is accessing a Translation Control Entry (TCE) in system memory, software must set the memory coherency bit (M) to a value of 1 for that page otherwise the hardware will not maintain coherency.

Engineering Note

Some system implementations might call for the i-cache to be kept consistent by the hardware. In such systems, the system design must take into consideration the data which is in transit at any given time (for example, data in system queues must be visible to the coherency mechanism).

Architects and designers (BUC and System) should be aware that consistency is no easy matter, and should be given careful consideration in the development process.

An example of a BUC ordering requirement is that the IOCC requires that data be strongly ordered; i.e., writes from a Micro Channel device must appear coherent in the same order as the data is written (that is the requirement is consistency, not just coherency). The IOCC also is required to make the data consistent to all mechanisms, including the i-cache fetch mechanism. For more information on the IOCC requirements, see the Section "IOCC Architecture," beginning on page 75.

This IOCC example, may not be representative of other BUC requirements.

Most BUC architectures will require that data be kept coherent by the hardware (the BUC hardware and/or the system hardware). When the hardware is required to keep the I/O data coherent, there is also a good chance that there will also be an ordering requirement (that is, the BUC will be required to keep the data consistent, and not just coherent).

In addition to the requirement of some BUCs to make the data coherent in the same order as was originally written, there may also be timing considerations relative to I/O operation completion event. For example, the I/O operation completion event might be an external interrupt or a polled entity like a status completion block in system memory or a location in the BUC's address space. Care must be taken in the system to assure that the I/O operation complete event which signals the completion of a data write operation does not get serviced, and the data accessed by the software, before the data which was being written becomes consistent to the mechanism which is going to use the data.

Care must be taken when designing a BUC which will be used to transfer instruction code pages. PowerPC processor hardware implementations are not required to keep the i-cache coherent with changes to memory or data caches, even if the page is marked as coherence required (the M bit in the PTE set to a value of 1). As a result, some processors will not indicate coherence required when they perform an i-cache fetch. The result is that the system may not even make the i-cache fetch visible to some BUCs in the system. Thus, if a BUC is going to be used to transfer code pages, it should have a mechanism to assure the data is in a place which is visible to the i-cache fetches of the processor(s) in the system before a processor tries to access that data via an i-cache fetch (which probably means it must be flushed into system memory). This mechanism must not be visible to the software (that is, the software shall not have to do anything special to flush the data from the I/O cache or buffer). If the operation is interrupt driven, then an acceptable mechanism is to keep the interrupt, which is signaling the completion of the operation, in order with the data; the interrupt is not presented to the software until the data is made visible to the i-fetch mechanism. If the operation is a polled operation (with the polled completion block being in system memory), then one mechanism which is acceptable is to make all data globally visible to all mechanisms in the same order as the device has written the data.

IOCC Architecture

The RISC System/6000 PowerPC Input/Output Channel Controller (IOCC) Architecture is a special case of the BUC architecture as it relates to the Micro Channel bus support functions for Load and Store instructions, interrupt, and channel control. A number of feature I/O slots are associated with the IOCC for pluggable I/O devices.

The IOCC Architecture allows certain variations of function and performance to optimize its usage across multiple IOCC designs and machine environments. The specific personalization is established with the contents of the IOCC Configuration register (See Section 7.4.5.2, "IOCC Configuration Register," on page 132).

7.1 System Structure

Figure 10 on page 78 illustrates a logical view of the RISC System/6000 PowerPC IOCC. Functions provided by the IOCC include data buffering, address translation, Direct Memory Access (DMA), and interrupt support.

The Operating System can access all system facilities, including, virtual memory, system memory, Micro Channel bus I/O, bus memory, and the IOCC. The IOCC contains special facilities needed by the system for translation, and other functions.

Mapping of a virtual address to a system memory address is managed via the translation mechanism associated with the processor chip set. The Operating

Note

This chapter uses the abbreviated signal names as they appear in the *IBM Personal System/2 Hardware Interface Technical Reference–Architectures* (S84F-9808) document; for example, 'cd chrdy' represents 'card channel ready'.

System grants conditional access authority to processes, allowing the processes to access the Micro Channel bus memory, the I/O, and to the IOCC facilities.

The IOCC Architecture includes the definition of 16 independent I/O channels. One channel (0xf) is used by the system master for Load and Store transfers, leaving 15 that can be programmed for bus master transfers. The number of channels that can be programmed for DMA slave transfers is implementation dependent. (See Section 7.4.5.2, "IOCC Configuration Register," on page 132). A "bus master" is a Micro Channel device that contains its own direct memory access controller. A "DMA slave" is a Micro Channel device that requires the system to provide the direct memory access control.

A bus master on the Micro Channel bus can access bus memory and bus I/O. Pages in the bus memory address space are mapped to system memory by the Bus Mapping register which allow for mapping ranges of pages to system memory (see Section 7.4.5.7, "Bus Mapping Register," on page 136). Mapped pages are checked for proper access authority (writes to read only pages are not allowed) before allowing an access to proceed. Since the IOCC cannot intercept or stop accesses from a bus master to bus attached memory or bus I/O devices, no access checking is performed when a bus master addresses devices on the Micro Channel bus.

The IOCC DMA slave controller provides a convenient mechanism for moving data between an I/O device and system or bus memory. It provides addressing and control functions on behalf of the I/O device.

Most processor accesses to system memory go through the processor data cache. When sharing system memory areas with I/O devices, hardware must maintain the consistency among the processor data cache, the system memory, and any I/O buffers or I/O cache for all I/O operations (Load and Store instructions and DMA). When the processor is accessing the same page as an I/O DMA operation or when it is accessing a Translation Control Entry (TCE) in system memory, software must set the memory coherent bit (M) to a 1 for that page otherwise the hardware will not maintain coherency. Valid combinations of the write through (W), cache inhibit (I), and M bits in these cases are 0b001, 0b011, or 0b101.

The fact that the hardware must keep the data consistent among the processor data cache, the system memory, and any I/O buffers or cache for all I/O operations has important implications. The following is meant to give an indication of some of the considerations for consistency, but should not be construed, in any way, to weaken the requirement of the hardware to keep the data consistent (with the only requirement of software being to set the wim bits appropriately). One implication of hardware enforced consistency is that hardware must guarantee that the data appears consistent in the same order that the device on the Micro Channel bus has written the data (for example, if the device writes to address x and then to address y, then the data written to address x must be guaranteed to be consistent to the software before, or at the same time as, the data written to address y). Another implication is that it is hardware's responsibility to keep the I/O data consistent under all conditions. PowerPC processor implementations are not required to keep the i–cache consistent with changes to memory or data caches, even if the page is marked as coherence required (the m bit in the PTE set to a value of 1). As a result, some processors will not indicate coherence required when they perform an i–cache fetch. The result is that the system may not even make the i–cache fetch visible to the IOCC. Thus, since the IOCC is going to be used to transfer code pages, it must have a mechanism to flush the data to a point which is visible to the i–cache fetch mechanism (call it the point of global visibility) of the processor(s) in the system before a processor tries to access that data via an i–cache fetch. In most systems the point of global visibility will be system memory. This mechanism must not be visible to the software (that is, the software shall not have to do anything special to flush the data from the I/O cache or buffer). Additionally, the IOCC hardware must take into consideration the fact that the I/O operation complete event from the device, which signals completion of the write to the software, could be any of several mechanisms (for example, an external interrupt or a polled status completion block in system memory).

Programming Note

If the virtual mapping has real-time dependencies, then the software designer should consider "pinning" the appropriate pages, that is, forcing the appropriate pages to stay in system memory.

7.1.1 Virtual Memory

Virtual memory is a large address space containing logical system objects such as programs and data. Each object is assigned a unique address in the virtual memory space at the time of creation and this address is used thereafter to reference that object.

Virtual memory objects are mapped to system memory on a demand basis. At the time of reference by a system or user program, the translate unit associated with the processor chip set verifies whether that object is currently in system memory and, if so, supplies the appropriate (real) memory address. If not in system memory, the Operating System is called to obtain the requested object, place it in system memory, and update the tables used by the translate unit. The original faulting instruction is then retried and control is returned to the original system or user program.

The Translation Control Entry (TCE) mechanism in the IOCC provides a facility to translate accesses from the Micro Channel Address space into the real system memory address space. This allows data to be scattered throughout the real memory pages, but to have a contiguous virtual memory address space mapped to a continuous Micro Channel address space (that is, provides a scatter and gather type of operation).

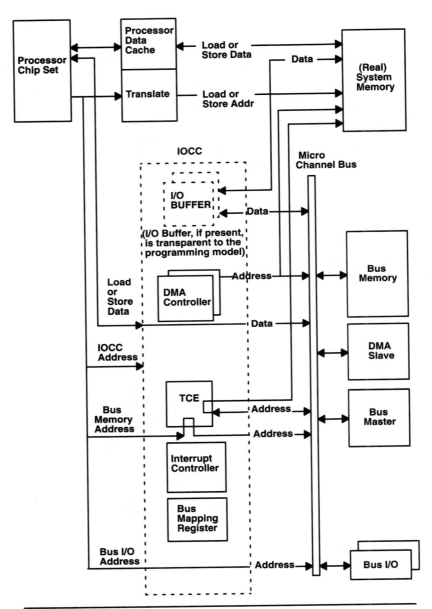

Figure 10.   **Programming model**

7.1.2 System Memory

System memory is that memory closely associated with the processor chip set complex. The RISC System/6000 PowerPC architecture provides for up to 4 GB of system memory in 32-bit machines, and up to 2^{52} bytes in 64-bit machines.

7.1.2.1 Load and Store Instruction Access to System Memory

System memory is accessible with normal processor accesses with the T bit in the SR (32-bit machines) or STE (64-bit machines) set to a 0; these T=0 accesses do not involve the IOCC.

7.1.2.2 Bus Master Access to System Memory

Bus memory references made by the bus master are redirected to system memory by the TCE mechanism and the Bus Mapping register. Accesses to system memory are translated before allowing them to proceed. This mapping of bus addresses to system memory is transparent to the requesting bus master. See Section 7.4.2, "Bus Master," on page 115 for more information, in general, and Figure 27 on page 117 for the address model for bus master operations.

7.1.2.3 DMA Slave Access to System Memory

DMA slave accesses are directed to system memory via the TCE mechanism and bits in the Channel Status Register (CSR). The Bus Mapping register does not get involved for DMA slave operations. See Section 7.4.3, "DMA Slave," on page 119 for additional information and Figure 31 on page 122 for the address model for DMA slave operations.

7.1.3 Bus Memory and Bus I/O Address Space

Bus memory is the memory that logically resides on the Micro Channel bus. The Micro Channel bus includes 32 address bits, providing up to 4 GB of addressability. Bus memory is generally packaged on feature I/O cards and is associated with specific devices. Devices are generally mapped into the bus memory space when they have large addressability requirements, such as video display buffers and floating-point work space.

The Micro Channel bus includes a special address space for accessing I/O control registers in Micro Channel devices. It includes 16 address bits and provides up to 64 KB of addressability. I/O devices do not decode address bits A31 to A16 and these address bits are considered undefined for I/O devices. Note that the addressing nomenclature for the Micro Channel bus is little-endian format (see Appendix "Big-Endian and Little-Endian Tutorial,"

on page 293 and Section 7.2, "Bit and Byte Numbering Conventions," on page
82.

7.1.3.1   Load and Store Instruction Access to Bus Memory and I/O

The IBM family compatible buses have separate address spaces for bus
memory addresses and bus I/O address spaces. When accessing bus memory
and I/O via Load and Store instructions in RISC System/6000 PowerPC
systems, these two address spaces are mapped together. Also mapped into this 4
GB address space are part of the IOCC facilities at addresses from 64 KB up to
(but not including) an address of 512 KB (see Section 7.1.4, "IOCC Facilities,"
on page 81 for more information about IOCC facilities, and Figures 23 on page
105 and 24 on page 105 to see how the Load and Store address space is mapped).
These address spaces are differentiated from each other via an address decode
as illustrated in Figure 23 on page 105. Bus memory is referenced when the
Load or Store instruction effective address is 512 KB and above and the
Alternate IOCC Address Space bit in the SR or STE is set to a 0. Bus I/O is
referenced when the Load or Store instruction effective address is less than 64
KB. See Section 7.4.1, "Load and Store Instructions," on page 104 for more
information about Load and Store operations.

The Micro Channel bus memory and I/O address space is accessible to Load
and Store instructions from the system processor with the T bit in the SR or STE
set to a 1. Load and Store accesses to bus memory and I/O are protected by
several protection mechanisms. See Section 7.4.1.3, "Load and Store
Authority Checking," on page 109 for more information on these protection
mechanisms.

7.1.3.2   Bus Master Access to Bus Memory and I/O

When a bus master is accessing bus memory and I/O, it has control of the
'M/IO' signal line on the Micro Channel bus, and therefore has access to the
entire 4 GB of bus memory address space, with the I/O space being entirely
disjoint from the bus memory space. Any bus master on the Micro Channel bus
has unconditional access to other devices on the Micro Channel bus if the access
is to bus memory and those devices have their memory address space marked as
not being mapped to system memory by the Bus Mapping register or if the I/O
address space is being accessed. In such cases, accesses are unprotected; the
IOCC just acts as a bus monitor (looking for address parity errors), allowing the
operation to continue if the channel is enabled. See Section 7.4.2, "Bus
Master," on page 115 for more information.

7.1.3.3   DMA Slave Access to Bus Memory and I/O

The address map for DMA slaves accessing Bus Memory is illustrated in Figure
31 on page 122. On DMA slave accesses to the Micro Channel bus, the access

shall always be to the bus memory address space of 0 to 4 GB. Bus I/O space is not accessible to DMA slave operations. See Section 7.4.3, "DMA Slave," on page 119 for more information about DMA slave operations.

7.1.4 IOCC Facilities

IOCC Facilities are special addresses in the IOCC Load and Store instruction address space (for specifics, see Section 7.4.1.1, "Address Spaces and Effective Addresses," beginning on page 104). The IOCC facilities are only accessible to Load and Store instructions from the system processor. Load and Store accesses to IOCC facilities are protected by several protection mechanisms. See Section 7.4.1.3, "Load and Store Authority Checking," on page 109 for more information on these protection mechanisms. These facilities are not accessible to bus master or DMA slave devices on the Micro Channel bus and the address space of these facilities does not reside in the address space of the bus master or DMA slave devices (see Figure 24 on page 105 for the Load and Store address model, Figure 27 on page 117 for the address model for bus master operations, and Figure 31 on page 122 for the address model for DMA slave operations).

7.1.4.1 IOCC Registers

IOCC registers are IOCC facilities managed by the system supervisor that control all aspects of the Load and Store instructions, channel, and interrupt operations. Refer to Section 7.4.5, "IOCC Registers," on page 130 for a description of these registers and Section 7.4.1.1, "Address Spaces and Effective Addresses," on page 104 for a description of how these registers are addressed.

7.1.4.2 IOCC Commands

IOCC commands are IOCC facilities used to change the state of the IOCC or control special bus actions. They take the form of Load and Store instructions to special (effective) addresses, where the addresses specify the actions to be taken. In most cases, the Load or Store processor instruction can be either string or non-string instructions. See Section 7.4.4, "IOCC Commands," on page 128 for more information.

7.2 Bit and Byte Numbering Conventions

Note

For a tutorial on big-endian and little-endian, see Appendix "Big-Endian and Little-Endian Tutorial," on page 293 and also the appendix of *PowerPC Architecture* (book I).

This section describes the big-endian and little-endian impacts on the IOCC Architecture.

7.2.1 Big-Endian and Little-Endian Mode Concurrency

The LE bit in the processor Special Purpose register controls the current mode of operation of the processor (LE=0 for big-endian and LE=1 for little-endian). There is also the concept of being able to change this bit on a more dynamic basis, namely at an interrupt boundary. In this book, however, only the requirement of switching the mode at boot time is being addressed.

7.2.2 Two Processor Implementations of Little-Endian Mode

There are currently two defined implementations of the PowerPC Architecture for the processor for the little-endian mode. For convenience, they are denoted as the True Little-Endian (TLE) and the Little-Endian via Address Modification (LE/AM) processor implementations. It is assumed, for discussion here, that what the IOCC sees, from the system perspective, is the same for both types of processors; namely, the TLE view. That is, for systems using LE/AM processors, the system shall store the data in memory in TLE format and Loads and Stores (to the IOCC, Micro Channel bus, or to system memory for data which will be accessed via DMA) shall look to the IOCC like Loads and Stores from a TLE processor.

7.2.3 I/O Load and Store Access from the Processor to the I/O

This section describes the big-endian and little-endian considerations when I/O is accessed via I/O Load and Store instructions.

7.2.3.1   I/O Load and Store Operations with LE=0 (Big-Endian Mode)

When performing I/O Load and Store instructions with LE=0, the *system* should be designed so that the Micro Channel bus and IOCC facilities are treated as big-endian entities. For example, for a 1-word Store operation, byte 0 of the register gets directed to byte 0 of the target (the Micro Channel bus or IOCC facility). Notice that if the target is a little-endian target (a little-endian register on a Micro Channel adapter, for example), then the software may need to make use of the Load or Store *Reverse* instructions to get the right data between the big-endian program and the little-endian target (see Section 7.2.3.3, "Programming Considerations," on page 87 for more details).

Figure 11 shows how the bytes get steered from the processor register to the bytes of an IOCC register internal to the IOCC, and Figure 12 on page 84 shows examples of how the bytes get steered from the processor register to the Micro Channel bus space. Figure 13 on page 85 is similar to Figure 12 except that it shows the effect of dynamic bus sizing when issuing a 4-byte Load or Store instruction to a 2-byte Micro Channel device. Dynamic bus sizing is described in Section 7.3.2.2, "Dynamic Bus Sizing" on page 98.

Note in Figure 12 that although the data bits require renaming in going from the big-endian format of the processor register to the little-endian format of the Micro Channel bus, the bits remain in the same sequence within the byte.

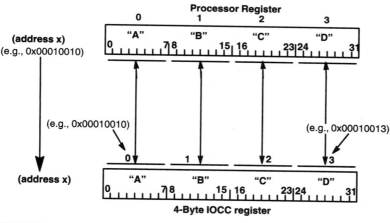

Figure 11. **Byte steering for an I/O Load or Store to an IOCC register (LE=0)**

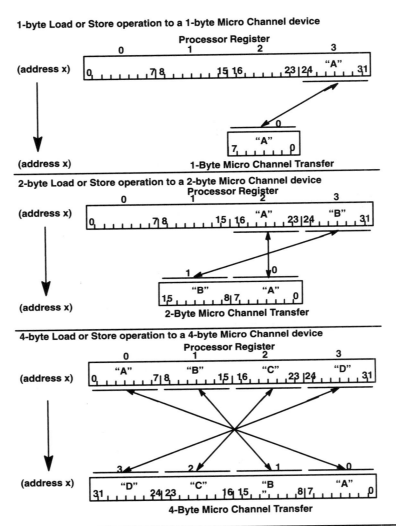

Figure 12. **Byte steering for an I/O Load or Store to a Micro Channel device (LE=0)**

4-byte Load or Store operation to a 2-byte Micro Channel device

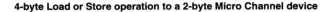

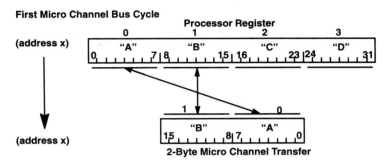

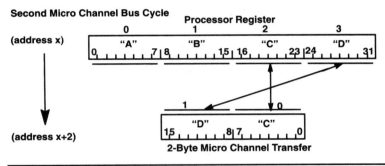

Figure 13. **Byte steering for an I/O Load or Store to a Micro Channel device (LE=0), showing dynamic bus sizing**

7.2.3.2   I/O Load and Store operations with LE=1 (Little-Endian Mode)

For I/O Load and Store operations performed with LE=1, the *system* should be designed so that the Micro Channel bus and IOCC facilities are treated as little-endian entities when the processor is running in the little-endian mode (LE=1). For example, for a 1-word Store operation, the left-most byte of the register (byte 0 of the register in big-endian format, byte 3 in little-endian format) gets directed to byte 3 of the target. Notice that if the target is a big-endian target (a register, for example), then the software may need to make use of the Load or Store *Reverse* instructions to get the right data to or from the little-endian register to the big-endian target (see Section 7.2.3.3, "Programming Considerations," on page 87 for more details). Since the TLE processor implementation itself does some of the byte steering, the byte steering that is done by the IOCC should be the same (given that everything else in the system is the same) as the IOCC steering required for the LE=0.

Note

The cross-over of data in the case of the IOCC registers is done for consistency with Micro Channel bus big-endian registers. See also Section 7.2.3.3, "Programming Considerations," on page 87.

Figure 14 on page 86 shows how the bytes get steered from the processor register to the bytes of an IOCC register internal to the IOCC, and Figure 15 on page 87 shows examples of how the bytes get steered from the processor register to the Micro Channel bus space. Note that the byte steering in Figure 14 looks different from the Figure 11 on page 83, but this is not due to a difference in the steering required by the IOCC, but rather it is due to the difference in steering provided by the processor.

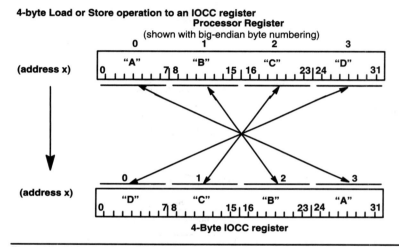

Figure 14. **Byte steering: I/O Load or Store to IOCC registers for LE=1**

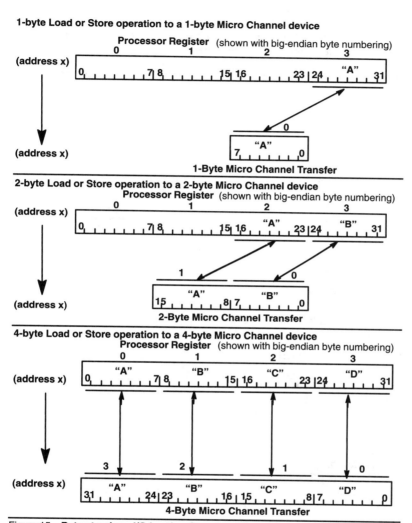

Figure 15. **Byte steering: I/O Load or Store to a Micro Channel device for LE=1**

7.2.3.3   Programming Considerations

There are two I/O Load/Store models for PowerPC, one for writing big-endian programs and one for writing little-endian programs. These two models are largely the same. The difference is that when running with LE=0, the hardware shall direct processor byte 0 to byte 0 of the Micro Channel bus, byte 1 to byte 1, etc., but when running in LE=1, the hardware shall assume a little-endian device or register and shall direct the bytes appropriately. Thus, when running in little-endian mode (LE=1), a Load or Store to a little-endian device on the Micro Channel would *not* require the Load or Store *Reverse* instructions, but a Load or Store to a big-endian device would not. This is shown in Table 30.

Target	LE=0	LE=1
IOCC register (big-endian)	Load or Store	Load or Store *Reverse*
TCE (big-endian)	Load or Store	Load or Store *Reverse*
Big-endian Micro Channel device	Load or Store	Load or Store *Reverse*
Little-endian Micro Channel device	Load or Store *Reverse*	Load or Store

Table 30. **Programming Considerations**

7.2.4   DMA Data Interchange Between I/O and Memory

This section deals with the DMA data paths and addressing for all DMA operations. DMA Slave and DMA for bus masters are treated the same.

Input/output, such as writing the contents of a memory page to disk, transfers a byte stream on both big-endian and little-endian systems. For a disk transfer, for example, byte 0 of the page is written to the first byte of the disk record and so on. Figure 16 on page 89 shows how the structure **s** would be mapped onto a disk device for the big-endian and true little-endian cases (assume that structure **s** starts at address 0).

For a PowerPC system running in big-endian mode with a big-endian memory, I/O transfers happen "naturally" because the byte that the processor sees as byte 0 is the same one that the storage subsystem sees as byte 0. Figure 16 shows that for a system with a TLE memory implementation with LE=1, that transfers would happen "naturally," also.

Example of a C structure (s), showing values of the elements

```
struct {
    int    a;    /*  0x11121314                        word        */
    long   b;    /*  0x2122232425262728                doubleword  */
    int    c;    /*  0x31323334                        word        */
    char   d[7]; /*  'A', 'B', 'C', 'D', 'E', 'F', 'G' array of bytes */
    short  e;    /*  0x5152                            halfword    */
    int    f;    /*  0x61626364                        word        */
} s;
```

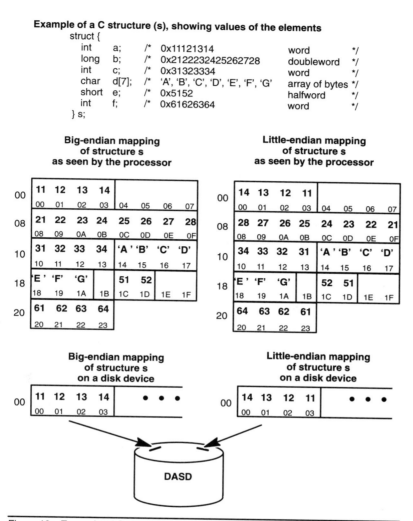

Figure 16. **Example of C structure, and the mapping of that structure on to a disk device**

7.2.4.1   DMA of LM=0 Stored Data

For the big-endian mode, during DMA, no translation is required; byte 0 is transferred to byte 0, and so on. Figure 17 on page 90 shows how the system must transfer data when handling big-endian format data.

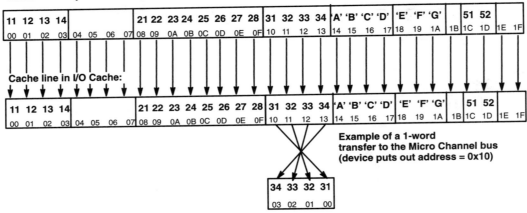

**Big-endian structure s
in big-endian memory or cache with LM=0**

Example of a cache line transfer to an I/O cache line in the IOCC and then to the Micro Channel device

Figure 17.   **Transfer of an LM=0 data structure via DMA**

7.2.4.2   DMA of LE=1 Stored Data

For systems where the memory controller or processor assures that the data gets stored in memory as true little-endian format when LE=1 (as shown in Figure 16 on page 89) and where there is no modification in going from the memory to the IOCC, then DMA transfers occur the same as for the LE=0 case (see Figure 18 on page 91).   No translation is required; byte 0 is transferred to byte 0, and so on.

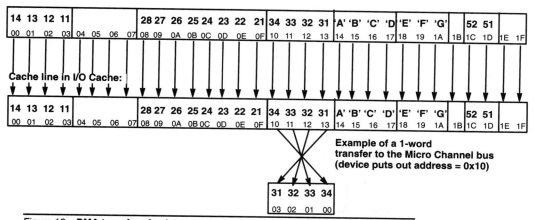

Figure 18. DMA transfer of a data structure written with LE=1 via a TLE processor

7.2.4.3   DMA Access of the TCE table

The TCE table is stored as a series of 1-word or 2-word scalars in big-endian format. The transfer of the TCE data occurs the same as it would for any data (see previous sections on DMA of stored data). Figure 19 on page 92 shows examples of accessing 1-word TCEs for LE=0 and LE=1 and Figure 20 on page 93 shows examples of accessing 2-word TCEs.

Programming Note

TCEs are always assumed to be in big-endian format in memory. That means software should use Load and Store *Reverse* instructions when building the TCE table in LE=1 mode (see Section 7.2.3.3, "Programming Considerations," on page 87).

Example of a 1-word TCE table structure (t1) showing values of the elements

```
struct {
   int    a;    /*  0x11121314        word    */
   int    b;    /*  0x21222324        word    */
   int    c;    /*  0x31323334        word    */
   int    d;    /*  0x41424344        word    */
   int    e;    /*  0x51525354        word    */
   int    f;    /*  0x61626364        word    */
   int    g;    /*  0x71727374        word    */
   int    h;    /*  0x81828384        word    */
} t1
```

**Structure t1 in big-endian memory
for LE=0 or for LE=1
with a TLE proc. implementation**

	11	12	13	14	21	22	23	24
00	00	01	02	03	04	05	06	07
	31	32	33	34	41	42	43	44
08	08	09	0A	0B	0C	0D	0E	0F
	51	52	53	54	61	62	63	64
10	10	11	12	13	14	15	16	17
	71	72	73	74	81	82	83	84
18	18	19	1A	1B	1C	1D	1E	1F

**(LE=1 tables built
with Store *Reverse*
Instructions)**

Example of accessing the third TCE in the table (offset 0x08 into the table)

Table in system memory:

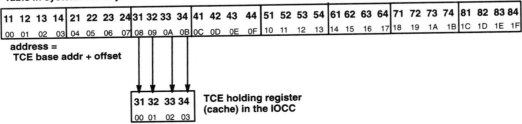

address =
TCE base addr + offset

31 32 33 34
00 01 02 03

**TCE holding register
(cache) in the IOCC**

Figure 19.   **TCE table access for 1-word TCEs**

Example of a 2-word TCE table structure (t2) showing values of the elements

```
struct {
    long   a;    /*  0x1112131415161718      doubleword   */
    long   b;    /*  0x2122232425262728      doubleword   */
    long   c;    /*  0x3132333435363738      doubleword   */
    long   d;    /*  0x4142434445464748      doubleword   */
} t2
```

**Structure t2 in big-endian memory with LE=0
or for LE=1 and TLE proc. implementation**

00	**11** 00	**12** 01	**13** 02	**14** 03	**15** 04	**16** 05	**17** 06	**18** 07
08	**21** 08	**22** 09	**23** 0A	**24** 0B	**25** 0C	**26** 0D	**27** 0E	**28** 0F
10	**31** 10	**32** 11	**33** 12	**34** 13	**35** 14	**36** 15	**37** 16	**38** 17
18	**41** 18	**42** 19	**43** 1A	**44** 1B	**45** 1C	**46** 1D	**47** 1E	**48** 1F

Example of accessing the third TCE in the table (offset 0x10 into the table)

Table in system memory:

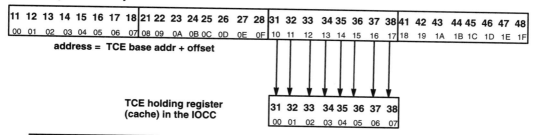

address = TCE base addr + offset

**TCE holding register
(cache) in the IOCC**

Figure 20.   **TCE table access for 2-word TCEs**

7.3 Micro Channel Bus Protocols

The RISC System/6000 PowerPC IOCC is optimized to use the Micro Channel. The IOCC Architecture fully complies with all requirements of the Micro Channel Architecture.

A brief description of the Micro Channel protocols is summarized in this section. For more details, see the *IBM Personal System/2 Hardware Interface Technical Reference–Architectures* (S84F-9808).

This section uses the abbreviated signal names as they appear in the *IBM Personal System/2 Hardware Interface Technical Reference–Architectures* (S84F-9808) document; for example, 'cd chrdy' represents 'card channel ready'.

7.3.1 Micro Channel Arbitration

Arbitration is the resolution of multiple bus requests, awarding use of the bus to the highest priority requester. It applies to all devices that request bus use such as processors, bus master devices, and DMA slave devices. Characteristics of the Micro Channel arbitration mechanism include:

- One to 16 bus masters

- Parallel prioritization

- Asynchronous operation

- Programmable priority levels

- Programmable fairness mode

- Mixable linear and fairness modes

- Preemptive burst capability

- Extendable to multiple buses

The arbitration mechanism distributes prioritization among the adapters but retains control and clocking functions within the IOCC.

Parameters such as arbitration level and burst characteristics are programmable via the Configuration registers in each device. There are no restrictions on changing operating modes following system startup.

Figure 21 illustrates an arbitration cycle. Devices request service by activating the 'preempt' signal. The IOCC responds by deactivating the 'arb/gnt' signal when the current bus owner completes its bus activity. Each requesting arbiter then presents its arbitration level on the arbitration bus. The IOCC then reactivates the 'arb/gnt' signal, and the device with the highest priority (lowest arbitration level value) on the arbitration bus is granted use of the bus. Device Request (Drq) and Device Acknowledge (Dack) are signals (internal to each of the device arbiters) which signal a request to arbitrate for the bus, and acknowledgement of being granted the bus, respectively.

At the end of the bus cycle, the arbitration cycle is repeated if the 'burst' signal is not active. If there are no requesters, control is returned to the default arbiter at the arbitration bus level 0xf.

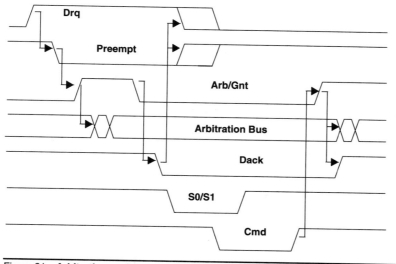

Figure 21. **Arbitration cycle**

Both DMA slave and bus master devices utilize the arbitration mechanism to initiate bus cycles. The difference is that once granted use of the bus, the bus master device controls bus cycles, while the IOCC controls the bus cycles for DMA slave devices.

7.3.1.1   Micro Channel Priority Assignment

At startup, each device supporting arbitration is assigned a unique priority level ranging from 0x0–0xf. This priority level establishes the selection criteria to be used when contention exists. If multiple requests occur simultaneously, the device with the lowest numbered priority level is awarded use of the bus.

Arbitration level 0xf is always assigned to the system processor. If there are no other bus requesters, bus ownership defaults to level 0xf. Thus, the IOCC *owns* the Micro Channel bus during idle conditions. Since Micro Channel bus utilization is normally low, the IOCC does not normally have to arbitrate for the bus for I/O Load and Store instructions. Some IOCC implementations execute any pending I/O Load or Store instruction during the arbitration cycle (that is, when the 'arb/gnt' signal is in the 'arb' state), and shall extend the arbitration cycle as needed to complete the I/O Load or Store instruction.

Micro Channel I/O devices with long bursting characteristics should be designed using the Fairness (rotational) Arbitration Protocol, without which it is possible to lock out system processor I/O Load or Store instructions until the I/O device transfer is complete. If a lockout occurs for an extended period of time, a bus timeout error is posted, the 'arb/gnt' signal is set to the 'arb' state, and the 'reset' signals are activated to all slots. While the bus timeout error is active, all system processor I/O Load and Store instructions are guaranteed access to the bus.

7.3.1.2   Non-Preemptive Burst

Devices can force non-preemptive burst operations if it is necessary to retain control of the bus for short periods of time. Examples include use of a read-modify-write sequence in setting locks and use of a burst to allow the completion of a word-organized transfer sequence. The device signals the arbiter that a forced burst is required by activating the 'burst' signal to the arbiter. When the burst sequence is complete, the device must deactivate the 'burst' signal.

7.3.1.3   Preemptive Burst

This function allows a device to use consecutive bus cycles without any arbitration overhead, as long as no other device is requesting bus service. It takes advantage of the low average utilization of I/O buses in general, and increases the effective data rate of a device. Devices programmed for preemptive burst mode conditionally activate the 'burst' signal when the 'preempt' signal is inactive. A device can remain temporarily non-preemptive for up to 7.8 microseconds following a preemption request. This allows completion of, for example, block transfers.

7.3.1.4   Fairness Modes

Devices operating in burst mode or devices with high bus request rates can cause severe interference to devices assigned lower priority levels. The problem is compounded when multiple high-bandwidth devices are present in the system. The programmable *fairness* mode is provided to make these high-bandwidth devices subject to preemption by any device. If multiple high-bandwidth devices are active simultaneously, service is rotated in a priority sequence, and each receives a percentage of bus cycles inversely proportional to the number of active bus requesters. Two devices with *fairness* turned off can totally monopolize a Micro Channel bus, causing other device operations to fail.

To meet wide variations in device operating requirements, arbiters are programmable to operate in either linear or fairness mode. Operating modes can be mixed on the same bus. Linear priority mode is provided to meet low latency requirements of unbuffered devices, while fairness mode provides a more equitable distribution of bus cycles in a high-demand environment, for example, with two or more high-bandwidth bus masters.

Fairness mode is a special case of preemptive burst. If there is only one bus requester, the current bus owner can utilize all of the bus bandwidth. As with preemptive burst, a device programmed in fairness mode can remain temporarily non-preemptive for up to 7.8 microseconds following a preemption request.

7.3.1.5   DMA Slave Selection

A DMA slave on a Micro Channel bus is selected either by its arbitration level or, optionally, by its I/O address (but not both). In RISC System/6000 PowerPC systems, the method supported for selection of DMA slave devices is by its arbitration level, status ('s0' exclusive-ored with 's1'), and an I/O cycle ('M/IO' signal in the IO state and 'arb/gnt' is in the 'gnt' state).

7.3.2   Basic Transfer Cycle

Although the RISC System/6000 PowerPC IOCC Architecture is generic and can attach a number of unique buses, the intended design point is the Micro Channel bus. These bus protocols are illustrated in Figure 22.

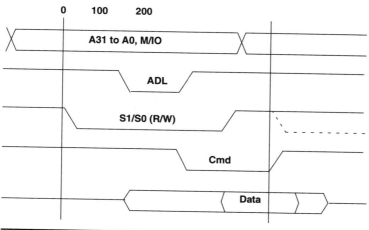

Figure 22.   **Micro Channel bus cycles**

The Micro Channel bus offers a 32-bit or, optionally, 64-bit (in implementation using 8-byte Streaming Data Protocol) data path and 4 GB of address space. It includes extensive support for reliability, availability, serviceability, extendability, and configurability. The physical package and connector are designed to improve electrical characteristics.

Two status lines, 's0' and 's1', define the initiation of bus write and read cycles respectively, while the 'M/IO' line differentiates between I/O memory and I/O devices. All addresses for the next cycle are overlapped with the processing of the current cycle. The Micro Channel bus architecture includes a special protocol for transferring sequential blocks of data. This is known as the Streaming Data Protocol, and is described in the next section.

7.3.2.1   Streaming Data

The Streaming Data Protocol is a single-address, multiple-data protocol that improves bus efficiency by amortizing bus cycle arbitration and address setup across multiple data cycles. It has particular value in transferring data between a memory and a processor cache or between a memory and a high-performance I/O device.

Streaming data begins with a cycle similar to a standard basic transfer cycle, but switches to a clock synchronous transfer protocol.

The IOCC supports streaming data operations for bus master operations. In addition, IOCC implementations may support streaming data operations for DMA slave and Load and Store string operations.

Following the activation of the 'cmd' signal, the bus master indicates Streaming Data Protocol capability by starting a bus clock called the 'sd strobe' signal. This clock is used by both the bus master and slave to clock data onto and off of the bus. The operation proceeds with new data being placed on the bus every time the 'sd strobe' signal makes a high-to-low transition. The frequency of the 'sd strobe' signal supported by the master and the slave in the Micro Channel operation is implementation dependent, and is communicated between the master and slave as part of the Micro Channel protocol. For additional information on the Streaming Data Protocol, refer to *IBM Personal System/2 Hardware Interface Technical Reference–Architectures* (S84F-9808).

7.3.2.2   Dynamic Bus Sizing

Micro Channel bus read or write operations do not necessarily have to match the physical width of the device. The Micro Channel architecture requires that discrepancies in data transfer widths be automatically managed by the current bus master. The IOCC is considered to be the current bus master for processor initiated I/O Load and Store instructions, and thus, must manage logical data-width transformations.

A Load or Store instruction issued to a device of lesser width than the command causes multiple I/O cycles to be taken until the transfer width is satisfied. This automatic data-width matching is referred to as dynamic bus sizing in the Micro Channel architecture. The multiple I/O cycles complete as a preemptable operation in the RISC System/6000 PowerPC IOCC, allowing bus master and DMA slave cycles to break in for service. As such, bus master or DMA slave latency is unaffected by use of dynamic bus sizing.

Protocols and sequencing of dynamic bus sizing are described in the *IBM Personal System/2 Hardware Interface Technical Reference–Architectures* (S84F-9808).

It is generally recommended that the programmer writing an I/O device driver be aware of the physical characteristics of the target device. One should be aware when dynamic bus sizing is invoked by IOCC hardware since this operation requires more time to complete. See Section 7.4.1.6, "String Operations," on page 114 for details on when this could be a problem.

7.3.2.3 Partial Transfer Cycles

Partial write operations, for example, writing one byte of a 2-byte device, or two bytes of a 4-byte device, are permitted in the bus architecture and are useful in performing unaligned moves. The Micro Channel supports partial write operations when operating with both memory and I/O devices.

Bus write operations issued on address boundaries matching the device width allow completion of the operation in the minimum number of bus cycles. Operations issued to non-aligned addresses transfer the data to the device using multiple (partial write) cycles. These write operation use the bus 'sbhe'/'a0' and 'be0 to be3' protocols to write the desired portion of the word. Partial transfers apply to I/O Load and Store instructions and (potentially) to bus master and DMA slave operations when operating with bus memory.

Partial transfers can take two to four times the normal number of bus cycles and caution should be exercised in their use. Non-aligned I/O Load and Store instructions slow the processor for a longer period of time than aligned I/O Load and Store instructions, adding latency to system interrupt service. See Section 7.4.1.6, "String Operation," on page 114 for details on when this could be a problem.

7.3.2.4 Micro Channel Bus Refresh

Bus refresh cycles are provided as a convenience to I/O devices with embedded random access memory (RAM).

A refresh cycle is similar to an I/O memory read operation, except that the 'refresh' line is also activated. Address bits 0 through 11 (using the Micro Channel little-endian notation) are incremented by one, and are placed on the bus during the refresh cycle.

7.3.3 Micro Channel Bus Errors

Four different kinds of errors are detectable on the Micro Channel bus:

■ Invalid address

■ Parity

■ Channel check

■ Bus timeout.

When an error occurs, an error status is either logged in IOCC registers (in the case of a bus master or DMA slave operation) or is is sent back to the processor which issued the I/O Load or Store instruction for logging into that processor's DSIER (in the case of an error during an I/O Load or Store instruction) as an aid in error recovery. For bus master operations, individual error status is kept for each arbitration level to assist in recovery of multiple errors and is stored in the Channel Status Register associated with that device.

7.3.3.1 Invalid Address

The Micro Channel architecture requires a positive response to all addresses. Address response is signalled on the Micro Channel by driving the 'cd sfdbk' signal low. Some conditions which could cause a lack of 'cd sfdbk' to occur are:

■ If the device is not present

■ If the device is not seated in the card slot properly

■ If the device is not enabled

■ If there is bad address parity on the bus and there is no detection of the bad address parity on the bus, and if the resulting bad address does not select any device

When an I/O Load or Store instruction is issued, the IOCC checks for this address response. If none is received, a DSI is issued and a Micro Channel bus error code is sent to the system for logging into the DSIER.

When a bus master gets on the Micro Channel bus, it is the responsibility of the bus master to check for a 'cd sfdbk' signal.

7.3.3.2 Micro Channel Parity Errors

The Micro Channel architecture definition includes address and data parity functions. Data parity checking is performed only when both the bus master and slave support data parity. Address parity checking is performed when the bus master supports address parity and *any* slave on the bus supports address parity. Since the IOCC acts as a bus master for I/O Load and Store operations, and since the IOCC supports address parity checking, if any Micro Channel device (not necessarily the target slave of the Load or Store operation) supports address parity, address parity shall be checked on an I/O Load or Store instruction (and therefore a device driver which uses I/O Load and Store instructions to the Micro Channel should always provide an exception handler for address parity error). Refer to Section 7.3.4, "Exception Reporting and Handling," on page 102 for details of the RISC System/6000 PowerPC I/O parity support.

7.3.3.3 Micro Channel Channel Check ('chck')

The Micro Channel includes a 'chck' signal which is driven by Micro Channel slave devices and indicates an unusual event occurred during the bus cycle. Examples include data or address parity error and page fault.

For details on the use of the 'chck' signal in reporting exception conditions within the RISC System/6000 PowerPC system, see Section 7.3.4, "Exception Reporting and Handling," on page 102.

It is important to note that RISC System/6000 PowerPC systems are designed to recover from synchronous channel checks on the Micro Channel bus (see the *IBM Personal System/2 Hardware Interface Technical Reference–Architectures* (S84F-9808) manual for a definition of 'synchronous' in relation to the 'chck' signal). Adapters that use the 'chck' signal asynchronously, shall force the system to initiate an Initial Program Load (IPL) in order to prevent data integrity exposures.

7.3.3.4 Micro Channel Bus Timeout

A number of conditions can result in a *hung* bus or in grossly extended Micro Channel bus cycles. These errors can result in overrun conditions to other devices on the Micro Channel bus and are checked by the IOCC using a bus timeout mechanism. Although the minimum architected bus timeout value is 7.8 microseconds, the IOCC does not attempt to check that finely and shall implement a timeout that varies between 15 and 120 microseconds.

Bus hang problems are caused by either hardware or software errors. These errors are generally associated with arbitration for the Micro Channel bus followed by failure to complete the bus cycle.

On a bus timeout error, the IOCC deactivates the 'arb/gnt' signal, sets bit 1 (the bus timeout bit) in the IOCC Miscellaneous Interrupt register, see Table 46 on page 141, and generates an interrupt. This error is considered to be uncorrectable and the master enable control in the IOCC Configuration register is reset. This disables all interrupt and channel requests. Also, a 'reset' signal is applied to all I/O slots. In addition, if an I/O Load or Store instruction is pending in the IOCC when the bus timeout occurs and the target of that Load or Store instruction is the Micro Channel bus, a DSI is sent for the terminated Load or Store Instruction. If an I/O Load or Store instruction is pending in the IOCC when the bus timeout occurs and the target of that Load or store instruction is an IOCC facility, then the Load or Store instruction shall be completed after the Micro Channel bus is cleared by the IOCC. IOCC architected registers (except if targeted by a pending Store instruction) remain unchanged, so that channel conditions at the time of the error can be logged. As an aid in determining the cause of the error, the state of some of the Micro Channel bus signals at the time of the error are also captured in the Bus Status Register.

Incorrect programming of the DMA controller can result in a hung bus. The DMA controller includes multiple channels; each can be personalized to control either a bus master or DMA slave device. Personalization can be dynamically performed. If a programmer were to personalize a channel for bus master operation, but the device was actually a DMA slave device, the bus would hang on the first DMA request that the device makes.

7.3.4 Exception Reporting and Handling

The *IBM Personal System/2 Hardware Interface Technical Reference–Architectures* (S84F-9808) manual contains a section entitled "Exception Condition Reporting and Handling" that defines the data and address parity on the Micro Channel.

The following are guidelines that should be followed in designing RISC System/6000 PowerPC systems and adapters:

■ Full parity support should be provided for all address and data buses for all RISC System/6000 PowerPC adapter boards, internal boards, and internal devices (such as Standard I/O devices, NVRAM, and System registers). Full address and data parity support is defined as traversing the complete paths of the address and data busses (generate parity at the signal source and check parity at each destination point where the address and data is used).

■ Internal RISC System/6000 PowerPC boards (Standard I/O and I/O Boards) should provide both address and data parity support to each of their devices.

Note

Suitable pull-up resisters should be utilized as appropriate (see the *IBM Personal System/2 Hardware Interface Technical Reference–Architectures* (S84F-9808) manual).

■ Adapter boards to be supported for RISC System/6000 PowerPC should provide both address and data parity support at the board connector and on all *internal* data and address buses.

– 8- and 16-bit devices should provide the 32–bit board connector to gain access to all the required parity signals.

– 8- and 16-bit devices, must also implement a notch in the board tab so they can be installed in a 16-bit board slot.

- Adapters that do not use the 32-bit board connector (8- and 16-bit data), should support data parity as a minimum. The objective is to include the 32-bit connector described previously to allow address parity, also, if possible.

- Existing adapter boards that may be useful in RISC System/6000 PowerPC that do not support parity will be addressed on an individual basis to correct over time.

- Devices and boards should meet the signal timing specifications described in the "Exception Condition Reporting and Handling" section of the *IBM Personal System/2 Hardware Interface Technical Reference–Architectures* (S84F-9808).

7.3.5 Micro Channel Interrupts

Eleven Micro Channel interrupt lines are supported by the IOCC. Interrupts on the Micro Channel are level-sensitive, active-low, and exhibit natural interrupt-sharing capabilities. The I/O Planar provides pull-up resistors on all Micro Channel interrupt signals so that unused lines float to the inactive state. Refer to Section 7.4.6, "IOCC Interrupt Structure," on page 137 for additional details.

7.4   IOCC Programming Model

The following section describes the programming model for the Micro Channel bus support functions provided by the IOCC.

7.4.1   Load and Store Instructions

The Load and Store instructions can be issued to devices on the Micro Channel bus in a similar manner that they are issued to system memory. The programmer specifies a SR (32-bit machines) or STE (64-bit machines) identifying a specific address space and supplies an offset into that space. The offset is obtained from the effective address and is not translated prior to being applied as a Micro Channel bus address. Figure 23 on page 105, in conjunction with Figure 4 on page 66 and Figure 5 on page 66, illustrates this process.

I/O Load and Store instructions are under control of the SRs or STEs. A command is directed to the IOCC when the type (T) bit of the SR or STE is set to a 1 (a direct-store segment) and the Bus Unit ID (BUID) in the SR or STE is set to select an IOCC (see Section 7.4.1.2, "IOCC SR (32-bit machines) and STE (64-bit machines) Definitions," on page 106 for the definition of the SRs, STEs, and BUIDs). All I/O operations require that the applicable K bit in the SR or STE be set to a 0 (the privileged mode).

For details on how the I/O address is generated, see Figure 4 on page 66 (for 32-bit machines) or Figure 5 on page 66 (for 64-bit machines).

7.4.1.1   Address Spaces and Effective Addresses

Figure 24 on page 105 illustrates the RISC System/6000 PowerPC address space which can be accessed by I/O Load or Store instructions. The addressing view from a device on the Micro Channel bus is slightly different and is shown in Figure 27 on page 117.

The I/O effective address provides for 32-bit addressing of the Micro Channel bus and IOCC facilities. Load and Store accesses are protected by several protection mechanisms. See Section 7.4.1.3, "Load and Store Authority Checking," on page 109 for more information on these protection mechanisms. Attempts to access addresses which are undefined (that is, unarchitected and unimplemented) in the IOCC control address space shall cause a DSI with an invalid operation error code and this is sent to the processor which issued the I/O Load or Store instruction for logging into that processor's DSIER.

The 32-bit Micro Channel bus memory address is formed by concatenating 28 bits of the effective address with the 4 EXTent (EXT) bits from the SR or STE. This partitions the bus memory device space into 16 segments of 256 MB each (4 GB of total address space), and separate SRs or STEs must be used to address adjacent segments.

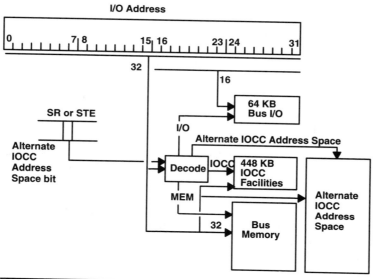

Figure 23. **I/O Load and Store instruction addressing**

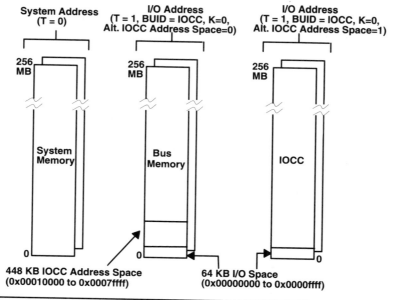

Figure 24. **Addressing model for I/O Load and Store instructions**

Results of crossing a T=1 segment boundary with a single Load or Store operation is implementation dependent, and may be dependent both on the implementation of the processor and the BUC. For implementations which DSI the operation, an invalid operation error code shall be sent to the processor issuing the Load or Store for logging in that processor's DSIER.

Although Micro Channel bus memory and Micro Channel bus I/O are disjoint in PC products, RISC System/6000 PowerPC systems map these two address spaces together. I/O requires 64 KB of addressing and this address space maps into the low addresses of the (4 GB) bus memory address space. When the Alternate IOCC Address Space bit in the SR or STE is set to a 0, part of the IOCC facilities are mapped into the address space from 64 KB up to (but not including) 512 KB. In addition, when the Alternate IOCC Address Space bit in the SR or STE is set to a 1, part of the IOCC facilities are mapped into the address space from 64 KB up to (but not including) 4 GB. The architecture of PC products is such that no bus memory feature cards may be hardwired in the address range of 0 to 640 KB, and no address conflicts exist. Effective addresses are not translated, but are used as *real* addresses into the Micro Channel and IOCC address spaces.

Table 31 on page 107 and Table 32 on page 108 summarize the RISC System/6000 PowerPC I/O addresses. The I/O address is obtained from the processor general purpose register and is under software control. The 32-bit address is formed by concatenating 28 bits of the effective address with the 4 extent (EXT) bits from the SR or STE before being used by the IOCC.

EXT bits from the SR or STE get concatenated with the least significant 28 bits of the processor effective address (value of EXT bits shown here). Addresses which are not architected are reserved, see Section 1.2.1 on page 2.

7.4.1.2   IOCC SR (32-bit machines) and STE (64-bit machines) Definitions

SRs (32-bit machines) or STEs (64-bit machines) provide access authority to the Micro Channel and IOCC address spaces for I/O Load and Store instructions. They are protected resources within the system and generally cannot be changed except by the Operating System. Certain bits of the SR or STE are passed from the processor to the IOCC during an I/O Load or Store instruction. For the definition of the BUC common fields of the SRs and STEs see Section 6.1.1.1, "SR (32-bit machines) and STE (64-bit machines) definitions for T=1," on page 62. Table 33 on page 109 defines the fields of the SR or STE which are passed by the processor and used by the IOCC and may only be applicable to IOCC and Micro Channel bus applications (not to other BUC implementations).

0 7	8 15	16 23	24 31	Description
0000 0000	0000 0000	I/O Device Address		Bus I/O
	x000	0 0 0 0 1 1 1 0	0 r r r	time delay command
			1 0 x x	Reserved (see time delay)
	0001 0000	0 0 0 0 1 0 0 0	0 0 0 0	IOCC Configuration Reg
			1 0 0 0	IOCC Personalization Reg
		1 0 0 1	0 0 0 0	Bus Status Reg
			1 0 0 0	TCE Address reg Word 0
			1 1 0 0	TCE Address reg Word 1
		1 0 1 0	0 0 0 0	Component Reset Reg
			1 0 0 0	Bus Mapping Reg
	0 0 0 1	1 0 0 0	0 0 0 0	Interrupt Enable Reg
			1 0 0 0	Interrupt Request Reg
		1 0 0 1	0 0 0 0	Misc. Interrupt Reg
	0 0 1 0	0 0 intrpt #	0 0	External Interrupt Vector Reg's
	0 0 1 1	1 0 ctrl reg#	0 0	DMA Slave Control Reg's
	0 1 0 0	0 0 chnl #	0 0	Channel Status Reg's. Accesing 0xf is implementation dependent
		1 0 Intrpt #	0 0	End of Interrupt command
	0 1 0 1	0 0 chnl #	0 0	Enable and Disable Channel (Arb Lvl) command
	0111 1111	1 0 1 1 1 1 1 1	1 x x x	Reserved (for implementation dependent use)
		1 1 x x x x x x	x x x x	Reserved (for implementation dependent use)
Bus Memory Address (0x00080000 and above)				Bus Memory

Table 31. **I/O Load and Store Instruction Addresses as Seen by the IOCC (Alternate IOCC Address Space Bit in SR or STE = 0)**

0	7	8	15	16	23	24	31	Description
0000	0000	0000	0000	I/O Device Address				Bus I/O
			x000	0 0 0 0	1 1 1 0	0 r r r		time delay command
						1 0 x x		Reserved (see time delay)
		0001	0000	0 0 0 0	1 0 0 0	0 0 0 0		IOCC Configuration Reg
						1 0 0 0		IOCC Personalization Reg
					1 0 0 1	0 0 0 0		Bus Status Reg
						1 0 0 0		TCE Address reg Word 0
						1 1 0 0		TCE Address reg Word 1
					1 0 1 0	0 0 0 0		Component Reset Reg
						1 0 0 0		Bus Mapping Reg
				0 0 0 1	1 0 0 0	0 0 0 0		Interrupt Enable Reg
						1 0 0 0		Interrupt Request Reg
					1 0 0 1	0 0 0 0		Miscellaneous Interrupt Reg
				0 0 1 0	0 0	intrpt #	0 0	External Interrupt Vector Reg's
				0 0 1 1	1 0	ctrl reg#	0 0	DMA Slave Control Reg's
				0 1 0 0	0 0	chnl #	0 0	Channel Status Reg's. Acceesing 0xf is implementation dependent
					1 0	Intrpt #	0 0	End of Interrupt command
				0 1 0 1	0 0	chnl #	0 0	Enable and Disable Channel (Arb Lvl) command
		0111	1111	1 0 1 1	1 1 1 1	1 x x x		Reserved (for impl. dependent use)
				1 1 x x	x x x x	x x x x		Reserved (for impl. dependent use)
		0100	slot #	0000	0 0 0 x	0 0 0 0	0 r r r	Board Configuration register (rrr=reg #; see Table 42 on page 132)

Table 32.   I/O Load and Store Instruction Addresses as Seen by the IOCC (Alternate IOCC Address Space Bit in SR or STE = 1)

SR bit	STE bit (Dword 0) (Dword 1)		Description
0	57	–	T bit (see definition in Table 25 on page 64)
1	58	–	K_s bit (see definition in Table 25 on page 64)
2	59	–	K_p bit (see definition in Table 25 on page 64)
3–4	60–61	–	BUID (see definition in Table 25 on page 64)
5–11	–	25–31	BUID (see definition in the Table 25 on page 64)
12–13	–	32–33	Reserved: These bits are reserved and should be set by any new software which is written to a 0, see Section 1.2.1 on page 2. PowerPC IOCC hardware implementations should ignore these bits for compatibility with POWER software, which might set these bits to something other than 0. Software can make use of operating system kernel services in order to provide compatibility of code from POWER to PowerPC (the kernel services shall hide the differences).
14–16	–	34–36	Reserved: See Section 1.2.1 on page 2.
17–23	–	37–43	Authority Mask: This field is used to give conditional access to various effective addresses. See Section 7.4.1.3, "Load and Store Authority Checking," on page 109 for more information.
24	–	44	Alternate IOCC Address Space: This bit, when set, provides additional IOCC facility address space. This bit was the 'IOCC Select' bit in the POWER I/O Architecture.
25–26	–	45–46	Reserved: These bits are reserved and should be set by any new software which is written to a 0. PowerPC IOCC hardware implementations should ignore these bits for compatibility with POWER software, which might set these bits to something other than 0. Software can make use of operating system kernel services in order to provide compatibility of code from POWER to PowerPC (the kernel services shall hide the differences).
27	–	47	Reserved: See Section 1.2.1 on page 2.
28–31	–	48–51	EXT (see definition in the Table 25 on page 64)

Table 33. **IOCC SR and STE Definition for T=1**

7.4.1.3   Load and Store Authority Checking

Load and Store access to the IOCC is limited by several protection mechanisms in the IOCC. These mechanisms are controlled by the K bit and the authority mask field which reside in the SR or STE. All accesses to the IOCC must have the appropriate K bit set to a 0. Accesses made to the IOCC with the appropriate

K bit set to a 1, shall cause a DSI with invalid operation error code to be logged into the DSIER of the processor which issued the I/O Load or Store instruction.

In addition, the authority mask field is used as an additional level of access protection for Load and Store instructions to I/O and bus memory address spaces. This works as follows:

■ A Load or Store instruction is targeted at the I/O or bus memory address spaces with a non-0 authority mask field

■ The IOCC accesses the TCE for the given effective address

— If the protection class (or one of the classes, if more than one class) that the SR or STE contains, matches with the page protect key in the TCE, then the IOCC allows the access

— If there is no match, this causes a DSI with an authority error code to be sent to the processor which issued the I/O Load or Store instruction for logging into that processor's DSIER

Programming Note

The applicable K bit of the SR or STE must be set to a 0 before the Load or Store instruction execution shall proceed to this authority check.

A mask of all 0's says that the process issuing the Load or Store instruction has unconditional access to all protection classes, and the IOCC shall not access the TCE (and therefore it doesn't matter if a TCE even exists). Accesses to the IOCC address spaces (with the Alternate IOCC Address Space either a 0 or a 1) require that the mask be all-0's or else causes a DSI with an invalid operation status and this is sent to the processor which issued the I/O Load or Store instruction for logging into that processor's DSIER. The exception to the authority mask checking is for accesses to the **time delay** command. For the **time delay** command, the authority mask is treated as though it is all 0's, even when it is not all 0's. The authority mask protection mechanism is independent of the K bit protection mechanism; both mechanisms must indicate that the access is permitted in order for the access to proceed. Table 34 on page 111 summarizes the protection mechanisms.

The authority mask protection mechanism is shown in Figure 25 on page 112. Table 35 on page 112 shows how the authority mask compares against the TCE key.

If the data accessed by a Load or Store instruction crosses a page boundary, then the I/O Load and Store Access Authority Checking shall be performed on both pages, and the instruction shall fail if the authority check fails for either page. Note that on a Store instruction, if the authority check fails for the second page, then data for the first page shall have already been sent to the device.

Bits from SR or STE			Address Range	Actions
K bit	Authority Mask	Alt. IOCC Address bit		
1	xxxxxxx	x	don't care	DSI; all accesses to the I/O, IOCC, or bus memory address spaces must have K=0
0	0000000	x	0 up to (but not including) 64 KB (except time delay command address)	Allow accesses to the Micro Channel I/O address space
0	non-zero	x		Access the TCE for the given effective address and compare the TCE page protect key to the authority mask field from the SR or STE and allow access if there is a match. If no match, then DSI the access and return an authority error code back to the processor issuing the Load or Store for logging into that processor's DSIER. See also Figure 25 on page 112 and Table 35 on page 112.
0	xxxxxxx	x	time delay command address	Allow access to the time delay command
0	0000000	x	64 KB up to (but not including) 512 KB	Allow accesses to the the IOCC facilities in both the primary and Alternate IOCC Address Spaces.
0	non-zero	x	64 KB up to (but not including) 512 KB	DSI the access and return an invalid operation status back to the processor issuing the Load or Store for logging into that processor's DSIER. Accesses to IOCC facilities must have an all-0 authority mask.
0	0000000	0	512 KB and up	Allow accesses to bus memory address space.
0	non-zero	0	512 KB and up	Access the TCE for the given effective address and compare the TCE page protect key to the authority mask field from the SR or STE and allow access if there is a match. If no match, then DSI the access and return an authority error code back to the processor issuing the Load or Store for logging into that processor's DSIER. See also Figure 25 on page 112 and Table 35 on page 112.
0	0000000	1	512 KB and up	Allow accesses to the IOCC facilities in the Alternate IOCC Address Space at 512 KB and above
0	non-zero	1	512 KB and up	DSI the access and return an invalid operation status back to the processor issuing the Load or Store for logging into that processor's DSIER. Accesses to IOCC facilities must have an all-0 authority mask.

Table 34. **Load and Store Instruction Authority Checking**

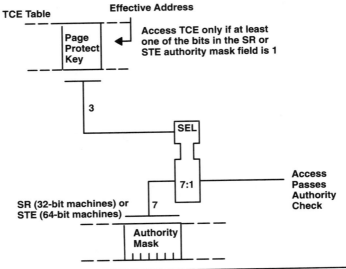

Figure 25.   I/O Load and Store access authority checking

TCE page protect key field value	SR or STE authority mask field which gives access to the corresponding page protect key (x = don't care about setting of bit)
0	none; key of 0 corresponds to a bus master or DMA slave
1	0b1xxxxxx (bit 17 = 1)
2	0bx1xxxxx (bit 18 = 1)
3	0bxx1xxxx (bit 19 = 1)
4	0bxxx1xxx (bit 20 = 1)
5	0bxxxx1xx (bit 21 = 1)
6	0bxxxxx1x (bit 22 = 1)
7	0bxxxxxx1 (bit 23 = 1)

Table 35.   **Load and Store Access Authority Checking**

7.4.1.4   I/O Load and Store TCE

The TCE layout for use with I/O Load and Store operations is illustrated in Figure 26 on page 113, and Table 36 on page 113 shows the bit definitions. The TCE table has a one-to-one correspondence with the first *n* pages of direct-store (T=1) address space. The first TCE controls access for Micro Channel bus addresses 0x00000000 to 0x00000fff; the second entry controls access for addresses 0x00001000 to 0x00001fff, and so on.

TCEs are located in system memory, and the memory must be continuous, real, and pinned. For the proper setting of the Page Table Entry bits for TCE pages, see Section 7.1, "System Structure," on page 75. Any error while the IOCC is accessing this memory may or may not be recoverable, depending on the implementation (see Section 7.4.7, "Non-Recoverable Errors," on page 141 and Section 7.4.8, "Recoverable Errors," on page 143). The size of the address space that can be mapped depends on how much system memory is allocated to the TCE area. A field in the TCE Address register is used to specify the amount of TCE RAM supplied. Refer to Section 7.4.5.5, "TCE Address Register," on page 135 for details.

Engineering Note

The data in the TCEs at startup time is indeterminate. The IPL ROM code should initialize the TCEs before turning on the master enable bit in the IOCC Configuration register.

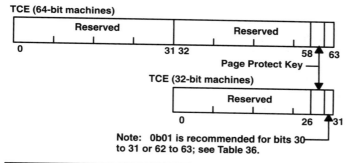

Figure 26. IOCC TCE layout for I/O Load and Store operations

32-bit TCE	64-bit TCE	Description
0–26	0–58	Reserved: See Section 1.2.1 on page 2.
27–29	59–61	Page protect key: These bits determine the protection class of the page for which the particular TCE is associated.
30–31	62–63	Reserved: These bits are reserved. These bits correspond to the page mapping and control field when a TCE is used for bus master operations, and therefore these bits can never be used for future changes to the architecture. By setting these bits to a 0b01 a bus master accessing this TCE in error shall receive a 'chck' (channel Check) error indication on the bus.

Table 36. IOCC TCE Definition for I/O Load and Store Operations

7.4.1.5   Address and Data Alignment

Except for string instructions, data for Load and Store instructions is normally right-justified in the processor register. One-byte operands are located in byte 3.

Two-byte operands are located in bytes 2 and 3. String operands are left-justified in the processor register.

Target I/O device addresses should be aligned on boundaries equal to the device width. This maintains optimal performance when performing Load and Store instructions. If this rule is not observed, the IOCC performs the operation using multiple (narrower) Micro Channel bus cycles. This can take up to four times longer to complete the Load or Store operation. Refer to Section 7.3.2.3, "Partial Transfer Cycles," on page 99 for additional details.

7.4.1.6   String Operations

String operations allow the issuance of Load or Store instructions with data widths from 1 to 128 bytes. The Micro Channel bus protocol used in the data transfer is dependent on the I/O device. String operations are applicable to any addressable device on the Micro Channel address space and to the IOCC address space. However, applicability of string operations may be limited by the device or facility itself. For example, string operations to IOCC facilities which do not match the length of the facility exactly shall cause a DSI with an invalid operation error code being logged into the DSIER of the processor which issued the I/O load or store instruction (however, the facility may have been modified). Also, string operations to IOCC address space which start in a reserved/unimplemented address space and spill over into an implemented facility shall be treated as though the operation was entirely to the reserved space (that is, the data is ignored on a Store instruction and returned as 0 on a Load instruction).

String operations issued to normal PC devices are performed using standard Micro Channel bus protocols. Multiple bus cycles are issued, using dynamic bus sizing, until the transfer length is satisfied. These multiple cycles operate under preemptive burst arbitration rules and Load or Store string instructions shall be momentarily suspended if any I/O device requests DMA slave or bus master operation.

String operations issued through IOCC implementations which support Load and Store streaming data operations, to devices supporting the streaming data transfer protocol, use that protocol where appropriate. This protocol operates under non-preemptive burst arbitration rules. It is up to the IOCC to guarantee that a bus timeout condition does not occur during an I/O Load or Store instruction due to conditions which are under its control.

If the data accessed by a string operation crosses a page boundary, then the Access Authority Checking shall be performed on both pages; the instruction shall fail if the authority check fails for either page. If the authority check fails for the second page for a store instruction, then data for the first page shall have already been sent to the device.

It is generally recommended that the programmer writing an I/O device driver be aware of the physical characteristics of the target device when using string operations. One should be aware of the effects of dynamic bus sizing and partial transfers, since these operations require more time to complete. Refer to Section 7.3.2.2, "Dynamic Bus Sizing," on page 98 and Section 7.3.2.3, "Partial Transfer Cycles," on page 99 for details of these functions. Slower than expected I/O instruction processing can have detrimental effects on system performance. For example, the system processor can not accept an interrupt while I/O Load or Store instructions are in process. Both dynamic bus sizing and unaligned moves (partial transfers) take longer to complete, adding latency to system interrupt service. Although most devices are reasonably fast and do not cause any problems, this latency can be large if extended string operations are performed against slow devices.

In an SMP environment, string operations are not atomic.

7.4.1.7 Load or Store Multiple Instructions

If an I/O Load or Store multiple instruction is issued, then this gets treated like a string operation of the same length, and the same rules apply (see Section 7.4.1.6, "String Operations," starting on page 114.

7.4.2 Bus Master

Bus master transfers refer to data transfers between a bus master I/O device and bus memory, I/O, or system memory where the bus master device supplies the memory addresses and controls all aspects of the data transfer. RISC System/6000 PowerPC systems, for performance reasons, put the system memory on a separate bus from the Micro Channel bus. Transfers from a bus master shall be directed to either bus memory (for bus to bus operations) or to system memory. The Bus Mapping register provides a means to specify that certain blocks of bus address space are allocated for bus to bus data transfers by bus masters. For more information, see Section 7.4.5.7, "Bus Mapping Register," on page 136. If the target of a bus master operation is the Micro Channel bus, and if the channel is enabled via the Channel Status Register (CSR), see Table 37 on page 118, for that device, then the IOCC does not participate in the bus transaction, it only acts as a monitor. During this monitor activity, the IOCC looks for address parity errors. In addition, if the prevent channel disable on error bit in the CSR is set to a 0, the IOCC also monitors for the card selected feedback error. In addition, only the parity on the low order 16 bits of the address (Micro Channel address bits 0 to 15) is checked if the bus master is doing an operation to the 64 KB I/O space. For more information on bus master error checking, see Section 7.4.8.2, "Bus Master Error Conditions," on page 146.

7.4.2.1   Bus Master Addressing Model

Engineering Note

Software should ensure
that no device on the
Micro Channel bus is
configured in the
address range of 0 up to
(but not including) 512
KB.

The addressing model for bus master accesses is shown in Figure 27 on page 117. The Bus Mapping register determines whether the address is an address targeted for system memory or if it is a bus to bus operation. If the operation is targeted for system memory, the TCE table is used to translate the address from the Micro Channel address to the system memory (real) address.

Note that for bus master operations, the Micro Channel I/O space is disjoint from the bus memory address space (unlike Load and Store operations and DMA slave operations where it is mapped into the bus memory address space); that is, the bus master controls the 'M/IO' signal line on the Micro Channel bus and this signal effectively gives the bus master the choice of making the I/O address space an entirely disjoint address space.

7.4.2.2   Bus Master Control Registers

Engineering Note

The data in the CSRs at
startup time is
indeterminate. The IPL
ROM code should
initialize these registers
before turning on the
master enable bit in the
IOCC Configuration
register.

The bus master Channel Status Register (CSR) is illustrated in Figure 28 on page 117 and the field definitions are in Table 37 on page 118. Channel number 0xf does not have a CSR; the results of accessing a CSR with the channel number of 0xf is implementation dependent. This register contains status and some personalization controls. Each of the other 15 channels has its own CSR.

Following device arbitration, the appropriate CSR is selected and the information in this register is used to control various aspects of the transfer.

7.4.2.3   Bus Master Operations to System Memory

Figure 29 on page 118 illustrates the bus master operations to system memory.

7.4.2.4   Bus Master Use of TCEs

TCEs are used by the IOCC to map Bus Master Micro Channel Bus addresses into System Memory Addresses.

The IOCC uses TCEs to provides address translation for all bus master operations to system memory. Translation allows the organizing of I/O buffers within the context of the processor's virtual page map and assists in eliminating a subsequent move operation. The processor maps discontiguous system memory pages into a contiguous virtual address space for use by the software. The TCEs do a similar task for the I/O; they map discontiguous system memory pages into a contiguous Micro Channel address space. The TCE table is an IOCC analogue of the system translation tables, and is generally managed in concert with those tables. Address translation mechanisms apply to 4 KB memory pages, matching the system page size. Although the TCEs contain a page fault code point, the intent of this is not to allow dynamic paging during I/O, but rather to allow for error isolation.

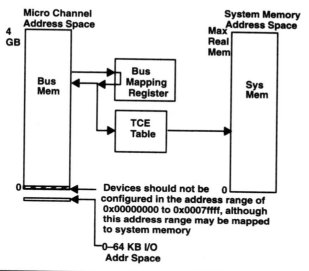

Figure 27. Addressing model for bus master operations

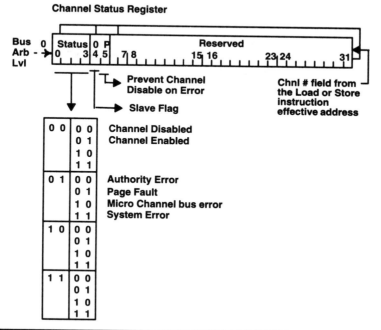

Figure 28. Channel Status Register

Bits	Description
0–3	Status: This field contains channel status, and may be set by the software or the IOCC. A 0x0 indicates the channel is disabled and a 0x1 indicates that the channel is enabled. Values between 0x2–0xf are error codes. Refer to Section 7.4.8.2, "'Bus Master Error Conditions," on page 146 for a description of bus master error conditions. Bit 3 is controlled by channel **enable** and **disable** commands. Refer to Section 7.4.4.3, "Enable and Disable Commands," on page 130 for more information on the **enable** and **disable** commands. Logging of errors and disabling of the channel on errors can be inhibited during bus to bus operations by use of the prevent channel disable on error bit (see the description of this bit in this register, below).
4	DMA Slave Flag: This bit is set to 0 to use an I/O Store instruction to personalize a channel for bus master data transfer operation. The IOCC never changes this bit.
5	Prevent Channel Disable on Error: If set to a 1, this bit shall disable the logging of errors during the bus monitoring function (that is, during a bus to bus operation) and shall also ensure that the channel remains enabled. This bit only affects the operation during bus to bus data transfers, and does not affect operations during transfers to system memory (errors that occur when the IOCC is involved in the transfer shall always log an error and shall always disable the channel). For cases where the hardware cannot tell whether the access is to system memory or not (for example, an address parity error which makes access to the Bus Mapping registers uncertain), when this bit is set to a 1 the hardware shall assume the access is bus to bus, and this bit shall prevent the logging of the error.
6–31	Reserved, see Section 1.2.1 on page 2.

Table 37. **CSR Definition for Bus Master Operations**

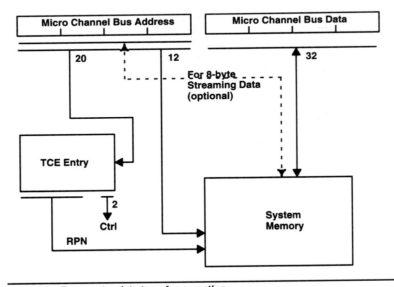

Figure 29. **Bus master data transfer operation**

System memory translate and protection information is contained in the TCE table. Following device arbitration, the appropriate CSR is selected, and the Micro Channel bus address is used to select the appropriate TCE. The RPN from the TCE and 12 bits from the Micro Channel bus address are used to address system memory. Each TCE identifies whether that page is mapped to system memory. If a page is mapped, the TCE also contains mapping information.

The TCE layout for bus master operations is illustrated in Figure 30 and Table 38 on page 120 details the usage of the TCE bits for bus master operations.. The TCE table has a one-to-one correspondence with the first *n* pages of Micro Channel bus memory addresses. The first TCE maps Micro Channel bus addresses 0x00000000 to 0x00000fff; the second entry controls mapping of addresses 0x00001000 to 0x00001fff, and so on.

TCEs are located in system memory, and the memory must be continuous, real, and pinned. For the proper setting of the Page Table Entry bits for pages which are mapped to system memory, see Section 7.1, "System Structure," on page 75. Any error while the IOCC is accessing this memory shall result in a TCE access error. The number of bus memory addresses that can be mapped depends on how much system memory is allocated to the TCE area. This amount is product dependent. A field in the TCE Address register is used to specify the amount of TCE RAM supplied. Refer to Section 7.4.5.5, "TCE Address Register," on page 135 for details.

Engineering Note

Data coherency and TCE coherency are related. If software issues a Store instruction to a TCE such that the IOCC must invalidate any copy of that TCE in an IOCC cache or buffer, then if any data associated with the page represented by that TCE is in an IOCC cache or buffer, it must be written to system memory, if modified, and invalidated if modified or not. Only after any associated data in the cache is flushed and/or invalidated can the TCE be invalidated.

The data in the TCEs at startup time is indeterminate. The IPL ROM code should initialize the TCEs before turning on the master enable bit in the IOCC Configuration register.

TCE (64-bit machines)

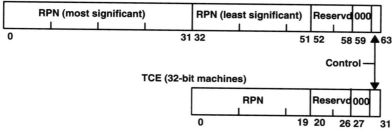

Figure 30. **TCE layout for bus master operations**

7.4.3 DMA Slave

The IOCC contains a DMA controller ("DMA controller" is the name given to a system-supplied resource that mediates data transfers between memory and DMA slaves) for the Micro Channel bus. Three parties are involved in this type of DMA operation: the DMA slave, the system memory, and the DMA controller.

32-bit TCE	64-bit TCE	Description
–	0–31	RPN: These bits compose the most significant bits of the Real Page Number (RPN) when operating with a 64-bit TCE. In certain IOCC implementations, all of these bits may not be required. Software should ensure that the RPN is valid (for example, is not outside the range of real memory).
0–19	32–51	RPN: These bits compose the least significant bits of the RPN when operating with 64-bit TCEs, or the entire RPN when operating with 32-bit TCEs. This field in the TCE contains the real page number that the bus address is mapped to in system memory. Software should ensure that the RPN is valid (for example, is not outside the range of real memory).
20–26	52–58	Reserved: See Section 1.2.1 on page 2.
27–29	59–61	Reserved: These bits are reserved and should be set to a 0. These bits correspond to the page protect key field when a TCE is used for Load and Store instruction authorization checking, and therefore these bits can never be used for future changes to the architecture. By setting these bits to 0, this guarantees that a bus master TCE cannot be used for a Load or Store instruction access (there is no bit in the authorization field which corresponds to a key of 0).
30–31	62–63	Page Mapping and Control: These bits define page mapping and read-write authority. They are coded as follows: 00 Reserved 01 Page Fault (no access) 10 System Memory (read only) 11 System Memory (read/write) Code points 0b0X signify that the page is not mapped to system memory. Code point 0b00 is reserved and should not be coded by the software. If c,de point 0b00 is programmed in error, the hardware shall treat this as a page fault. Code point 0b01 should be set when a page is not mapped at that address. It causes a synchronous channel check response to a bus master on a bus master operation. Bus master devices designed to take advantage of this function are expected to cause an interrupt and to halt and wait for the system to take corrective action. Code point 0b1X signifies that the page is mapped to system memory. Code point 0b10 signifies that the page is a read-only page while code point 0b11 is for a page which can be written to as well as read from.

Table 38. IOCC TCE Definition for Bus Master Operations

Each DMA slave channel includes a pair of 32-bit registers containing the current memory address, the length of the transfer remaining, and the control information corresponding to the current page being accessed. The IOCC implements up to 15 DMA slave channels. Each DMA slave channel can be associated with one of 15 Micro Channel bus arbitration levels. The number of DMA slave channels is implementation dependent (see Section 7.4.5.2, "IOCC Configuration Register," on page 132).

Bit 4 of the Channel Status Register must be set to a 1 when controlling a DMA slave device. Software should program unallocated channels as bus master channels. After the system supervisor loads the DMA slave control registers and enables the channel, the IOCC is ready to control DMA operations on behalf of the DMA slave device.

Software supports assignment of DMA slave channels to arbitration levels on a first come first serve basis. If a channel is not available the resource request is rejected. Hardware does not check for the mapping of a DMA slave channel to more than one arbitration level at a time. This must be controlled by the software.

If the DMA slave operation completes without error, the IOCC terminates the DMA slave operation and disables the channel. If an error occurs during the DMA slave operation, the IOCC sets a code identifying the class of error into the CSR status field and terminates the DMA slave operation. No additional DMA slave requests or **enable** commands shall be accepted by this channel until the error is cleared by a Store instruction. The DMA Slave Control registers are frozen, capturing details on channel status at the time of error. Refer to the "DMA Slave Error Conditions," on page 150 for details.

To suspend or terminate a DMA slave operation prior to its normal ending point, it is recommended that a DMA **disable** command be used. This command provides a soft termination of a DMA operation without destroying the current state of the DMA slave control registers. Refer to Section 7.4.4.3, "Enable and Disable Commands," on page 130 for details on these commands.

DMA slave termination is accompanied by the IOCC pulsing the 'tc' signal on the Micro Channel Bus. Devices are expected to post an interrupt when this occurs, notifying the system that the DMA operation is complete.

7.4.3.1 DMA Slave Addressing Model

The addressing model for DMA slave accesses is shown in Figure 31 on page 122. The CSR determines whether the address is an address targeted for system memory or if it is a bus to bus operation. If the operation is targeted for system memory, the TCE table contains the system memory (real) addresses. If the operation is a bus to bus operation, the DMA Slave Control register contains the Micro Channel bus address of the target device. Note that for DMA slave operations, the Micro Channel I/O space is not accessible and the access shall always be to the bus memory address space at addresses of 0 to 4 GB.

TCEs provide support for page level scatter and gather DMA slave operations to system memory. The DMA Slave Control register is initialized with the first page TCE number; the rest of the TCEs involved in the transfer are sequential. Figure 32 on page 122 illustrates DMA slave operations. Notice that the memory address consists of a TCE number and an offset.

Programming Note

Software should ensure that no device on the Micro Channel bus is configured in the address range of 0 up to (but not including) 512 KB. The reason is that certain system implementations may place some IOCC facilities on the Micro Channel bus in that address range and may not isolate those devices from the other Micro Channel devices. Devices configured in this address range, then, could pose an addressing conflict with IOCC facilities.

DMA slave operations cannot access Micro Channel I/O address space, only bus memory and system memory address spaces.

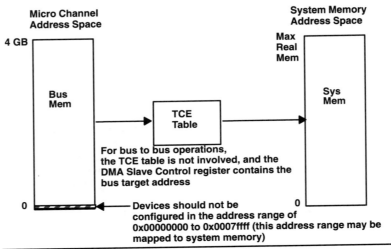

Figure 31. **Addressing model for DMA slave operations**

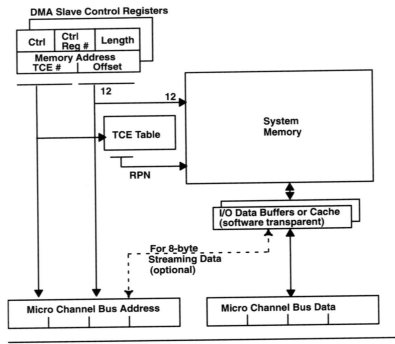

Figure 32. **DMA slave operations**

7.4.3.2 DMA Slave Control Registers

Figure 33 on page 124 shows the registers used for DMA slave operations. Figure 34 on page 124 illustrates the TCE table entry.

The following are the detailed definitions for the registers used in controlling DMA slave operations.

■ Channel Status register

There are 15 CSRs each having a one to one correspondence to one of 15 arbitration levels (level 0xf is not included; the results of accessing a CSR with the channel number of 0xf are implementation dependent. The bit assignments for this register are in Table 39 on page 125.

■ DMA Slave Control register

The DMA Slave Control register contains the system or bus memory address for the DMA slave operation. The number of DMA Slave Control registers is equal to the number of DMA slave channels implemented. (See Section 7.4.5.2, "IOCC Configuration Register," on page 132). The number of DMA Slave registers implemented is defined in the IOCC Configuration register field maximum number of DMA slave channels. Trying to access a control register number greater than the number of DMA slave channels supported by the implementation will produce results which are implementation dependent. This register is dynamically associated to the arbitration level based on the Control register number field assigned in the CSR. Software must ensure that the same channel number is never assigned to more than one CSR a time.

If the DMA transfer is to or from bus memory (CSR bit 5 equal to 0) the DMA Slave Control register is applied as a 32-bit address directly to the I/O address bus. If the transfer is to or from the system memory, this register is defined in Table 40 on page 125.

The DMA address is incremented by the size of the transfer and the length count is decremented by the same amount. Each time the TCE number is incremented in the DMA Slave Control register, the next sequential TCE entry is fetched from system memory so that the IOCC can complete the translation to a system memory address. Note that only one DMA slave channel can be assigned per arbitration level.

Engineering Note

The data in the CSRs and DMA Slave Control registers at startup time is indeterminate. The IPL ROM code should initialize these registers before turning on the master enable bit in the IOCC Configuration register.

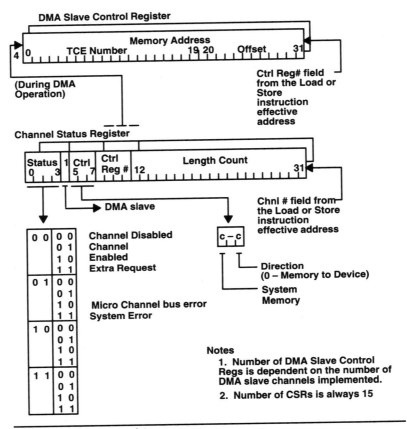

Figure 33.   **DMA slave registers**

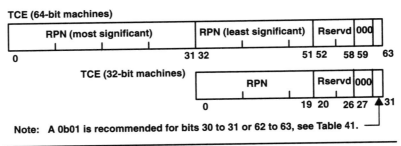

Figure 34.   **TCE layout for DMA slave operations**

Bits	Description
0–3	Status: This field contains channel status, and may be set by software or the IOCC. A 0x0 indicates the channel is disabled and a 0x1 indicates that the channel is enabled. Values 0x2 to 0xf are error codes. Refer to Section 7.4.8.3, "DMA Slave Error Conditions," on page 150 for a description of DMA slave error conditions. This field is controlled by channel **enable** and **disable** commands. Refer to Section 7.4.4.3, "Enable and Disable Commands," on page 130 for more information on the **enable** and **disable** commands. Once the transfer is complete (after transferring the number of bytes indicated by the length count field plus one), the IOCC shall disable the channel.
4	DMA Slave Flag: This bit is set to a 1 using an I/O Store instruction to personalize a DMA channel for DMA slave operation. The IOCC never changes this bit.
5	System Memory Flag: This bit selects whether system memory or bus memory is to take part in a DMA slave transaction. This bit is set to a 1 for DMA slave transfers to or from system memory and set to a 0 for DMA slave transfers to bus memory.
6	Reserved, see Section 1.2.1 on page 2.
7	Direction Flag: This bit selects the direction (device to memory or memory to device) of a DMA slave transfer. This bit is set to a 0 to transfer data from memory to the I/O device and is set to a 1 to transfer data from the I/O device to memory.
8–11	Control Register Number: This field is used to assign a DMA Slave Control register to a specific CSR. Setting of this field with a control register number greater than the number of DMA slave channels supported by the implementation minus 1 (as indicated by the maximum number of DMA slave channels field of the IOCC Configuration register) will produce results which are implementation dependent.
12–31	Length Count: This field is used to indicate the length of the DMA slave transfer (byte count minus 1). The IOCC shall pulse the 'tc' signal on the Micro Channel bus when this field goes from all 0's to all 1's, that is, when the IOCC is transferring the last byte of data to the device. This field is updated by the IOCC during the transfer to reflect the number of bytes remaining to be transferred minus 1.

Table 39. CSR Definition for DMA Slave Operations

Bits	Description
0–19	TCE Number: The TCE number in the memory address provides an index into the TCE table where the TCE information (RPN) is obtained if the channel is mapped to system memory. When mapped to system memory, the address used to address system memory consists of the RPN from the TCE concatenated with the offset.
20–31	Offset: These bits are the lower 12 bits of the memory address.

Table 40. DMA Slave Control Register Definition

7.4.3.3 DMA Slave Use of TCEs

The TCE layout for DMA slave operations is illustrated in Figure 34 on page 124 and the fields are defined in Table 41 on page 126.

32-bit TCE	64-bit TCE	Description
–	0–31	RPN: These bits compose the most significant bits of the Real Page Number (RPN) when operating with a 64-bit TCE. In certain IOCC implementations, all of these bits may not be required. Software should ensure that the RPN is valid (for example, is not outside the range of real memory).
0–19	32–51	RPN: These bits compose the least significant bits of the RPN when operating with 64-bit TCEs, or the entire RPN when operating with 32-bit TCEs. This field in the TCE contains the real page number that the bus address is mapped to in system memory. Software should ensure that the RPN is valid (for example, is not outside the range of real memory).
20–26	52–58	Reserved: See Section 1.2.1 on page 2.
27–29	59–61	Reserved: These bits are reserved and must be set to a 0. These bits correspond to the page protect key field when a TCE is used for Load and Store instruction authorization checking, and therefore these bits can never be used for future changes to the architecture. By setting these bits to a 0, this guarantees that a DMA slave TCE cannot be successfully used for a Load or Store instruction access (there is no bit in the authority mask field which corresponds to a key of 0).
30–31	62–63	Reserved: These bits are reserved. These bits correspond to the page mapping and control field when a TCE is used for bus master operations, and therefore these bits can never be used for future changes to the architecture. By setting these bits to a 0b01, a bus master accessing this TCE in error shall receive a 'chck' error indication on the bus.

Table 41.   IOCC TCE Definition for DMA Slave Operations

TCEs are located in system memory, and the memory must be contiguous, real, and pinned. For the proper setting of the Page Table Entry bits for TCE pages, see Section 7.1, "System Structure," on page 75. Any error while accessing TCE memory results in a TCE access error.

7.4.3.4   DMA Slave Bus Protocols

Conventional Micro Channel bus protocols are used in DMA operations and are documented in Section 7.1, "Basic Transfer Cycle," on page 97.

I/O devices request DMA service on a demand basis by arbitrating for the bus using the 'preempt' line. This causes the 'grant' line to be deactivated, causing an arbitration cycle. When the 'grant' line is reactivated, the IOCC inspects the Control register associated with the bus requester to determine if any DMA service is required. If it is, the IOCC performs a DMA slave sequence on behalf of the requester.

When service is granted to a device, data is transferred between the device and memory. The sequence to be used depends on whether the memory is bus or system memory. The number of bytes transferred is generally equal to the data width of the device. The DMA address is incremented by the size of the transfer and the length count is decremented by the same amount.

If the specified DMA address does not have the same boundary as the I/O device data width, the operation proceeds using a Partial Transfer Protocol as described in Section 7.3.2.3, "Partial Transfer Cycles," on page 99. For example, a DMA transfer involving a 2-byte I/O device and a buffer starting on an odd address results in two 1-byte DMA sequences being performed. This retains the functional integrity of the operation, but requires additional time to complete the operation. As a result, it is suggested that buffers in system memory be located on address boundaries matching the physical width of the I/O device.

7.4.3.5   DMA Slave Transfers to Bus Memory

DMA slave transfers between a device and Micro Channel bus memory consist of two bus cycles: one to read the data from the source and one to write the data to the target. An input operation consists of an I/O device read cycle followed by a bus memory write cycle. An output operation is reversed.

There is no buffering on transfers to or from bus memory.

7.4.3.6   DMA Slave Transfers to System Memory

DMA slave transfers between a device and system memory have only one apparent Micro Channel bus cycle: an I/O device read or write. The memory operation does not appear as a bus cycle.

7.4.3.7   Special Sequences

Special mechanisms are provided to improve the relative data transfer efficiency of highly buffered devices.

The Micro Channel supports preemptive burst operations to take advantage of low average Micro Channel bus loading. A device starts this mode by activating the 'burst' line prior to the end of the DMA slave cycle. No arbitration cycle occurs, and the DMA controller concatenates successive DMA sequences until the 'burst' line is deactivated. Micro Channel arbitration rules require preemptive burst devices to deactivate the 'burst' line request if any other device requires bus service.

The DMA controller also supports a special transfer mode called streaming data transfer. This mode is a single-address, multiple-data protocol, and is described in Section 7.3.2.1, "Streaming Data," on page 98.

7.4.4   IOCC Commands

IOCC commands are used to change the state of the IOCC or control special bus actions. They take the form of Load and Store instructions to special (effective) addresses (see Table 31 on page 107 and Table 32 on page 108), where the addresses specify the actions to be taken. In most cases, the Load or Store instruction can be either a string or non-string operation, however, the length of the operation must exactly match the length of the target facility or else the IOCC shall cause a DSI with invalid operation error code and this is sent back to the processor which issued the I/O Load or Store instruction for logging into that processor's DSIER. Commands supported by the IOCC include:

- **Time delay**

- **End Of Interrupt**

- **Enable** and **disable**

The IOCC commands are only accessible to Load and Store instructions from the system processor. The IOCC commands are protected by several protection mechanisms. See Section 7.4.1.3, "Load and Store Authority Checking," on page 109 for more information on these protection mechanisms.

All IOCC commands are 4-byte operations except for the **time delay** command.

7.4.4.1   Time Delay Command

A number of Micro Channel devices have strict rules regarding minimum periodicity of Programmed I/O commands. "Programmed I/O (PIO)" commands are commands that are issued using processor reads and writes. Using program path lengths for timing is not a good programming practice, since program performance varies widely by processor type and (current) operating environment. To assist in programming devices with real-time dependencies, the IOCC supports a special time delay command that can guarantee separation of bus I/O commands.

Execution of this command is overlapped with succeeding processor instructions as long as they do not attempt to access the same IOCC. If, however, another I/O Load or Store instruction is issued to the same IOCC before the time delay has expired, that command is held off until the pending delay is completed. This command affects only Programmed I/O and has no effect on DMA or other I/O operations run by hardware.

Although the time delay command can be coded as a 1-, 2-, or 4-byte Load or Store instruction, the multi-byte Loads and Stores in the time delay command are provided for POWER compatibility (with the POWER delays of 2 to 7 microseconds becoming IOCC induced delays of 8 microseconds minimum and 32 microseconds maximum), and should be avoided for new code or rework of existing code. When writing new code or reworking existing code, only the 1 microsecond time delay command should be used. There are two reasons for this. First of all, the PowerPC Architecture of the processor does not guarantee atomic operations for unaligned Load and Store operations and may break multi-byte unaligned time delay commands into multiple time delay commands. Some processors may keep the operation atomic, and will not break the operation into multiple operations (the 601 processor implementation is one example). Note that the delay specified here only reflects the IOCC induced delay; there may be other significant delays introduced by the system which will add on to the total delay.

The second reason for using only the 1 microsecond version in all new and reworked code is that all versions except the 1 microsecond version are for POWER compatibility, and may be removed from the PowerPC IOCC Architecture in the future.

The 1 microsecond time delay command is coded as a Load or Store instruction with the last four address bits of the command address equal to 0b0000 and a length of one byte, and has a tolerance of minus zero and plus one microsecond. Details on the POWER time delay commands which are implemented in the IOCC for compatibility purposes, can be found in the POWER I/O Architecture documentation. The Alternate IOCC Address Space bit is a don't care for the time delay command.

Implementations of the IOCC for systems where the processor will break unaligned time delay commands into multiple commands shall decode the addresses immediately following the time delay command so that valid unaligned POWER time delay commands are guaranteed not to cause a DSI on those machines.

If a Load instruction is used to call the time delay command, the data returned is indeterminate. If a Store instruction is used, the data is ignored.

7.4.4.2   End Of Interrupt

Following presentation of an I/O interrupt to the system, the IOCC automatically masks off that particular interrupt signal so the presentation is only made once. An **End Of Interrupt** command unmasks a particular interrupt signal so that it can interrupt again, when it is active. On a Store instruction, the data is ignored. On a Load instruction, the data is indeterminate. This command should be issued following the interrupt service, once the interrupt has been reset at the device.

The interrupt number field in the address of this command indicates the level of interrupt to be unmasked (see Table 31 on page 107).

7.4.4.3 Enable and Disable Commands

The **enable** and **disable** commands allow system initiation and suspension of DMA slave and bus master operations for devices attached to the Micro Channel. Each command is directed to a specific channel as specified by the channel field in the effective address. The effective address of the command specifies the channel to be started or stopped.

The **enable** command initializes a channel to accept requests by changing the channel status in the Channel Status Register from the disabled (0b0000) state to the enabled (0b0001) state. This command is coded as a Load instruction and returns the original contents of the selected CSR to the target processor register. The channel status field must initially be 0b0000 for this command to update the channel status to the enabled state. This command always returns a status consisting of the full contents of the associated CSR prior to the operation of this command. The status field is the only field changed by this command.

The **disable** command disables operation for a particular channel by changing the channel status from the enabled state (0b0001) to the disabled (0b0000) state. The disable command is coded as a Store instruction (the store data is ignored). It does not disrupt any other data in the channel registers, allowing restart of the operation if the device is designed accordingly. The channel status field must initially be 0b0001 for this command to update the status field. If it is not a 0b0001, then the operation shall be ignored by the IOCC.

A request from a DMA slave when the channel is disabled is considered to be an error and sets an extra request error code in the CSR associated with that device. The 'tc' signal on the Micro Channel bus is pulsed in an attempt to shut off the device.

If a bus master makes a request to a disabled bus master channel, the IOCC shall not activate the 'sfdbkrtn' signal and synchronously activates the 'chck' signal, but does not update the error code.

The disable command issued to channel 0xf is ignored by the IOCC (on a Store instruction, data is ignored, on a Load instruction, data returned is indeterminate).

7.4.5 IOCC Registers

The IOCC registers are only accessible to Load and Store instructions from the system processor. The IOCC registers are protected by several protection mechanisms. See Section 7.4.1.3, "Load and Store Authority Checking," on page 109 for more information on these protection mechanisms.

All IOCC registers except the Board Configuration Registers are 4-byte registers and should be accessed only with 4-byte Load and Store instructions. IOCC implementations may take either one of the following two choice of actions in the case where the software accesses the 4-byte registers with something other than a 4-byte Load or Store (implementation dependent):

1. Complete the operation correctly as specified by the software.

2. DSI the instruction with an invalid operation error code and send this back to the processor which issued the I/O Load or Store instruction for logging into that processor's DSIER.

7.4.5.1 Board Configuration Register (BCR)

The Micro Channel defines a slot select mechanism for accessing board-unique configuration data. This data is called the Programmable Option Select (POS) data by the Micro Channel Architecture and is accessed through the BCRs in the IOCC. The Micro Channel Architecture defines this data to be accessible only with 1-byte operations, and therefore, software should assure that only 1-byte Load and Store instructions are used in accessing this data. Eight bytes of addressing (eight 1-byte registers) are provided per board, which includes a unique 2-byte board identification and up to 4 bytes of programmable parameters. This mechanism is called setup, and is used at startup time to determine the boards in the system and to set configuration parameters on each board. Support is provided for up to 16 boards. The definition of the BCRs and their addressing are shown in Table 42 on page 132.

Refer to the *IBM Personal System/2 Hardware Interface Technical Reference–Architectures* (S84F-9808) manual for more information on the POS registers and a description of the setup mechanism. Even though the Micro Channel architecture specifies that only Micro Channel address bits 0 to 2 are to be used in the address decode operation, some boards are developed with a dependency on setup addresses being between 0x0100 and 0x0107. To accommodate these boards, bit 23 of the processor effective address is allowed to be either a 1 or 0, giving two different processor effective address ranges (see Table 31 on page 107). Address bits 29 to 31 designate the byte being addressed within the 2-word field.

Board Configuration register data is unique to each specific board. Refer to each board specification for details.

The BCRs are only accessible with the Alternate IOCC Address Space bit in the SR or STE set to a 1. See Table 32 on page 108.

Engineering Note

For compatibility with device drivers written for POWER, IOCC designs should allow multi-byte access to Micro Channel adapters for setup cycles to the BCRs when the Micro Channel adapter signals appropriately that it can accept such accesses.

For compatibility with PS/2 systems, **adapters** should *not* be designed to allow multi-byte access during Micro Channel setup cycles to the POS registers. Adapters which allow multiple byte access to the POS registers will probably not work in PS/2 systems.

Some of the data in the Board Configuration registers at startup time is indeterminate. The IPL ROM code should initialize these registers before turning on the master enable bit in the IOCC Configuration register.

Least Significant 3 Bits of the Effective Address	Operation	Processor Register Contents				POS Data Meaning
		Byte 0	Byte 1	Byte 2	Byte 3	
000	Load or Store String	POS 0	(note 1)	(note 1)	(note 1)	Board ID, LSB
001	Load or Store String	POS 1	(note 1)	(note 1)	(note 1)	Board ID, MSB
010	Load or Store String	POS 2	(note 1)	(note 1)	(note 1)	Device Unique
011	Load or Store String	POS 3	(note 1)	(note 1)	(note 1)	Device Unique
100	Load or Store String	POS 4	(note 1)	(note 1)	(note 1)	Device Unique
101	Load or Store String	POS 5	(note 1)	(note 1)	(note 1)	Device Unique
110	Load or Store String	POS 6	(note 1)	(note 1)	(note 1)	Sub-Addressing, LSB
111	Load or Store String	POS 7	(note 1)	(note 1)	(note 1)	Sub-Addressing, MSB
000	Load or Store Byte	(note 2)	(note 2)	(note 2)	POS 0	Board ID, LSB
001	Load or Store Byte	(note 2)	(note 2)	(note 2)	POS 1	Board ID, MSB
010	Load or Store Byte	(note 2)	(note 2)	(note 2)	POS 2	Device Unique
011	Load or Store Byte	(note 2)	(note 2)	(note 2)	POS 3	Device Unique
100	Load or Store Byte	(note 2)	(note 2)	(note 2)	POS 4	Device Unique
101	Load or Store Byte	(note 2)	(note 2)	(note 2)	POS 5	Device Unique
110	Load or Store Byte	(note 2)	(note 2)	(note 2)	POS 6	Sub-Addressing, LSB
111	Load or Store Byte	(note 2)	(note 2)	(note 2)	POS 7	Sub-Addressing, MSB

1. On a Load String instruction, unloaded bytes are undefined, on a Store String instruction, unused bytes are don't cares.
2. On a Load Byte instruction, the upper bytes of the register are dependent on which instruction form is used, and on a Store Byte instruction the upper bytes are don't cares.

Table 42. **BCR Addressing for Load and Store Instructions**

7.4.5.2   IOCC Configuration Register

The IOCC Architecture allows for certain variations of function and performance that optimize its usage across multiple IOCC designs and machine environments. This personalization is established via the IOCC Configuration register.

Figure 35 on page 133 illustrates the organization of the IOCC Configuration register and Table 43 on page 133 defines the fields.

Configuration Data

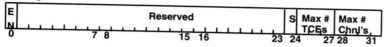

Figure 35. **IOCC Configuration register**

Bits	Description
0	Master Enable: This bit functions as a master enable control for channel and interrupt operations only. When set to a 0, this bit shall inhibit external interrupts from being passed to the system and shall prevent any device arbitration cycle on the Micro Channel bus. This bit is intended to disable channel operations until the system has initialized the Channel Control registers and TCE table, but also could be used following startup to assist recovery from catastrophic errors. The only time that hardware changes this bit is during startup and on a bus timeout error, and in both cases it sets the bit to a 0. Normally, this bit is set to a 1 following initial program load (IPL) and is never changed thereafter.
1–26	Reserved, see Section 1.2.1 on page 2.
24	64-bit Mode: This bit is set to a one by the hardware at startup if the IOCC hardware can operate in the 64-bit mode. The following are the differences when this bit is on: • 64-bit TCEs are used instead of 32-bit TCEs • The IOCC TCE Address register is larger For 64-bit implementations, this bit is setable by software; if this bit is set to a 0 by the software then the IOCC shall use 32-bit TCEs instead of 64-bit TCEs (the IOCC TCE Address register remains at 2-words, however). For 32-bit implementations, this bit is ignored on a Store instruction.
25–27	Maximum Number of TCEs: These bits indicate the maximum number of TCEs that can be programmed by software into the TCE Address register for the particular hardware configuration. For the legal values to which these bits can be set, see the description for the number of TCE table entries field in the TCE Address register table 28 on page 70; the number of TCE table entries field of the TCE Address register should not be set to a value greater than reported by the hardware by these bits, or the results will be implementation dependent (the number of TCE table entries field *can* be set to any value *less than or equal to* the value of these bits). These bits are read-only to the software, and on a Store instruction issued to the IOCC Configuration register, the data will be ignored for these bits.
28–31	Maximum Number of DMA Slave Channels: These bits indicate the maximum number of DMA slave channels (that is, the number of DMA Slave Control registers) that can be programmed by software for the particular hardware configuration. 0b0000 indicates that none are available and 0b1111 indicates that 15 channels are supported. The Micro Channel Architecture requires that at least 2 channels be configurable for DMA slave operations. The minimum required by the IOCC Architecture is the number of slots plus the number required by the Standard I/O devices. The number of DMA slave channels supported is implementation dependent. However, the number of arbitration levels supported is not implementation dependent and must be equal to15. These bits are read-only to the software, and on a Store instruction issued to the IOCC Configuration register, the data will be ignored for these bits.

Table 43. **IOCC Configuration Register Definition**

The IOCC Configuration register shall be initialized by hardware, including IPL ROM code and, with the exception of the master enable bit, this register shall be treated as a read-only register by the Operating System.

The data in the IOCC Configuration register at startup time shall be all 0's, except for bits 24 and 28 to 31, which indicate the mode of operation (32-bit/64-bit) and maximum number of DMA slave channels that the implementation will support. The IPL ROM code should ensure that all IOCC facilities are initialized before turning on the master enable bit in this register.

7.4.5.3   IOCC Personalization Register

This register allows various IOCC implementations to have a place where implementation variables can be established. Examples of the types of things which might be in this register are system arbitration time, bus memory refresh rate, and so on.

This register shall be initialized by hardware and IPL ROM code and shall be treated as a read-only by the Operating System. On a Store instruction, unimplemented bits shall be ignored. Unimplemented bits shall be returned by the hardware as a 0 on a Load instruction (software note: unimplemented bits are only guaranteed to be 0 as long as this field remains unimplemented; if these bits are redefined in the future, software may get back something other than 0).

This register is totally implementation dependent.

7.4.5.4   Bus Status Register (BSR)

The Bus Status Register (BSR) is a diagnostic facility that aids in I/O error isolation. It is comprised of one read-only register and provides the ability to sample certain signals on the Micro Channel bus when a bus timeout error occurs.

Figure 36 on page 135 illustrates the organization of the Bus Status Register.

The 'arb' bus lines, 'burst' signal, 'cd chrdy' signal, and 'sdr (0)' and 'sdr (1)' signals are latched in the BSR latches when a bus timeout error occurs. The 'arb' bus bit 0 is the least significant and bit 3 is the most significant bit. If a bus timeout error occurs during an I/O cycle, further bus errors shall not be trapped until the error interrupt is cleared out of the Miscellaneous Interrupt register. As such, the BSR contains a copy of the sampled Micro Channel bus signal lines at the time of the first error. No provision is made for saving bus states for successive errors.

On a Store instruction, data is ignored. On a Load instruction, the data returned is the contents of the register as described, if an error has occurred (bit 1 of the Miscellaneous Interrupt register is on); bits 0 to 23 are returned as a 0.

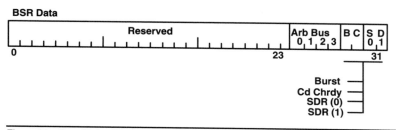

Figure 36. **Bus Status Register**

7.4.5.5   TCE Address Register

This register specifies the starting address and size of the TCE table in system memory. This register shall be initialized by the hardware and the IPL ROM code before the master enable bit in the IOCC Configuration register is enabled and shall not be changed thereafter.

Implementations which have the 64-bit mode set to a 1 at startup require that the IPL ROM code treat this register as 2 words, regardless of whether or not the 64-bit mode bit has been turned off prior to setup of this register. 32-bit implementations do not implement word 0 and an access to word 0 in 32-bit implementations shall result in a DSI with an invalid operation error code and this is sent to the processor which issued the I/O Load or Store instruction for logging into that processor's DSIER.

For information about this register, see Section 6.1.5, "BUC TCE Address Register," on page 69.

The data in this register at startup time is indeterminate. The IPL ROM code should initialize this register before turning on the master enable bit in the IOCC Configuration register.

7.4.5.6   Component Reset Register (CRR)

The Component Reset Register (CRR) is comprised of one register and provides the ability to individually drive the resets to each I/O slot. Writing a 0 into a bit position resets that slot, and writing a 1 removes the reset.

The use of the bits in this register are implementation dependent. The usage includes the reset of the standard I/O devices as well as the Micro Channel slots. On a Load instruction from this register, the value of the unimplemented bits is indeterminate. On a Store instruction, unimplemented bits are ignored.

The CRR is initialized to a 0 by the hardware at startup. This sets and holds a bus reset to all the I/O boards until explicitly enabled by a startup diagnostic utility.

After a reset operation occurs, the software removes the reset by writing a 1 to the board slots. To ensure proper timing relationships, the software must make sure the reset is held a minimum of 100 milliseconds before removing the reset.

Software can determine if a slot exists and contains a board by removing the reset to the slot and reading the board identification. A board identification of 0xffff means that no slot exists, or that the slot is empty.

On a bus timeout error, hardware sets the implemented CRR bits to a 0.

7.4.5.7   Bus Mapping Register

The Bus Mapping register provides a means to specify which blocks of bus memory address space are allocated for bus to bus data transfers by bus masters. This register allows for the flexibility of directing some of a bus masters transfers to bus memory and some to system memory.

Table 44 on page 137 shows the address ranges mapped by the Bus Mapping register bits. If a bit in the Bus Mapping register is set to a 0, then the corresponding range of bus address space shall NOT be mapped to system memory for bus master operations (that is, a bus master access to an address in this range shall result in a bus to bus transfer cycle). If a bit in the Bus Mapping register is set to a 1, then the corresponding range of bus address space is mapped to system memory for bus master operations. Notice that not only is the mapping granularity is different for the first 16 bits than it is for the second 16 bits, but also that the address range for bit 16 of this register is not the same as for bits 17 to 31. The address range for bit 16 is not a full 256 MB due to the overlap with the address range mapped by bits 0 to15.

7.4.5.8   Other IOCC Registers

The following IOCC registers are described elsewhere in this document, and are listed here for completeness:

- Interrupt Enable Register, see Section 7.4.6.1 on page 139.

- Interrupt Request Register, see Section 7.4.6.2 on page 139.

- Miscellaneous Interrupt register, see Section 7.4.6.3 on page 140.

- External Interrupt Vector Register, see Section 7.4.6.4 on page 141.

- DMA Slave Control registers, see Section 7.4.3.2 on page 123.

- Channel Status Registers, see Table 37 on page 118.

Note

I/O address space accesses by bus masters are always assumed to be bus to bus operations.

Engineering Note

The data in the Bus Mapping register at startup time is indeterminate. The IPL ROM code should initialize this register before turning on the master enable bit in the IOCC Configuration register.

Register bit	Address range mapped	Size of address range (MB)
0	0x00000000–0x000fffff	1
1	0x00100000–0x001fffff	1
2	0x00200000–0x002fffff	1
• • •		
15	0x00f00000–0x00ffffff	1
16	0x01000000–0x0fffffff	240
17	0x10000000–0x1fffffff	256
18	0x20000000–0x2fffffff	256
• • •		
31	0xf0000000–0xffffffff	256

Table 44. **Bus Mapping Register**

7.4.6 IOCC Interrupt Structure

This section describes the IOCC interrupt structure. The system level interrupt structure is described in Chapter 9, "External Interrupt Architecture," beginning on page 157.

The IOCC supports 11 bus I/O interrupts, 3 native I/O interrupts, 1 miscellaneous interrupt, and 1 reserved interrupt level. The miscellaneous interrupts are collected together and are presented as one logical level. This results in a total of 16 IOCC interrupt levels.

The IOCC interrupt structure is shown in Figure 37 on page 138.

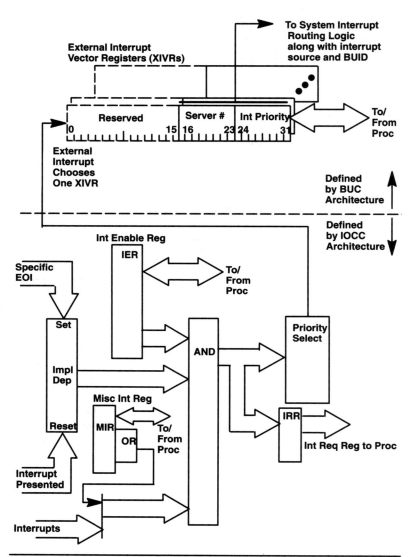

Figure 37.   **IOCC interrupt structure**

The registers which are IOCC unique are described briefly, below, and in more detail beginning on page 139.

- Interrupt Enable Register (IER)

  - One per IOCC

  - Allows for masking off of unused interrupts

- Interrupt Request Register (IRR)

  - One per IOCC

  - Allows the software to read which interrupts are pending in the IOCC

- Miscellaneous Interrupts Register (MIR)

  - One per IOCC

  - Contains several miscellaneous interrupts which get combined and presented to the system as one interrupt priority

- EXternal Interrupt Vector Register (XIVR)

  - 16 registers (one per interrupt source)

  - Provides a table lookup of the interrupt priority for each external interrupt

  - Provides a processor affinity field for each external interrupt (for MP implementations)

7.4.6.1   IOCC Interrupt Enable Register (IER)

This register provides the ability to enable or disable any of the interrupt request signals. Each bit in this register is defined to enable or disable the interrupt in the same corresponding bit position in the IOCC Interrupt Request Register, described in the next section. Unimplemented bits shall be set to 0 by a Store instruction. On a Load instruction, the value of the unimplemented bits are indeterminate. No dynamic management of the IER is necessary during interrupt service. It is provided primarily to allow disabling of unused, potentially noisy interrupts.

The data in the IER at startup time is indeterminate. The IPL ROM code shall initialize this register before turning on the master enable bit in the IOCC Configuration register.

7.4.6.2   IOCC Interrupt Request Register (IRR)

This register provides access to the device interrupt sources after they are masked by the IER, and can be read using an I/O Load instruction. On an I/O Store instruction to this register, data is ignored. A detailed description of each bit is in Table 45 on page 140.

Bits	Description
0	Miscellaneous Interrupt: The IOCC presents miscellaneous interrupts as a class interrupt, consuming one logical level. This appears in bit 0, and is an OR of all the bits in the Miscellaneous Interrupt register. If this interrupt is posted, the system is required to read the Miscellaneous Interrupt register to determine the cause of the interrupt. Bit 0 is set to 1 when any miscellaneous interrupt occurs and bit 0 in the Interrupt Enable Register is set to 1. This bit is reset to a 0 when the Miscellaneous Interrupt register is set to a 0.
1	Keyboard Interrupt: This bit is set to a 1 when a keyboard interrupt occurs and bit 1 in the Interrupt Enable Register is set to a 1. This interrupt is level-sensitive and must be reset within the device prior to a return from interrupt.
2	Serial Port Interrupts: This bit is set to a 1 when a board serial port 1 or serial port 2 interrupt occurs (Shared Interrupt) and bit 2 in the Interrupt Enable Register is set to a 1. This interrupt is level-sensitive and must be reset within the device prior to a return from interrupt.
3–7 9–12 14–15	I/O Bus Interrupts: These bits are set to a 1 when I/O bus interrupts occur and their corresponding bits in the Interrupt Enable Register are set to a 1. These bits reflect the current signal level of each of the Micro Channel interrupt lines and are not latched. It is not necessary to reset these bits as part of interrupt service.
8	Reserved, see Section 1.2.1 on page 2.
13	Parallel Port Interrupt: This bit is set to a 1 when a Standard I/O parallel port interrupt occurs and bit 13 in the Interrupt Enable Register is set to a 1. This interrupt is level-sensitive and must be reset within the device prior to an interrupt return.
16–31	Reserved, see Section 1.2.1 on page 2.

Table 45. **IOCC Interrupt Request Register Definition**

7.4.6.3   Miscellaneous Interrupts Register (MIR)

The first two bits of the MIR contain IOCC errors not reported in the Channel Status Registers. These errors are caused by asynchronous events or are associated with situations where no device interrupt is posted. As such, the IOCC reports these errors via its own interrupt.

The summary OR of the MIR is presented as bit 0 of the Interrupt Request Register.

The data in the MIR at startup time is indeterminate. The IPL ROM code shall initialize the MIR before turning on the master enable bit in the IOCC Configuration register.

This register is accessible by both Load and Store instructions. Store instructions function only as a masked reset. Writing a 0 to a bit position resets that bit, while writing a 1 does nothing. A detailed description of each bit is in Table 46 on page 141.

Bits	Description
0	Channel Check: This bit is set if the I/O bus 'chck' line is active during a Micro Channel operation (Bus master, PIO or DMA slave) at the beginning of a cycle (after 'arb/gnt' signal falls and before the first time the 'cmd' signal falls). There should be no devices that asynchronously report errors by activating the 'chck' signal. However, if this occurs, the channel check posts an asynchronous IOCC error interrupt. Normally, in RISC System/6000 PowerPC systems, the 'chck' signal is presented as a synchronous exception and a DSI is posted instead. Refer to Section 7.3.4, "Exception Reporting and Handling," on page 102 and Section 7.3.3.3, "Micro Channel Channel Check," on page 101 for more information.
1	Bus Time-out: This bit is set if an I/O bus timeout occurred. See Section 7.3.3.4, "Micro Channel Bus Timeout," on page 101 for additional details. While this bit is active, the 'arb/gnt' signal is forced high, bus arbitration is suspended, and control of the I/O bus is unconditionally given to the IOCC.
2	Auxiliary Processor Interrupt: This bit is defined for use in systems that have some form of auxiliary processor (for example, a bring-up processor or service processor). This bit is implementation dependent. This bit can be used by systems to allow an auxiliary processor to interrupt a system processor. This bit, if implemented, shall be ORed with the other bits of this register to form bit 0 of the IOCC Interrupt Request Register. If this bit is not implemented, or is implemented but not used by a system, then this bit should be set to a 0 by the software with a Store instruction.
3–31	Reserved, see Section 1.2.1 on page 2.

Table 46. **Miscellaneous Interrupts Register Definition**

7.4.6.4 IOCC External Interrupt Vector Register (XIVR)

This register is described in more detail under Section 6.2.2, "External Interrupt Vector Register (XIVR)," on page 72. There are 16 of these registers in the IOCC, one per interrupt source.

7.4.6.5 Interrupt Source Sent to the XISR

The External Interrupt Source Register (XISR) is a 3-byte system level register that contains the address of the physical source of an interrupt. Each processor has its own XISR. The low order 4 bits define up to 16 sources within a BUC and the upper 20 bits specify the system address (route) of the BUC. For interrupts from the IOCC, the XISR is defined in Table 47 on page 142.

7.4.7 Non-Recoverable Errors

Non-recoverable errors are defined as errors which, due to hardware limitations, software limitations, or both, have corrupted the system state such that it is not possible, by use of standard (known) procedures, to continue to the state that should have resulted if the operation had completed without error.

Bits	Description
0–10	Hardware Implementation Dependent Field 1, refer to Table 59 on page 168 for more information regarding this field.
11–19	BUID: These bits are the BUID of the interrupting IOCC.
20–23	IOCC Interrupt Number: This field represents the interrupt number of the interrupt that the IOCC has selected to present to the system and corresponds to a bit number of the IOCC IRR; for example, 0x0 in these bits indicates that bit 0 of the IOCC IRR is on (the Miscellaneous Interrupt), 0x1 indicates that bit 1 is on (the keyboard interrupt), and so on. For the definition of the IOCC IRR, see Section 7.4.6.2, "IOCC Interrupt Request Register (IRR)," on page 139.

Table 47. IOCC XISR Definition for IOCC Interrupts

Examples of non-recoverable errors include:

■ Errors which cannot be associated with a particular device driver

■ Errors which can be associated with a particular device driver, but cannot be associated with a particular application

■ Errors which are reportable back to the correct application, but may, if left unchecked until handled by the software, allow data corruption to propagate past the initial point of corruption

   – For example, onto the disk or onto the LAN

   – Initial point of corruption might be in data from another application

The general characteristic of non-recoverable errors is that they pose risks to further system operations. Since the potential for propagation of corrupted data must be minimized, it is important that hardware stop the propagation. How this is handled is system and IOCC implementation dependent. In some systems, this may mean the IOCC may need to checkstop.

See also Section 7.4.8, "Recoverable Errors," on page 143.

7.4.7.1   Non-Recoverable Load and Store Error Conditions

Error conditions that arise in Load and Store instructions issued to the IOCC include bus errors, programming errors, and hardware errors. The following errors may fall into the non-recoverable or recoverable category, depending on the IOCC, the system hardware, and Operating System implementations:

■ An attempt to cross a segment boundary with a single Load or Store instruction

■ TCE reload error

If it is possible for the IOCC to report these as recoverable errors, then they should be reported as recoverable errors, not as non-recoverable ones. If reported as a non-recoverable error, then the implementation should not report an error code in the DSIER.

Errors which are always non-recoverable include:

- Bus time-outs

- Errors on I/O Load and Store instructions issued to the IOCC facilities (for example, CSRs)

7.4.7.2 Non-Recoverable Bus Master and DMA Slave Error Conditions

Error conditions that arise in bus master and DMA slave operations include Micro Channel bus errors, programming errors, and hardware errors. The following errors may fall into the non-recoverable or recoverable category, depending on the IOCC and Operating System implementations:

- TCE Reload error

- System Address error

- System Data error

If it is possible for the IOCC to report these as recoverable errors, then they should be reported as recoverable errors, not as non-recoverable ones. If reported as a non-recoverable error, then the implementation should not report an error code in the Channel Status Register for that device.

Errors which are always non-recoverable include:

- Bus time-outs

7.4.8 Recoverable Errors

Recoverable errors are defined as errors which allow the system to keep operating and have the following characteristics:

- For Load and Store operations, can be reported to the device driver in such a way that the device driver can either retry the operation or can shut down the operation cleanly, without allowing any propagation of corrupted data.

- For a bus master or DMA slave operation, can be reported to the device and to the device driver in such a way that the device driver can retry the operation or can shut down the operation cleanly, without allowing any propagation of corrupted data. In the bus master case, this implies the capability of reporting the error to the device as a synchronous channel check.

It is the intent of this architecture to have all errors which can reasonably be reported as recoverable errors, to be reported as recoverable errors, and not non-recoverable ones.

See also Section 7.4.7, "Non-Recoverable Errors," on page 141.

7.4.8.1   Recoverable Load and Store Error Conditions

Error conditions that arise in Load and Store instructions include bus errors, programming errors, and hardware errors. Micro Channel bus errors such as address or data parity errors can be caused by hardware malfunctions or transient electrical noise (refer to Section 7.3.4, "Exception Reporting and Handling," on page 102 for more information). Software should try to distinguish between transient and hard failures by retrying the operation. The recommended approach is for the software to retry the operation three times before terminating the recovery procedure.

The class of errors which fall into the recoverable category include:

- Invalid operation

- Authority error

- Channel check

- Data parity error

- Card selected feedback error

The following errors may fall into the non-recoverable or recoverable category, depending on the IOCC and System implementations:

- An attempt to cross a segment boundary with a single Load or Store instruction

- TCE reload error

If it is possible for the IOCC to report these as recoverable errors, then they should be reported as recoverable errors, not as non-recoverable ones. If reported as a recoverable error, then the implementation should deliver a DSI to the processor and report an error code in the DSIER.

Load and Store instruction errors that are synchronous on the Micro Channel bus generate a DSI to the processor with an error code which gets logged into the DSIER of the processor which issued the Load or Store instruction. DSIs are ordered and precise.

No device should report errors by activating the 'chck' signal asynchronously. However, if this occurs, the error is reported as an miscellaneous interrupt (see

Section 7.4.6.2, "IOCC Interrupt Request Register (IRR)," on page 139). In addition, if the asynchronous channel check is present at the start of a Load or Store operation on the Micro Channel bus, a DSI shall also be reported and an error code shall be logged into the DSIER. Load and store error codes that get logged into the DSIER and are summarized in Table 48 which starts on this page, and continues to the next page.

No provision is made to capture status for multiple errors.

Error code (DSIER bits 12–15)	Description
0b0000	Reserved.
0b0001	Invalid Operation: This error occurs for one of the following conditions:
	When an attempt is made to access an IOCC facility (register or command) or Micro Channel address space (bus memory or I/O) without the applicable K bit in the SR (32-bit machines) or STE (64-bit machines) being set to a value of 0.
	When an attempt is made to access undefined address in the IOCC control address space.
	When an attempt is made to access a bus address for which a TCE does not exist and the authority mask in the SR or STE requires a TCE access (that is the mask is not all 0's).
	When an attempt is made to access an IOCC facility (command or register) with a length inappropriate for that facility and IOCC implementation.
	When an attempt is made to access an IOCC facility (command or register) with the authority mask in the SR or STE not set to all-0's.
	When an attempt is made to cross a segment boundary with a single Load or Store instruction. This error is implementation dependent; some implementations may not detected it or may detect it but produce an non-recoverable error (see Section 7.4.7, "Non-Recoverable Errors," on page 141).
0b0010	Reserved.
0b0011	Reserved.
0b0100	Reserved.
0b0101	Authority Error: This error occurs for accesses for which the page protect key in the TCE and authority mask in the SR or STE do not agree, including the case where the page protect key in the TCE field is set to a 0.
0b0110	Reserved.
0b0111	Reserved.

Table 48. **Load and Store Error Condition Descriptions**

Error code (DSIER bits 12–15)	Description
0b1000	Channel Check: This error occurs if a device responds with a synchronous channel check indication during a Load or Store operation, or if an asynchronous channel check is present at the start of the operation. For example, a device might respond with a channel check for a write operation to that device where there is bad parity on the data or address, or for other device detected errors during an operation to that device.
0b1001	Data Parity: This error occurs if the IOCC detects bad parity on a Load operation from an I/O device.
0b1010	Reserved.
0b1011	Card Selected Feedback Error: This error occurs if, after a device is addressed, it does not respond by driving the 'cd sfdbk' line. Some conditions which could cause this to occur are: • If the device is not present • If the device is not seated in the card slot properly • If the device is not enabled • If there is bad address parity on the bus and there is no detection of the bad address parity on the bus, and if the resulting bad address does not select any device.
0b1100	Reserved.
0b1101	Reserved.
0b1110	TCE Reload Error: This error occurs if the authority mask in the SR or STE requires a TCE access (that is the mask is not all 0's) and the IOCC receives an uncorrectable data parity or ECC error response from the system interconnect (for example, system bus) during the TCE access. The results of this error are implementation dependent. In some implementations, this error may be non-recoverable (see Section 7.4.7, "Non-Recoverable Errors," on page 141).
0b1111	Reserved.

Table 48. **Continued**

7.4.8.2   Recoverable Bus Master Error Conditions

Error conditions that arise in bus master operations include Micro Channel bus errors, programming errors, and hardware errors. Micro Channel bus errors, such as an address or data parity error, may be caused by hardware malfunctions or transient electrical noise. Refer to Section 7.3.3.2, "Micro Channel Parity Errors," on page 100 and Section 7.3.3.3, "Micro Channel Channel Check," on page 101 for a description of these errors. Errors have the potential of being handled differently depending on whether or not the channel is mapped to system memory. These different cases are described below.

In general, all recoverable errors shall result in the IOCC activating the 'chck' signal to the device at the time the error occurred (that is, synchronous to the operation which caused the error). The class of errors which fall into the recoverable category include:

- Authority Error

- Page Fault

- Data Parity

- Address Parity

- Card Selected Feedback Error

- TCE Extent

The following errors may fall into the non-recoverable or recoverable category, depending on the IOCC and system implementations:

- TCE Reload error

- System Address error

- System Data error

If it is possible for the IOCC to report these as recoverable errors, then they should be reported as recoverable errors, not as non-recoverable ones. If reported as a recoverable error, then the implementation should deliver a synchronous channel check to the device and report an error code in the device's Channel Status Register.

If the transfer is to or from system memory (that is, the channel is mapped to system memory and the IOCC is involved in the transfer), then on an error, an error code identifying the class of error is set into the Channel Status Register (bits 0 to 3) corresponding to that channel. The CSRs capture the channel status until the error code is reset by a Store instruction. All errors cause the 'chck' signal to be pulsed. In addition, on TCE extent and address parity errors, the IOCC shall not activate the 'sfdbkrtn' line. When a bus master device sees this error condition, it should suspend operations and post an interrupt. For additional information refer to Section 7.3.4, "Exception Reporting and Handling," on page 102. After the error condition, if the bus master device tries to continue accesses with the channel effectively disabled (also, if the bus master tries to make an access and the channel was never enabled), the IOCC activates 'chck' and shall not activate 'sfdbkrtn'. If the access is directed to the IOCC, the IOCC shall not take or supply data, and continued read accesses by the device after the error results in the IOCC bus drivers being disabled which results in all ones on the Micro Channel data bus.

If the transfer is a bus to bus operation and the prevent channel disable on error bit is set to a 1, then the IOCC shall still monitor the bus for address parity errors,

Programming Note

Not all Micro Channel Adapters look at the 'chck' (channel check) signal. Device drivers which are written for adapters which do not look at the 'chck' signal must read the CSR for that adapter, even if even if that adapter reports successful completion of the operation with no error.

but shall not log that error or disable the channel on an error (the 'chck' signal is still pulsed). Note that if the prevent channel disable on error bit is set to a 1 for a particular bus master, then that bus master must have the capability to detect and report (to the system) address parity and card selected feedback errors.

If the transfer is a bus to bus operation, and if the prevent channel disable on error bit is set to a 0, then this is treated like the mapped case, and on an error an error code identifying the class of error is set into the CSR (bits 0 to 3) corresponding to that channel. The CSRs capture the channel status until the error code is reset by a Store instruction. All errors cause the 'chck' signal to be pulsed. In addition, on address parity errors, the IOCC shall not activate the 'sfdbkrtn' line. When a bus master device sees this error condition, it should suspend operations and post an interrupt. For additional information refer to Section 7.3.4, "Exception Reporting and Handling," on page 102. After the error condition, if the bus master device tries to continue accesses with the channel effectively disabled (also, if the bus master tries to make an access and the channel was never enabled), the IOCC activates 'chck' and shall not activate 'sfdbkrtn'.

Table 49 on page 148 summarizes the various IOCC actions for errors that occur during bus to bus (non-mapped) operations. Table 50 on page 149 summarizes the actions for operations involving system memory (operations mapped to system memory). Table 51 on page 149 summarizes the actions for operations involving a disabled channel or an access to a channel with an error pending. More details on these error codes are shown in Table 52 on page 151.

Error	CSR Prevent Channel Disable on Error Bit	Pulse 'chck'?	Log Error in CSR?	Disable Channel?
Address Parity	0	yes	yes	yes
(On an address parity error, bus to bus versus bus to system memory operation is indeterminate, therefore assume bus to bus)	1	yes	no	no
Card Selected	0	yes	yes	yes
Feedback	1	no	no	no

Table 49. **IOCC Actions on Errors during Bus to Bus Operations**

Error	CSR Prevent Channel Disable on Error Bit	Pulse 'chck'?	Log Error in CSR?	Disable Channel?
Authority	don't care	yes	yes	yes
Page Fault	don't care	yes	yes	yes
TCE Extent	don't care	yes	yes	yes
Data Parity	don't care	yes	yes	yes
Address Parity	0	yes	yes	yes
(On an address parity error, bus to bus versus bus to system memory operation is indeterminate, therefore assume bus to bus)	1	yes	no	no
Card Selected Feedback	don't care	yes	yes	yes
ECC	don't care	yes	yes	yes
System Address	don't care	yes (if synchronous)	yes	yes
TCE Reload	don't care	yes	yes	yes

Table 50. IOCC Actions on Errors during Transfers to or from System Memory

CSR Status on Bus Master Access	CSR Prevent Channel Disable on Error Bit	Pulse 'chck'?	Log Error in CSR?
Disabled	don't care	yes	no
Error Previously Logged	don't care	yes	no

Table 51. IOCC Actions on a Bus Master Access when the Channel Is Not Enabled

7.4.8.3 Recoverable DMA Slave Error Conditions

Error conditions that arise in DMA operations include bus errors, programming errors, and hardware errors. The class of error is coded and set in the status field (bits 0 to 3) in the CSR. The 'tc' signal is then pulsed, which should cause the I/O device to suspend DMA operations and post an interrupt. If it does not stop DMA, but continues to request DMA service, the IOCC services the DMA requests with dummy cycles, pulsing the 'tc' signal on every cycle.

The class of errors which fall into the recoverable category include:

■ Extra request

■ Channel check

■ Data Parity error

■ Card selected feedback error

■ TCE extent error

The following errors may fall into the non-recoverable or recoverable category, depending on the IOCC and system implementations:

■ TCE Reload error

■ System Address error

■ System Data error

If it is possible for the IOCC to report these as recoverable errors, then they should be reported as recoverable errors, not as non-recoverable ones. If reported as a recoverable error, then the implementation should pulse the 'tc' signal on the Micro Channel bus and report an error code in that device's Channel Status Register.

Error codes are summarized in Table 53 on page 152.

Error code (CSR bits 0–3)	Description
0b0100	Authority Error: This error code is set if an attempt is made to write to a read-only page in system memory.
0b0101	Page Fault: This error code is set if an attempt is made to access a page in system memory and TCE page mapping and control bits are set to 0b01. This can occur in normal operation. Devices attempting to take advantage of this function must present an interrupt after receiving a 'chck' signal on the Micro Channel bus.
0b0110	Error on the Micro Channel bus: This error code is set for the following detected errors: Data Parity: This error occurs if the IOCC detects bad parity when operating as a slave on the bus (when the transfer is from device to system memory). This error shall not occur on a bus to bus data transfer. Address Parity: This error occurs if the IOCC detects bad parity on Micro Channel address bus and the prevent channel disable on error bit in the CSR for the device on the bus is set to a 0. This error code is not set if the prevent channel disable on error bit is set to a 1 and the operation is a bus to bus operation. Card Selected Feedback Error: This error occurs if, after a device is addressed by a bus master, it does not respond by driving the 'cd sfbk' line and the prevent channel disable on error bit in the CSR for the bus master on the bus is set to a 0. This error code is not set if the prevent channel disable on error bit is set to a 1 and the operation is a bus to bus operation.
0b0111	System Access Error: This error code is set if the operation is to system memory and one of the following errors is detected: TCE Extent: This error occurs if the bus master is attempting to access system memory and an attempt is made to access a bus address for which a TCE does not exist. System Data Error: This error occurs if the IOCC received an uncorrectable data parity or ECC error response from the system interconnect (for example, system bus) during a bus master transfer request to system memory. The results of this error are implementation dependent. In some implementations, this error may be non-recoverable (see Section 7.4.7, "Non-Recoverable Errors," on page 141). System Address Error: This error occurs if the real page number in the address is invalid. Software should make sure that the real page number in the TCE is valid. The results of this error are implementation dependent. In some implementations, this error may be non-recoverable (see Section 7.4.7, "Non-Recoverable Errors," on page 141). TCE Reload Error: This error occurs if the IOCC detects a parity or uncorrectable ECC error during a TCE access. This results of this error are implementation dependent. In some implementations, this error may be non-recoverable (see Section 7.4.7, "Non-Recoverable Errors," on page 141).

Table 52. **Bus Master Error Condition Descriptions**

Error code (CSR bits 0–3)	Description
0b0011	**Extra Request:** This error code is set if a DMA slave request is received by a DMA slave channel when the channel is disabled. Receipt of an unsolicited DMA request is an error unique to a DMA slave. This error is generally caused by I/O device malfunctions after the IOCC pulses the 'tc' signal in an attempt to shut off the DMA slave. This error can also occur with incorrect programming of the channel.
0b0110	**Error on the Micro Channel bus:** This error code is set for the following detected errors:
	Channel Check: This error occurs if the device responds with a channel check indication during a DMA slave operation or if an asynchronous channel check is present at the start of the operation.
	Data Parity: This error occurs if the IOCC detects bad parity on the Micro Channel data bus when the IOCC is reading data. (See Section 7.3.4, "Exception Reporting and Handling," on page 102 for details.)
	Card Selected Feedback Error: This error occurs if, after a device is addressed, it does not respond by driving the 'cd sfbk' line. Conditions that could cause this to occur are: if the device is not present; is not seated in the card slot properly; is not enabled or detects bad address parity and does not respond to that address. This error can only occur on the second cycle of a bus to bus operation.
0b0111	**System Access Error:** This error code is set for the following errors on operations to system memory:
	TCE Extent Error: This error occurs if a DMA slave request is received and the DMA slave control register 4 contains a TCE number for which there does not exist a corresponding TCE.
	System Data Error: This error occurs if the IOCC receives an uncorrectable parity or ECC error response from the system interconnect (for example, system bus) during a DMA slave request to system memory. The results of this error are implementation dependent. In some implementations, this error may be non-recoverable (see Section 7.4.7, "Non-Recoverable Errors," on page 141).
	System Address Error: This error occurs if the real page number in the address is invalid. The results of this error are implementation dependent. In some implementations, this error may be non-recoverable (see Section 7.4.7, "Non-Recoverable Errors," on page 141).
	TCE Reload Error: This error occurs if the IOCC detects a parity or uncorrectable ECC error during a TCE access. The results of this error are implementation dependent. In some implementations, this error may be non-recoverable (see Section 7.4.7, "Non-Recoverable Errors," on page 141).

Table 53. **DMA Slave Error Condition Descriptions**

System Resources 8

System Resources are those facilities which are present on all PowerPC systems and are necessary to configure and operate the system, especially at Initial Program Load (IPL) time. These resources are accessed through the high real memory addresses reserved for them.

8.1 Operator Interface

The operator interface is used primarily at IPL time to provide a means for the operator to indicate the mode and path for IPL, as well as a means for the system microcode and IPL software to display messages on the progress of IPL/or abnormal conditions. A means is also provided for the operator to generate a reset to the processor which may be independent of a keyboard.

8.1.1 Display Interface

The operator interface display is accessed via the memory mapped word at address 0xf...ff600300. The minimum display capability is three characters as defined in Table 54 and Table 55. This capability is defined to be compatible with the LED display on the Risc System/6000 POWERstation Model 320.

This capability is defined to be compatible with the three position Key Mode Switch on the Risc System/6000 POWERstation Model 320.

Bit(s)	Description
0–3	First Character (leftmost)
4–7	Second Character
8–11	Third Character
12–31	Reserved

Table 54. **Display Data Word Definition**

The characters displayed for each of the values stored in these three positions are defined in Table 55.

Value	Character displayed
0000	0
0001	1
0010	2
0011	3
0100	4
0101	5
0110	6
0111	7
1000	8
1001	9
1010	a
1011	b
1100	c
1101	d
1110	e
1111	f

Table 55. **4-Bit Character Values**

8.1.2 IPL/Operation Mode

There are three modes in which the system may be powered up and/or IPLed. The mode to be in effect at the time the system is powered-up or re-IPLed may be selected by the operator either via a Key Mode Switch or an equivalent system facility.

The system microcode shall determine the state desired by the operator by accessing bits 30 and 31 of the memory mapped word at location 0xff0000e4. The "Mode Name" and Icon are example representations and may be varied on different system implementations. The three modes are encoded as shown in Table 56.

Value	Mode Number	Mode Name	Icon
01	1	Secure	2
10	2	Service	(wrench icon)
11	3	Normal	[1]

Table 56. **IPL/Operation Modes**

8.1.3 Operator Reset

The operator may generate a reset to the processor via a reset button or equivalent facility. The System Reset Count in the Reset Status register (shown in Table 6 on page 12) and the IPL/Operation Mode (shown in Table 56) determine the Operating System's actions.

Note

The operator reset capability is defined to be compatible with the Rest Button on the RISC System/6000 POWERstation Model 320.

IPL/Operation Mode Number	System Reset Count Bit 31	Reset Generated When Operator Reset Activated
1	0	None
1	1	None
Not 1	0	Soft
Not 1	1	Hard

Table 57. **Operator Reset**

A soft reset causes the processor to perform a system reset interrupt. A hard reset causes the processor to perform a power-on reset cycle and IPL, if possible. The details of how the processor handles these signals may be found in the processor's Book IV.

8.2 Non-Volatile Random Access Memory (NVRAM)

Non-Volatile RAM (NVRAM) is used by PowerPC systems to allow the system bring-up routines to save system configuration and other information relating to system operation without having to access peripheral storage.   This information is used during bring-up to determine if the configuration has changed and/or an error occurred which caused the system to restart.

The NVRAM contents and mapping is described in Section on page 35.

8.3 Timer Facilities

Each PowerPC system provides facilities for the maintenance of clocks for timing and time of day purposes. Multiprocessor systems also provide means for the synchronization of these facilities among the various processors. This section describes those facilities which, if implemented, are common to all PowerPC systems implementing them.

8.3.1 Time of Day Clock

A non-volatile Time of Day (TOD) Clock reference is available through the memory mapped locations 0xff0000c0 – 0xff0000dc. The definition of the use of this area is system implementation specific.

8.3.2 Time Base Enable

Architecture Note

The Time Base Enable section does not apply to 601 based systems.

PowerPC systems shall incorporate support for the enabling and synchronization of the processor's local clock facility. *PowerPC Architecture* (book III) has defined a TBE_ pin (Time Base Enable pin) which enables a system clock circuit to be implemented.

8.3.3 Symmetric Multi-Processor (SMP) Synchronization

Through the use of the PowerPC TBE_pin, the local clocks on all the processors in the system can be stopped and set to the same time. When the clocks are restarted, they all start on the same cycle and count the same frequency, keeping them in sync.

External Interrupt Architecture

The term "interrupt" is used to mean the signalling of a processor that an "interrupt condition" exists at a given "source." When enabled (with the MSR EE) the processor starts "interrupt processing" as specified in the *PowerPC Architecture* (book III), continuing as directed by software.

9.1 External Interrupt Overview

The External Interrupt Architecture is separated into an Interrupt Routing Layer and an Interrupt Presentation Layer. The Interrupt Routing Layer is expected to route all interrupt conditions to the appropriate instance of an interrupt management area within the Interrupt Presentation Layer. The Interrupt Presentation Layer communicates the interrupt source to software. Software accepts the interrupt condition and is responsible for resetting the interrupt condition (via path(s) not specified in this section). Software is also responsible for indicating the acceptance of the interrupt and for notifying the Interrupt Presentation Layer that it has processed the Interrupt.

The architecture of the PowerPC external interrupt structure is required to span a wide range of system requirements; from the simple single user personal computer to multi-user systems consisting of a hierarchy of multiple processors. Identical implementations can not effectively address such a range. However, the programming interface and the logical view shall be consistent.

The logical view of the system is that of n (up to 256) queues of events. Within each queue there exists a prioritized list of events. Each queue is associated with a logical server. In the single processor system, there is one server and, therefore, one queue. In a multi-processor system there would be one queue associated with each processor and at least one global queue associated with the collection of processors viewed as one logical server. For multi-processor systems, the Available Processor Mask (APM) shall be supported to identify which processors are available in the system. The APM is expected to be placed in NVRAM in order to allow the turning off or on of a processor to be specified prior to system reset and reinitialization. The effect of the mask is required to be supported during initialization. Failure to support the updating of the APM mask after the Operating System has been initialized will prohibit the support of "Live Insertion" of a new processor, that is, the support of dynamically using a newly inserted processor. In addition, failure to support the updating of the APM mask after the Operating System has been initialized will prohibit the turning off of a processor. Because a processor could not be turned off, there would be no opportunity to support a graceful system degradation when a processor is no longer working properly. The complete architecture to allow the turning off or on of a processor is not included in this document, For multi-processor systems, the Global Queue Interrupt Routing Mask shall be supported to identify which processors are available for use for global queues. For multi-processor systems, the SMP EPOW XIVR shall be supported to allow the EPOW interrupt to be directed to a specific processor by the software. A system with a richer hierarchy might group subsets of processors into server groups and associate with each group a queue common to the group.

In PowerPC systems, the highest priority interrupt is 0x00 and the lowest is 0xff. Since 'higher priority' and 'lower priority' could be confusing (since they relate to a numerically smaller and numerically larger priority number, respectively), this document uses the terms more favored and less favored. Hence, interrupt level 0x55 is more favored than interrupt level 0xff and less favored than interrupt level 0x00. Similarly, 0x00 is the most favored interrupt level and 0xff is the least favored interrupt level.

Associated with each queue is a server number in the range of 0x00 through 0xff. The individual processors within the complex are assigned server numbers ascending from 0x00 and queues which serve multiple processors are assigned server numbers descending from 0xff. Queue lengths are implementation dependent, but have a minimum depth of one.

External interrupts are sourced from Bus Unit Controllers (BUCs), other processors in the complex, and from other sources in the system (for example, EPOW). While the different sources require different physical signalling mechanisms, the logical appearance to the server is as one queue headed by the most favored event.

The PowerPC External Interrupt architecture defines two layers; the interrupt presentation layer and the interrupt routing layer. These layers are shown in Figure 38 on page 161. The interrupt presentation layer consists of the registers associated with processors or servers to which the Operating System software interfaces to create and handle individual interrupts. The interrupt presentation layer's only option is the number of processors or servers within a system. The interrupt routing layer, routes the interrupts from the sources to the destinations and is by its nature far more implementation specific. Software may have to manage the configuration of the interrupt routing layer but does not have to interface to this layer on a per interrupt basis.

9.1.1 System Level Interrupt Register Overview

The registers used to manage interrupts are described, briefly, below, and in more detail beginning on page 165. The placement of these facilities is restricted to the upper four (4) gigabytes because on a 64-bit word machine, software shall assume that the upper 32-bits are all ones. For additional information regarding the location of the registers defined below, see Section 3.2 starting on page 10.

■ SMP Global Queue Interrupt Routing Mask (GQ_IRM)

- Required facility for each global queue supported by the interrupt routing layer hardware. The software uses this facility to tell the hardware which processors are available for a particular global queue. See Section 9.2.7 on page 171 for more details regarding the GQ_IRM.

■ Available Processor Mask (APM)

- Required facility for SMP systems to be used by the interrupt routing layer hardware to know which processors are available. The support for this facility is required at system initialization, but optional after IPL.

■ Global Queue Interrupt Request Register (G_QIRR)

- This register may be written as a single byte or as four bytes (a 32-bit word).

- Used in SMP systems as a non-processor specific server queue.

- Consists of two registers:

    ■ Global Most Favored Request Register (G_MFRR), which is an MFRR.

    ■ Interrupt Source Specification Register (ISSR)

        ○ Used in SMP systems to configure the source specification of a G_MFRR interrupt (see XISR).

■ Queued Interrupt Request Register (QIRR)

- This register may be written as a single byte or as four bytes (a 32-bit word).

- Consists of two registers:

Architecture and Programming Note

It is expected that many systems will typically support a single byte of the QIRR, that is, the MFRR byte with the second register, that is, the low order three bytes being unimplemented.

- Most Favored Request Register (MFRR)

    - At least one per processor plus one per non–processor specific server queue

    - Holds the priority of the most favored request on the queue

    - This register can be read back by the software to verify that the write has taken place

- Interrupt Source Specification Register (ISSR) or reserved or unimplemented

■ External Interrupt Request Register (XIRR)

  – One per processor

  – Consists of two registers:

    - Current Processor Priority Register (CPPR)

        - This register is updated by the software to contain the current processor priority

        - This register is updated when the software issues a Load instruction to the XIRR at a certain address and is updated to the priority of the interrupt represented by the XISR data which is delivered by the executed Load instruction.

    - External Interrupt Source Register (XISR)

        - Indicates the source of a pending interrupt (or a value of 0, if no pending interrupt)

■ EXternal Interrupt Vector Register (XIVR)

  – One per interrupt level in each BUC

  – Defined in section 6.2.2 on page 72

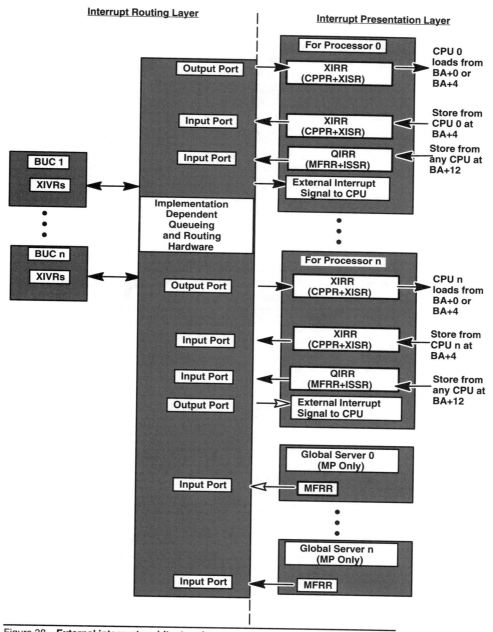

Figure 38. **External interrupt architecture layers**

9.1.2 Interrupt Routing Layer

Engineering Note

Those systems which
have processors which
externalize the EE bit of
the MSR are encouraged
to use it to override the
value in the CPPR in
interrupt routing
decisions.

The goal of the implementation dependent interrupt routing hardware within the interrupt routing layer is *to direct the most favored interrupt request to the processor operating at the least favored priority*. To the best of its ability, the interrupt routing layer shall avoid sending an interrupt to a processor which is running at a more favored level than the incoming request. Due to the range of system requirements, just one method of interrupt routing is not architected. Different implementations may approximate the above goal to different levels of accuracy and this will appear as a variable delay in the routing of interrupt requests. The greater the expected system load due to interrupts, the closer the interrupt routing hardware must approach the goal in order to achieve proper system performance. To fully achieve the goal, the interrupt routing hardware must be fully aware of the state of the system (that is, the exact per cycle processor priority, and the contents of all logical interrupt request queues). In practice this is not possible; there may be more potential interrupt requests than the queue manager logic can hold, and processor priority may take several cycles to propagate from the processor to the interrupt routing hardware. The depth of queue problem is handled by requiring the BUCs to resubmit interrupt request messages that are rejected by the interrupt routing hardware. This allows the interrupt routing hardware to implement a queue depth (minimum of one) to satisfy some percentage of the expected cases with the interrupt rejection mechanism used to handle any overflow cases. The software is unaware of the rejection mechanism which only exhibits a variable latency to affected interrupt requests. Since the interrupt routing hardware may be unaware of the true processor priority when it first routes a request toward a processor, the routing hardware shall be prepared for the priority to change after it has initially assigned a request to a specific processor. Failure to take changing processor priority into account can result in priority inversions and severe system performance degradation (priority inversion can occur if an interrupt is queued which has a less favored priority than the current processor priority, and if that queued interrupt prevents an interrupt with a more favored priority than the processor from getting in and interrupting the processor); the queued interrupt will not get serviced until the processor drops in priority below the queued interrupt priority. Again the interrupt rejection mechanism may be used to recover from queue resource problems.

When an interrupt source submits an interrupt request to the routing layer, the same instance of the request shall be resubmitted if and only if the interrupt condition has not been reset when either the interrupt is rejected by the routing layer or software issues the End Of Interrupt.

Various implementations are possible including a single element queue per processor consisting of an external interrupt priority and source, through multiple external interrupt source queue registers. The exact queueing implementation shall be transparent to the software interfacing to the Interrupt presentation layer.

At system configuration time, the configuration of the Interrupt routing layer shall include determining how many logical servers are supported, which processors support which logical server, and which interrupts are to be directed to which server. GQ_IRMs shall be used to specify which processors work against which logical server queue. The GQ_IRMs may be replicated in the BUCs or may be centralized. In addition, the interrupt routing layer shall use the APM to determine which processors are available for any interrupt routing.

9.1.3 Interrupt Presentation Layer

Each processor has associated with it a memory mapped Interrupt Management Area which contains the eXternal Interrupt Request Register (XIRR). The XIRR is a 4-byte facility and is composed of two fields: the Current Processor Priority Register (CPPR) and the External Interrupt Source Register (XISR). For more information on the XIRR, see Section 9.2.1, "External Interrupt Request Register (XIRR)," on page 165.

The CPPR contains the processor's operating priority. The CPPR may be written by software to prevent interruptions from less favored priority requests. The interrupt routing layer shall only direct an interrupt request to a processor if its CPPR field is less favored than the priority of the interrupt request. Software stores to the CPPR as a 1-byte register to inform the interrupt hardware of the current operating priority of the processor. For more information on the CPPR, see Section 9.2.2, "Current Processor Priority Register (CPPR)," on page 167.

To determine the source of the interrupt the software reads the XISR by issuing a Load instruction to the XIRR. The value in the XISR specifies the source of the interrupt (if a BUC, which BUID and level or, if a processor, which server queue). Based upon this information, the software can determine the location of the request parameters. The XISR presents the appearance of a read only register from the interrupt routing layer for Load operations, and a write only register to the interrupt routing layer for Store operations. That is, what is written is not automatically what is read. The XISR is only accessed atomically with the CPPR by 4-byte accesses directed to the XIRR. (PowerPC only supports atomic accesses to fields on their "natural" alignment.) For interrupts from BUCs, the upper bits of the XISR indicate the BUC BUID, and the low order 4 bits of the XISR field define up to 16 sources (or levels) within a BUC. Several values of this register have defined meanings. For more information on the XISR, see Section 9.2.3, "External Interrupt Source Register (XISR)," on page 167.

The interrupt presentation layer of the architecture is embodied through an Interrupt Management Area for each processor in the system. The Interrupt Management Area is within the system's System Management Memory Space, refer to Table 8 on page 15. The address of the processor's interrupt management area is referred to as its Base Address (BA) for the rest of this document. The BA is different for each processor (that is, there is a separate

Architecture Note

The hardware which implements the Interrupt Management Area is not required to participate in any cache coherency protocol. Software shall mark the corresponding page or pages as cache inhibited.

Programming Note

The inter-processor interrupt mechanism has associated with each logical queue, a physical queue of request blocks in system memory. This queue is maintained in priority order by the software. The implementation of the queue is not defined in the interrupt mechanism architecture but is left up to the Operating System software. The implementation of the various queues may be different depending upon the expected frequency of use. Associated with each queue is a Most Favored Request Register (MFRR) (in system memory space). When a program enqueues a request block to the queue, it determines if the new request is at a more favored priority, and if it is, the value of the new request's priority is written into the MFRR. When a process dequeues a request for service, the priority value of the next request on the queue is loaded into the MFRR. If the queue is empty after dequeue, the least favored value (0xff) is loaded into the MFRR. A value other than 0xff in the MFRR indicates to the interrupt hardware that an interrupt of that priority should be signalled to a (the) processor which services that queue.

Interrupt Management Area for each processor), and these areas can be accessed by any processor (there is no protection against it). The BA for a processor is setup at configuration time. The layout of the Interrupt Management Area is in Table 58.

Address	Byte 0	Byte 1	Byte 2	Byte 3	Comments
BA+0	CPPR	XISR			XIRR without side effects
BA+4	CPPR	XISR			XIRR with Load/Store side effects
BA+8	DSIER	DSIER			Data Storage Interrupt Error Register
BA+12	MFRR	ISSR or Reserved or Unimplemented			Required QIRR

Table 58. **Interrupt Management Area: Interrupt Presentation Layer Registers**

9.1.3.1   Interrupt Handling

When the interrupt routing layer wishes to signal an interrupt to a processor, it loads the XISR with the source of the interrupt. Any non zero value in the XISR field shall cause a interrupt to be signalled to the processor. This signal is masked by the processor's MSR EE bit prior to the processor generating the interrupt sequence. The loading of the XISR shall be atomic. If at a later time, a higher priority interrupt is made available to the interrupt routing layer, the interrupt routing layer may atomically change the value in the XISR to reflect the source of the higher priority interrupt. If a higher priority interrupt preempts a lower priority interrupt in this way, the interrupt routing layer shall insure that the lower priority interrupt shall be re-presented at a later time.

Once the processor has read the XIRR at BA+4, the interrupt routing layer may not "change its mind" and either preempt or cancel the request.

The XIRR facility appears twice in the external interrupt management area. Address BA+0 is designed to be used with interrupt polling. Address BA+4 has side effects when read or written, and is designed to allow efficient interrupt handler software by having the hardware assist the software in the interrupt queueing process. For more information on these side effects and how the external interrupt registers are used, see Section 9.2.1, "External Interrupt Request Register (XIRR)," on page 165.

9.1.3.2   Processor to Processor Interrupts

The Most Favored Request Register (MFRR) holds the priority of the most favored request queued on a software managed queue for this processor. When written to a value other than 0xff the MFRR competes with other external interrupts for the right to interrupt the processor. When the MFRR's priority is the most favored of all interrupt requests directed to the processor, an appropriate value is loaded into the XISR (see Section 9.2.3, "External

Interrupt Source Register (XISR)," on page 167) and an interrupt is signaled to the processor. When the processor reads the XIRR at BA+4, the value in the MFRR shall be loaded by the hardware into the CPPR. The MFRR may be read back by the software to ensure that the MFRR write has been performed.

During the processing of an inter-processor interrupt, the highest priority request is dequeued by the software from the software queue associated with the MFRR and the priority of the next favored request is loaded into the MFRR by the software.

9.1.3.3 Global Queues

In MP systems, the System Management Memory Space shall also contain one or more Global Queue MFRR's which are used by software to send inter-processor interrupts to any processor within some server group. The Global Queue MFRR's work just like the per processor MFRR described above except that the interrupt routing layer determines the processor to receive the request based upon its own algorithm, and the value loaded into the XISR is a BUID which indicates the Global Queue.

9.2 Interrupt Register Definition Details

This section describes the registers that shall be implemented by the interrupt routing layer hardware.

9.2.1 External Interrupt Request Register (XIRR)

The XIRR is a 4-byte register at addresses BA+0 and BA+4. Issuing a Load instruction to the XIRR at address BA+0 causes the CPPR and XISR to be Loaded into the processor with no side effects. This is designed for software polling of external interrupts. Issuing a Load instruction to the XIRR at address BA+4 has the following atomic side effects:

Prior to data transfer:

- Clear the interrupt signal to the processor, whose BA is being accessed, returning the load data to the requesting processor only after the time the processor will no longer respond to this instance of the interrupt.

After data transfers:

- The contents of the CPPR are set to the priority of the interrupt signalled in the XISR (if XISR was zero the CPPR field is unmodified).
- The XISR is reset to 0x000000. Subsequent interrupt requests of more favored priority shall now cause an interrupt to be signaled and presented in the XIRR.

Architecture Note

Software is not required to be aware of the high order XISR bits required to route an EOI to a given BUC. If a given BUC design needs software to generate an EOI (say to reset a BUC's hung interrupt routing logic) that is not associated with a presented XISR value, then the means for such an EOI shall be included in the BUC specific architecture.

Engineering Note

If the hardware elects to reject interrupts on a CPPR change from a more favored to a less favored level, then on a 4-byte Store to the XIRR, the hardware can do one of two things:
1. Do a multiple rejection (on both the CPPR change and the XISR write)
2. Do the rejection for the XISR write (using the fact that the write of the CPPR shall be of a less favored priority than the previous CPPR value; a requirement placed on the software).

The interrupt routing layer shall insure that all interrupt signal constraints of the processor are met. If, for example, the processor does not internally latch the interrupt signal, and were not able to guarantee proper operation if the interrupt signal was deactivated during the processor's interrupt presentation cycle, then the interrupt routing layer would have to externally latch the interrupt signal resetting the latch with the read of the XISR rather than as the result of an interrupt rejection.

Programming Note

At the end of the interrupt handler, writing the XIRR at BA+4 with the value read at the start of the interrupt handler has the combined effects of issuing an explicit End Of Interrupt to the BUC and returning the processor's operating priority to its pre-interrupt value. Software may keep the interrupt's operating priority in the interrupt source table structure for internal shadowing of the operating priority during the execution of the interrupt handler, or read the value of the CPPR at BA+0. (Alternatively, the interrupt handler software may update the value of the CPPR at BA+4 with an equal or less favored priority.)

When software is polling interrupts, after the software decides to take an interrupt, the software shall signal the hardware that the interrupt is being taken by issuing a Load to XIRR at BA+4. Software shall then compare the XISR with the value it read at BA+0 to make sure that the hardware did not change the XISR between the Loads.

Changing the CPPR is not a context synchronizing operation. Due to timing windows, the interrupt line to the processor may glitch as an interrupt is being rejected causing a phantom interrupt to the processor. The interrupt handler shall see an XISR value of zero for these interrupts and can ignore them.

This setting of the CPPR on the Load of the XIRR has the effect of rejecting all less favored or equal priority external interrupts from the time that the software issues a Load instruction to the XIRR until it issues a Store instruction to the CPPR with a new value.

Issuing a Store instruction to the XIRR facility at BA+0 is undefined (data is ignored). Storing to the XIRR at address BA+4 has atomic side effects and the effects are different for a 1-byte versus a 4-byte Store. When the Store instruction is a 1-byte Store, then this is a Store to the CPPR (see Section 9.2.2, "Current Processor Priority Register (CPPR)" on page 167). When the Store instruction is issued to the XIRR with a length of 4 bytes, an interrupt reset is sent to the source as indicated in the data that accompanies the Store to the XISR (not to the source indicated in the XISR at the time of the Store). This interrupt reset is said to indicate the End Of Interrupt (EOI) by the software. When issuing an EOI, software shall store the same XISR value (bits 0–23) to BA+4 that were read from the XISR when the associated interrupt was accepted. The results of an attempt to issue an EOI by storing into BA+4 without having previously read the XISR shall be unpredictable. The data that accompanies the Store to the XISR is not written into the XISR (and shall not be obtained if subsequently read with a Load instruction); it is used to indicate the source to be reset and provide other hardware implementation dependent information. Issuing a Store to the XISR at this address allows the source to present subsequent interrupts at the level indicated in the data accompanying the Store instruction. For a 4-byte Store, byte 0 is stored in the CPPR, but software shall ensure that this store of the CPPR is of a less favored or equal priority than the previous CPPR value, because hardware is not required to handle dual resets for this case (one for the change in CPPR value to a more favored or equal priority and one for a write to the XISR).

9.2.1.1 Interrupt Programming Considerations

When software begins to process an interrupt, the PowerPC Machine State Register (MSR) External interrupt Enable (EE) bit is off — masking off any subsequent external interrupts. During the interrupt processing sequence, the software shall set the EE bit to allow subsequent interrupts to be presented. Care shall be taken to insure that the contents of the XIRR at BA+4 have been returned to the processor prior to setting the EE bit, in order to avoid a race with interrupt routing layer's interrupt signalling termination. Such a race can produce undefined results. One way to insure the data has returned, in the face of potential processor speculative instruction execution, is to place an XIRR value data dependency in the code prior to the setting of the EE bit; as in the following code.

```
lwz  r4,BA+4    /* get XIRR */
mfmsr r5
xor  r6,r4,r4    /* create data dependency on the load of BA+4 & set r6=0 */
ori  r6,r6,EE    /* so will not be executed until the load of XIRR is complete */
or  r5,r5,r6
mtmsr r5        /* MSR = MSR+EE  */
```

9.2.2 Current Processor Priority Register (CPPR)

This register is a 1-byte register containing the current priority of the processor with which it is associated. This register is in real memory space at addresses BA+0 and BA + 4. Issuing a 1-byte Load to the CPPR (at either BA+0 or BA+4) has no side effects. The CPPR is a field in the XIRR register. Each processor has its own CPPR. When the processor changes state, such as entering or leaving a "critical section" of code, software may store the process priority of the processor into the CPPR. Hardware shall reject all interrupts for a processor that are at a priority less favored than the CPPR priority. Thus, keeping the CPPR current shall prevent an external interrupt from interrupting a process of more favored or equal priority.

The CPPR is a field in the XIRR and can be read or written as part of the XIRR. For more information, see Section 9.2.1, "External Interrupt Request Register (XIRR)," on page 165.

When the contents of the CPPR are changed, the interrupt routing layer shall insure that only interrupts of more favored level are signaled to the processor and are presented in the XIRR. It is acceptable to recompute (possibly by interrupt rejection) the most favored interrupt to present after any Store to the CPPR if the direction of change of priority is to a less favored priority, and it is mandatory if the Store to the CPPR is a more favored or equal priority to any queued interrupt. When an interrupt is removed from the XIRR because of a store to the CPPR, if there is no interrupt of higher priority (higher than the new CPPR value) waiting to replace it in the XISR, then the hardware shall set the XISR to a value of 0 (atomically, with the CPPR store), indicating that no interrupt is pending, and shall lower the interrupt request line to the processor.

The value of the data in this register at startup time is indeterminate. The ROM code should initialize this register before the processor MSR EE bit is set to allow interrupts.

9.2.3 External Interrupt Source Register (XISR)

This register is a 3-byte register that contains the identifier of the source of the interrupt. Each processor has its own XISR. This register is in real memory space at address BA + 1 and BA + 5. However, this register shall be accessed as part of the XIRR for purposes of atomicity. Issuing a Load instruction to the XIRR at address BA+0 causes the XISR to be Loaded into the processor with no side effects. This is designed for software polling of external interrupts. Issuing a Load instruction to the XIRR at address BA+4 has the side effects of resetting the XISR to 0x000000 atomically after the contents of the XIRR have been transferred to the processor. Subsequent interrupt requests of more favored priority shall then cause an interrupt to be signaled and presented in the XIRR. For more information see Section 9.2.1, "External Interrupt Request Register

Engineering Note

Because software will be issuing Load and Store instructions to the CPPR frequently, the performance of a Load and Stores to this register should be optimized.

The assignment of 4-bit interrupt source numbers to internal BUC conditions are device dependent. Normally the assignments will be contiguous starting with the value of 0.

Bits 0–10 of the XISR, the Hardware Implementation Dependent Field 1, may be used by implementations requiring BUID extension or routing bits. A system may use this field (or portions of this field) for routing an interrupt reset to a system bus on which a BUC resides. This field (or portions of this field) is expected to be used as a routing field in systems with a hierarchical MP structure where there are multiple buses. The BUID extension is not part of the address of the BUC, and the BUC does not need to look at the BUID extension field.

Engineering Note

The value of the data in the XISR at startup time is indeterminate. The IPL ROM code should initialize this register before the processor MSR EE bit is set to allow interrupts.

(XIRR)," on page 165. The value which gets written into this register by hardware is one of the following:

- For a BUC, an 11-bit "Hardware Implementation Dependent Field 1" concatenated with the BUID (assigned by the system at configuration time) concatenated with a 4-bit interrupt source number of the interrupt within the BUC.

- For an MFRR, a BUID (assigned by the system at configuration time).

A single physical BUC may be assigned multiple 4-bit interrupt source groups thus the architecture allocates interrupt sources in groups of 16. Thus, BUCs which need to specify more than 16 interrupt sources must use multiple sequential BUIDs. The BUIDs shall be allocatable in a compact form starting at 0 so that the content of the XISR may be used as a direct index into an interrupt source vector data structure (this implies a system configuration method that allows software to be able to set the BUID for any given BUC). Several values have special meanings in the XISR, see Table 59 for the XISR bit meanings and Table 60 for the special values.

XISR Bits	XIRR Bits	Meaning
0–10	8–18	Hardware Implementation Dependent Field 1: These bits are reserved for use by the hardware and have no other architected use. This field is not to be used as a communication vehicle between hardware and software, that is, hardware cannot expect software to take any actions as a result of values in this field.
11–19	19–27	BUID: These bits indicate the BUID of the interrupting BUC.
20–23	28–31	Interrupt Source: These bits indicate one of 16 possible caused of interrupts for the BUC.

Table 59. **XISR Content for T=0 and T=1 BUCs**

Value	Meaning
0x000000	Reset: This value indicates that there are no current external interrupts pending. The XISR takes on this value as a side effect of a load from the XIRR at location BA + 4.
0x000001	Early Power Off Warning (EPOW): This value indicates that an EPOW interrupt is pending, that is, a change to any non-keylock field in the power/keylock status register in table 7 on page 13.
0x000002 and up to but not including the first BUID value	Inter-Processor Interrupt (IP): These values indicate that an Inter-Processor Interrupt is pending (see the definition of the MFRR, below). There is one value allocated per MFRR. In an SMP System, each processor has an MFRR with its XISR value of 0x000002. The system configuration software shall set up the first BUID in the system such that the value loaded into the XISR for the lowest BUID shall be greater than the largest previously defined BUID values.

Table 60. **XISR Special Values**

Address	Byte 0	Byte 1	Byte 2	Byte 3	Comments
BA+0	G_MFRR	ISSR			Required QIRR for SMP Systems

Table 61. **Interrupt Management Area: Interrupt Presentation Layer Registers**

9.2.4 Queued Interrupt Request Register (QIRR)

The Queued Interrupt Request Register is a 4 byte register with the first byte being the Most Favored Request Register (MFRR) and the remaining low order 3 bytes as being either the ISSR or unimplemented or reserved. Software may write either a single byte, the MFRR or a full four bytes.

9.2.5 Most Favored Request Register (MFRR)

This is a 1-byte register. The content of this register is controlled by software and indicates the most favored Inter-Processor (IP) interrupt priority on an IP interrupt queue for the processor or server to which the particular MFRR is associated. If an MFRR for a processor is set to a value of 0xff, then there are no items in that IP interrupt queue for that processor, and the hardware is not to signal an IP interrupt to that processor. When software puts something on an IP queue for a processor, it shall also set this register to the priority of the most favored item on the IP queue. When this register is a value other than 0xff, it is treated by the interrupt routing layer as another interrupt request competing for presentation to the processor via the XIRR. When the value in an MFRR is the most favored of all interrupt requests directed to the processor, an appropriate value is placed into the XISR (see Section 9.2.3, "External Interrupt Source Register (XISR)," on page 167) and an interrupt is signaled to the processor. As with all other interrupt sources, an MFRR interrupt shall be resubmitted if and only if the interrupt condition has not been reset when either the interrupt is rejected by the routing layer or software issues the End Of Interrupt. The interrupt condition is taken to be an MFRR value other than 0xff, therefore, once the MFRR has a non-0xff value, and the interrupt routing layer has started to route the interrupt, the interrupt routing layer shall not reroute the interrupt request to the interrupt presentation layer because of a subsequent change of value in the MFRR. The only way that the interrupt routing layer will reroute the MFRR interrupt request is due to an interrupt rejection or an interrupt reset (given that the MFRR does not have the value 0xff). The MFRR's value is only changed due to a software store. Each processor has at least one MFRR. There is also one or more global MFRRs in an SMP system.

Hardware does not initialize the MFRR so software should initialize it prior to the first setting of the processor's MSR EE bit to allow interrupts.

The MFRRs associated with a specific processor's IP interrupt mechanism is located at an address of BA+12, BA+16, and so on. The addresses of the MFRRs associated with global queues are defined in Section 3.3 in Table 8 on page 15.

9.2.5.1   Programming Timing Considerations

Due to unpredictable delays of the queueing in the interrupt routing layer, software can make no assumptions as to when an interrupt caused by a store to an MFRR will occur. Nor can software assume that changing the value of the MFRR from one non-0xff value to another will have any direct/predictable affect upon the interrupt presentation sequence.

The value loaded into the MFRR is a guide to the interrupt routing layer, there is no architected mechanism to make it globally performed. When an inter-processor interrupt is signaled to the processor, the software shall rely upon the in storage request queue which can be maintained consistently via architected locking primitive operations.

Depending upon the software/hardware interactions, any of the following conditions could occur:

■ The priority of the incoming inter-processor interrupt may be more or less favored than the highest priority request on the queue – software should adjust the CPPR value according to the queue request priority.

■ If multiple queue requests are processed per inter-processor interrupt cycle, an inter-processor interrupt may be signaled to a processor when the request queue is indeed empty. Software should perform an XIRR load of BA+4/Store BA+4 sequence for each inter-Processor interrupt request it processes.

9.2.6 Global Queue Interrupt Request Register (G_QIRR)

The Queued Interrupt Request Register is a 4 byte register with the first byte being the Global Most Favored Request Register (G_MFRR), which is an MFRR, and the remaining low order 3 bytes as being the ISSR. Software may write either a single byte, the G_MFRR, or a full four bytes.

The ISSR (Interrupt Source Specification Register) contains the value to be loaded into the XISR when the interrupt associated with the corresponding MFRR is signalled to a processor.

9.2.7 SMP Global Queue Interrupt Routing Masks (GQ_IRMs)

Symmetrical multiprocessor (SMP) systems use the GQ_IRM as its communication mechanism for determining which processors are available for the use of global queues. The location of the software/hardware interface for the GQ_IRMs is defined in the IPLCB, which contains the number of global queues and a variable length structure for each global queue supported which allows for various placements for this support. See Section 3.3.3, "IPLCB/Global Queue Interrupt Routing Mask Location Interface," on page 16 for the software interface to the GQ_IRMs.

During initialization, the firmware initializes each supported GQ_IRM to no processors available for global queue routing. Software has the responsibility of assigning processors to service the global queues.

The hardware/software communication protocol allows the hardware to read from the GQ_IRM and software to both read and write the GQ_IRM. The mask is a 32-bit value with one bit set to a one and the rest of the bits set to zeros. Software is expected to read from the GQ_IRM using the loc_pN_raddr and to write to the GQ_IRM using the loc_pN_waddr as a 32-bit word. In order to turn on a specific processor, the software should read the GQ_IRM verification word associated with the processor OR in the mask associated with the processor and write back the word associated with the specific processor. Similarly, to turn off a specific processor, the complement of the mask would be ANDed with the word read and the new word would be written back.

9.2.8 Available Processor Mask (APM)

The Available Processor Mask (APM) facility is a required hardware facility for SMP systems. The APM is used by the interrupt routing layer hardware to know which processors are available for routing interrupts. The support for this facility is required at system initialization.

The read and write addresses are 32-bit word aligned addresses and software is expected to read and write on 32-bit word aligned boundaries. The processor number is expected to be used to form a mask to turn a processor off or on. The mask (constructed by software) is a 32-bit value with one bit set to a one and the rest of the bits set to zeros. This mask is constructed modulo 32, for example, access to the 35th processor would be formed by using a mask with the remainder of 35/32, which is 3 or the third bit or bit 2 (starting from 0) in the mask word set to one (0x2000). In order to turn on a specific processor, the software should read the APM verification word associated with the processor OR in the mask associated with the processor and write back the word associated with the specific processor. Similarly, to turn off a specific processor, the complement of the mask would be ANDed with the word read

Engineering Note

Although hardware could support a single address for the APM to be both written and read from software, it is recommended that hardware support two (2) separate addresses. This is especially true if the location(s) of the APM is(are) in NVRAM with the changes monitored by a Service Processor.

Architecture and Programming Note

In order to write machine independent software, software should poll for the change. In order to provide for software that runs efficiently on all machines, it is suggested that a time delay be used between reads that do not reflect the changed value. Because hardware may change the value immediately to indicate that all NEW interrupts shall use the new mask, software shall be prepared to handle interrupts that had previously been issued and that may still be in the pipeline.

Hardware documentation should specify the minimal, nominal, and worst case support for the change to take effect.

and the new word would be written back. Software should write using the write address and verify using the read address.

Software shall be able to verify that any change has taken place. The architected mechanism is for software to issue a read after a write. Once the read value reflects the value written, the hardware shall have guaranteed that the change has taken place; that is, all NEW interrupts shall use the new mask.

Software shall be able to verify that any change has taken place. The architected mechanism is for software to issue a read after a write. Once the read value reflects the value written, the hardware shall have guaranteed that the change has taken place; that is, all NEW global interrupts shall use the new mask.

9.2.8.1   IPLCB Interface for Available Processor Mask (APM) Format

It is recommended that the Available Processor Mask be kept in NVRAM with some type of CRC checking.

Byte	length (in bytes)	Identifier	Description
0	4	num_processors	Number of Processors (N)
4	4	access_id_waddr	Access Identification of type of Access for loc_waddr (IF (access_id_waddr == 0) then normal memory map access at loc_waddr) (IF (access_flag_waddr == 1) then machine DD access at loc_waddr)
8	4	loc_waddr	Real Address of First Processor 32-bit (software write address) start
12	4	access_id_raddr	Access Identification of type of Access for loc_raddr (IF (access_id_raddr == 0) then normal memory map access at loc_raddr) (IF (access_flag_raddr == 1) then machine DD access at loc_raddr)
16	4	loc_raddr	Real Address of First Processor Verification (software read address) start

Table 62. **IPLCB/Available Processor Mask Location Interface**

System Exception Processing

10

The following is the system architecture for the processing of system exception conditions. The architecture addresses exception detection and logging, and, specifically, does not support system recovery. The intent of the document is to specify the architecture for systems which elect to implement this function. It describes the architected system facilities required to support the architecture, and the actions the system elements are to take in response to system error conditions. The detection mechanisms rely on error detection logic, such as parity and Error Correction Code (ECC) checking, but must also cover protocol and time-out error conditions.

10.1 Exception Handling

In general, when there is no data integrity exposure, it is preferable to retry error conditions that may be transient to avoid end user interaction. In the remainder of this section, it is assumed that the errors under discussion are non-transient errors. Also, whenever there is no data integrity exposure, it is preferable to cause the least system (and thus end-user) impact.

The strategy for handling non-transient (errors that still occur after retry) errors is to record sufficient information to let the operating system recover from some set of problems, and to stop the system as close to the point of error, as possible, for other cases. With this in mind, a number of system exception facilities are defined by the architecture. State data, maintained in these facilities and others, must be accessible to isolate the failing components. Depending on the recoverability of the error, one of the interrupts, in Section 10.1.2 on page 174, shall be generated to signal the system to initiate its error handling sequence.

10.1.1 Target Market Categories

Appendix "Target Market Categories," starting on page 239, defines the minimum level of exception processing support, in terms of error checking, detection, logging, retry, and service and exception facilities, required for a given system implementation. In the error handling section of Table 75 on page 241, logging refers to recording system state into NVRAM or system registers for later processing by system software. The categories are defined to correlate to a system's market segment and price point. In general, when a given element is defined as being required, it is applicable to both the processor and Bus Unit Controllers (BUCs) of the system.

As you progress from the low-end, or Class-1 category, to the Class-6 category, the requirements are more stringent, and costly to implement. As an example, in the Class-1 category, there is:

■ Minimal error checking, or exception handling or registers required

At the other end of the spectrum, the Class-6 category demands:

■ All memory, bus, and caches must be ECC protected

■ Detection of processor and bus transaction time-out conditions

■ Detect, and not propagate, log, and attempt recovery from errors

■ Provide service processor interfaces

■ Provide exception facilities and I/O retry

With the preceding information as background, the remainder of this chapter defines the System Exception Architecture and facilities in support of this architecture. The categories of implementations are included here to clarify the basis for design.

10.1.2 Interrupts and Checkstop

In this section, interrupts and checkstop, which result from system exceptions, are presented along with the system actions which result. For details on interrupt processing internal to the system processor, reference the *PowerPC Architecture* (book III).

10.1.2.1 Checkstop

A checkstop condition causes the system to enter a state from which the only recovery sequence is to reset the hardware, presumably, after some service

Engineering Note

With increased operating frequencies (50+ Mhz), timing errors are more likely to occur, and, therefore it is recommended that additional debugging and isolation facilities be introduced into the designs. This assists not only in servicing the system, but in shortening the test cycle during development.

action. When this interrupt is signalled, the processor shall freeze its state to allow hardware, such as an Engineering Support Processor (ESP), to record the strings in nonvolatile memory and allow software to subsequently analyze the information collected. Examples of conditions which result in a checkstop are: address parity errors, internal parity, and instruction dispatch time-outs by the processor. Other sources may also signal this interrupt, whenever the ability of the processor to reliably process instructions is in doubt, and BUCs must be able to latch the condition, so as to permit the actions previously described.

10.1.2.2 Machine Check

Although, machine check interrupts may occur due to a variety of reasons, for example, address range errors and bus time out errors; the typical source for a machine check interrupt is associated with memory access errors. These may have been caused by hardware failures in the memory subsystem or, during DMA operations, when an invalid ECC may have been written with the data to indicate bad data parity on the store operation. If the processor detects a data parity error on a DSS load operation, it shall also signal this interrupt. In general, the system shall attempt to identify and log the cause of the error and resume execution. If this is not possible, it shall enter the checkstop state.

10.1.2.3 External

An external interrupt is used to signal either error conditions that are detected in the system logic or BUCs, or service requests from another processor or BUC. On uncorrectable memory errors, during DMA operations, this interrupt could also be used to notify the system of an error condition. It can also be generated by a time-out condition, and is an alternative to a checkstop or machine check condition, when in diagnostic mode.

10.1.2.3.1 Early Power Off Warning (EPOW) Interrupt

In the event that power must be dropped in an emergency, an early warning signal is given to the processor. This signal shall be activated at least 4ms prior to the loss of DC supply regulation. The cause of an EPOW interrupt can be seen in Table 7 on page 13.

In the event of an EPOW, the software can try to complete critical I/O operations prior to the loss of power. In the event of a false alarm transient, the system can be easily restarted. If power does totally fail, a full system restart shall be required.

10.1.3 Exception Conditions

The system response to the following exception conditions are outlined in Table 81, "System Exception Processing," on page 251. The errors associated with data and address parity in the table, refer to an error that occurs on the transfer across the bus. Parity errors that occur within the BUCs are marked as BUC internal errors and are presented as external interrupts.

Section E.4.2, "System Exception Processing," on page 249, refers to exception condition which can not be attributed to a specific system operation, but occur due to program or logic errors. References are made to diagnostic mode in this section, the definition and requirements associated with it are presented in Section 10.1.8 on page 180.

10.1.3.1   Hardware Correctable Memory Error

The system response to a hardware correctable memory error is to record the type of error in a status register, and save the referenced address. For systems with single Bit Error Correction/Double bit Error Detection (SBEC/DBED) ECC, single bit errors may be automatically corrected by the hardware, in memory or may be corrected on each access. If correction is not implemented a mechanism to protect against error propagation must be provided. No other system indication is required, although software may monitor and record occurrences. In diagnostic mode, if supported, an external interrupt is generated.

Engineering Note

These resources are provided to allow software to identify the memory errors and detect areas of storage with questionable reliability. By logging the errors and analyzing the log at a later time, software can identify storage areas that contain single bit hard failures or that are more susceptible to soft errors than is acceptable. The intent is to capture the information needed to isolate to the FRU (Field Replaceable Unit).

10.1.3.2   Hardware Uncorrectable Memory Error

Under this error condition, the memory controller shall log the type of error in a status register and save the referenced address. Signals on the system buses shall be sent by the memory subsystem to the processor, I/O, or other BUCs, as indication of an error condition. On some systems, if the error cannot be presented on the same bus tenure as the error, a checkstop shall be signalled. Additional information may be logged through system-specific exception registers to isolate memory errors to the failing component. In diagnostic mode, if supported, an external interrupt shall be generated for these cases.

10.1.3.3   Address Range Error

This exception is detected when a real address is presented which falls in the data space of the system address map, but is outside of its physical extents. The cause may be either a hardware malfunction, for example, an address in error being propagated or a device not responding, or by a software error in computing the address. This error is logged by the processor or BUC and an interrupt shall be signalled by the system. In diagnostic mode, if supported, the error shall be presented as an external interrupt.

With the introduction of real address memory mapped devices, an address range error is not, solely, within the province of the system memory controller. Therefore, unless specific facilities are implemented to detect this condition, it may go undetected for store operations and shall default to a time-out error for read operations. If the error is detected (as expected on the 60x bus which requires a response for a store), then the information to diagnose the errant address should be captured and logged.

10.1.3.4 Address Parity Error

For system implementations in categories above Class-2, an address parity error on the system bus shall ultimately result in a system checkstop condition. Since the information on the bus is corrupt, the target of the transaction on the bus is suspect. It is assumed that parity is checked at each BUC and each BUC is responsible for detecting and signalling a checkstop. Each BUC shall also save the parity bits associated with the address, and, additionally, the contents of the address bus are held for hardware access.

BUCs are to indicate this condition to the system, as a diagnostic aid, by all recording the occurrence in their status and address registers, but will not signal a checkstop. In diagnostic mode, the system will also be checkstopped.

10.1.3.5 Data Parity Error

For a write request where an uncorrectable data parity error is detected, the memory subsystem could signal an error condition or defer it by writing storage with invalid parity or an ECC code to indicate an error was detected on the write to memory. In this case, the operation is aborted and no interrupt is generated. As with the address parity condition, the parity fields associated with the data to indicate which byte(s) is in error are saved in an error status register. In diagnostic mode, if supported, an external interrupt is also generated.

10.1.3.5.1 Memory Mapped (T=0) Access

For system implementation in categories above Class-2, an uncorrectable data parity error shall result in a machine check or checkstop. This can occur as the error is detected or on a subsequent access to that data. In either event the error type and corresponding address must be logged.

10.1.3.5.2 Direct-Store (T=1) Access

On an access to a Direct-Store Segment (DSS) the controller shall indicate that the error occurred and the processor shall generate a Data Storage Interrupt (DSI).

10.1.3.5.3 DMA Access

A parity error on a DMA Read Request results in the operation being aborted and an external interrupt being generated.

10.1.3.6 Processor or BUC Error

For processor or BUC errors, other than internal processor errors or those resulting in a checkstop state, refer to Chapter "Bus Unit Controller (BUC) Architecture" starting on page 59, for requirements, and to Chapter "IOCC Architecture" starting on page 75 for IOCC specific examples. For DSS transactions these exceptions are reported as DSIs, all others may be reported as external interrupt. In diagnostic mode, if supported, a BUC internal error shall be reported as external interrupts.

For processor internal errors, the action taken by the processor will be implementation specific. However, the system requirement, when internal errors are detected, which result in a checkstop state are:

■ The processor/BUC signals the system when it enters the checkstop state.

■ The processor/BUC monitors a system checkstop signal and enters the checkstop state when asserted.

10.1.3.7 Time-out Error

In order to detect hung conditions caused by any number of sources, each transaction on the bus which expects a response, and internal processing within the processor must be protected by a timer. Table 82, "System Time-out Processing," on page 253 defines the time-out conditions and appropriate system response.

The bus master will usually control the time-out event and, if so, it is responsible for logging the event in a status register along with the corresponding address. Alternately, in systems where only one bus transactions is outstanding at a time, the time-out function could be centralized. The granularity and number of timers required is implementation dependent.

10.1.4 Processor Designs

A processor must have the following interfaces defined, when its intended use is in system implementations above category Class-1:

1. External interrupt

2. Checkstop input/output

3. System Reset input/output

4. Data Transfer error/Bus Check

The following shall be required for system implementations above category Class-2:

1. Data parity input/output

2. Address parity input/output

In addition to the interrupt mechanisms defined by the PowerPC processor architecture, the following internal detection mechanism must be supported:

1. Internal error detection (system implementation above category Class-2)

2. Instruction dispatch time-out (system implementations above category Class-3)

10.1.5 BUC Designs

A BUC must have the following interfaces defined, for system implementations above category Class-1:

1. Checkstop input/output

2. System Reset

The following are required for system implementations above category Class-2:

1. External Interrupt

2. Data parity input/output

3. Address parity input/output

In addition to the interrupt mechanisms defined by the BUC architecture, see Chapter "Bus Unit Controller (BUC) Architecture" starting on page 59, the following internal detection mechanism must be supported by system implementations above category Class-3:

1. Time-out Detection (master BUC only)

The following are required for system implementations above category Class-2:

1. Internal error detection

10.1.6 Real Address Memory Mapped I/O

There is, currently, no architected error detection or recovery mechanism for errors that occur during stores to real address memory mapped I/O.

10.1.7 Multiprocessor

The system actions which results from an error internal to the processor is implementation dependant. For example, a checkstop condition presented by any of the processors could cause the system to checkstop. Since data required by one of the other processors is likely isolated in the failing processor, it is best to preserve system state by checkstopping the system, and logging the error state.

10.1.8 Diagnostics

Systems, above category Class-2, must provide, for bring-up and debug purposes, a means for error conditions to be masked or presented in a less disruptive manner. A diagnostic mode bit may be defined for this purpose. In diagnostic mode, if supported, a checkstop condition may be presented as an external interrupt. The diagnostic mode bit indicates to a BUC that the system is operating in this mode. Since a checkstop state, would normally result in the system being halted, the type and the source of the error must be captured to be able to determine the source of the error.

10.1.9 System Exception Support Facilities

To assist in problem determination and isolation, a set of registers has been defined to maintain exception status and address information. The IPLCB is the machine-dependant method of identifying the location of system exception facilities. These are read-only registers that are set by hardware and are automatically reset when read by software. They contain the first occurrence of the highest priority event they monitor. The set of registers is defined on a per BUC basis. As an enhancement, a stack could be supported that maintains a history of the first n-events.

10.1.9.1 System Exception Registers

Each system BUC may have system exception register(s). The set may consist of registers documented in this book, and other system-specific registers, which are not documented in this book which are considered implementation dependant. If a "documented" register is implemented, its fields should be coded as defined in Appendix E.4 on page 248 to minimize the variations of system software needed to process the data. "Documented" registers which are not implemented shall return a value of zero.

10.1.10 System Exception IPLCB Interface

The IPLCB has data and pointer fields defined to locate the system exception registers. The placement of these facilities is restricted to the upper four (4) gigabytes because on a 64-bit word machine, software shall assume that the upper 32-bits are all ones. The IPLCB software interface must allow for the different machine dependent placements to be in NVRAM.

The IPLCB shall contains a structure of the form defined in Table 63.

The first field associated with the exception registers in the IPLCB holds the number of Identification, data length, and pointer fields which follow it. The pointer fields are used to address system exception register structures in memory mapped, I/O address spaces, or within NVRAM. This structure accommodates a variable number of BUCs, system exception registers, and system-specific exception register implementations. A value of zero in the first entry indicates that no exception facilities are implemented.

Byte	Length (in bytes)	Identifier	Description
0	4	num_except_fields	Number of Exception fields (N)
4	4	access_id_1	Identification of type of Access for 1st field (IF (access_id_1 == 0) then normal memory map for read_addr_1) (IF (access_id_1 == 1) then machine DD access for read_addr_1)
8	4	read_addr_1	Real read address for 1st field
12	4	num_words_1	Number of 32-bit words to read at the 1st real address
16	4	access_id_2	Identification of type of Access for 1st field (IF (access_id_2 == 0) then normal memory map for read_addr_2) (IF (access_id_2 == 1) then machine DD access for read_addr_2)
20	4	read_addr_2	Real read address for 2nd field
24	4	num_words_2	Number of 32-bit words to read at the 2nd real address
.	.	.	.
.	.	.	.
.	.	.	.
4+12(N–1)	4	access_id_N	Identification of type of Access for Nth field (IF (access_id_N == 0) then normal memory map for read_addr_N) (IF (access_id_N == 1) then machine DD access for read_addr_N)
8+12(N–1)	4	read_addr_N	Real read address for Nth field
12+12(N–1)	4	num_words_N	Number of 32-bit words to read at the Nth real address

Table 63. **IPLCB/System Exception Interface**

System Bus Architecture

11

There exists an interconnection between the various BUCs and system components, such as, main memory and the processors. This interconnection is called the "system bus." Refer to the Figure 2 on page 60 for an example of an interconnection via a system bus. The primary restriction on implementations of the bus and the various attachments is the requirement for software transparency. OS software should not be affected by the different attachments and configurations, including the hardware support for additional components, such as, a Level 2 cache. The following two sections are examples of two System Bus Architectures: the 60X bus and the 6XX bus. Compared to the 6XX System Bus, the 60X is limited in its ability to overlap pipe-lined snoops. Specifically, the 6XX System Bus is designed for more concurrency and better scaleability with frequency as compared to the 60X bus.

11.1 60X Bus Overview

The system perspective of the 60X bus is a processor independent interface that supports the memory model defined in the *PowerPC Architecture* (book III) for 32-bit implementations. The bus is synchronous, with all timing relative to the rising edge of the bus clock. Input are sampled and outputs are driven from this edge. Depending on processor implementation, the bus clock may run at the processor rate or it may be ratioed in some manner. The bus supports multi-master operation through arbitration provided by the system. The arbitration function is defined so that the arbiter can "park" any master on the bus, eliminating arbitration overhead. The 60X uses separate address and data busses and a variety of control and status signals. The address bus is 32 bits wide and the data bus is 64 bits wide.

11.1.1 60X Bus Memory Coherence

Note

A detailed description of the maintenance of the coherent memory system can be found in *PowerPC Architecture* (book II). 601 specific processor related information is contained in the corresponding *PowerPC 601 User's Manual.*

See *PowerPC Architecture* (book III), "Storage Segments," for information regarding direct-store segments.

The bus supports maintenance of a coherent memory system using the Modified Exclusive Shared Invalid (MESI) snoop protocol found in the 601, 604, and 620 processors and the Modified Exclusive Invalid (MEI) snoop protocol found in the 603 processor. Coherency of memory is maintained at a granularity of 32 bytes. In order to maintain a coherent memory system, each processor must broadcast the intention to read a sector that is not in its own cache as well as the intention to write to a sector that is not currently owned exclusively by the processor itself.

11.1.2 60X Bus Transfer Protocols

The bus supports two transfer protocols. The Basic Transfer Protocol is used for accesses to normal storage segments and supports transfer of any number of contiguous bytes within an aligned double word. It also supports transfer of aligned 32 byte blocks via a multi-beat (burst) transfer. The 60X bus provides a peak data bus bandwidth of 8 bytes per bus clock in the Basic Transfer Protocol that is a 264 MB peak throughput per second on a 33 MHz bus. The Extended Transfer Protocol, used for accesses to Direct Store Segments, provides an extended address, split transactions and a positive reply for each transaction. Because the performance of these transfer is limited compared to the basic protocol, this mode is only for compatibility with Power Architecture. Both transfers consist of an address and a data tenure each having three phases: arbitration, transfer and termination. Following are outlined the functions performed on the bus during each phase:

Address tenure:

- Arbitration – A master is trying to gain ownership of the address bus

- Transfer – The master drives the address and address related signals on the address bus

- Termination – The master terminates the address tenure or, if a condition in which the address tenure must be rerun is detected, the master issues another bus request.

Data tenure:

- Arbitration – A bus master is trying to gain ownership of the data bus

- Transfer – The master samples the data bus for reads or drives the data bus for writes

- Termination – The master terminates the data tenure unless a condition in which the data tenure must be retried is detected.

Furthermore, the 60X bus also supports address-only-transfers, which have an address tenure but no data tenure. This capability is used for a variety of broadcast operations useful in multiprocessor system.

11.2 6XX System Bus Overview

The 6XX bus is an interface for attachment of memory and high speed I/O devices expected to be used by future RISC System/6000 PowerPC System Architecture compliant systems. It provides the capability to build I/O data consistent systems as well as SMP (Symmetric Multi-Processing) systems. It is intended to support PowerPC system implementations. It assumes that one of the devices on this bus is an I/O controller chip that implements the BUC Architecture as defined starting on page 59.

This bus can be used as a high end Processor bus, an I/O mezzanine bus, or a MP system bus for mid range systems. It shall accommodate both 32-bit and 64-bit processors with real memory addressing beyond 32 bits. It supports the PowerPC asynchronous memory model, and the PowerPC synchronous direct-store segment model.

Logically this bus definition supports several functions:

■ Memory protocols

■ Arbitration protocols

■ Cache coherency protocols

■ Programmed I/O (PIO) load/store protocols

A device can support one or more of the above, or any combination of these. It does not need to attach to signals unless they are required to support the protocol it needs.

The bus consists of separate, i.e., non-multiplexed address bus and data buses. The address bus is 64 bits wide and supports addressing multiple address spaces. For example, multiple Microchannel I/O space of 32 bits, real memory spaces of 48 bits max, special purpose spaces to pass interrupts and processor commands, etc. The data bus width is defined to be 8 or 16 bytes (2 or 4 words).

These separate address and data buses, run mostly independent, thus allowing true split transactions. The requests and replies are tagged, allowing out of order replies, which are common for PIO to another bus or in a Non-Uniform Memory Access time (NUMA) environment.

Bring-Up Function and IPLCB

12

A global data structure, called the IPL Control Block (IPLCB), shall be created in main memory by IPL ROM after a sufficient amount of memory testing has been completed. This structure is re-created each time a system goes through a "hard initialization" (hard IPL), which is the equivalent of a power-on initialization. The structure is kept intact throughout the IPL process. On a "soft initialization" (soft IPL), the IPLCB shall be used in its existent state by the IPL ROM (i.e., it will not be recreated). The "official" definition of this structure is maintained in a C header file named iplcb.h which resides in both the AIX and the IPL ROM build environment. It also resides in the "/usr/include/sys" directory on systems that contain AIX. The structure is passed to the Operating System upon a successful IPL and contains information that is used by the Operating System. It is also passed from routine to routine in the IPL ROM execution environment as is explained later.

12.1 SMP Bring-Up Function

Initial Program Load (IPL) Read Only Memory (ROM) requires certain capabilities from 6xx hardware to be able to effectively boot a Symmetrical Multiprocessor (SMP) system. These requirements are listed below and are conditions that must be met before a Power-On Reset (POR) causes control to be passed to IPL ROM at IPL ROM offset location 0x100 from the IPL ROM start address, refer to Section 3.1, "Memory Map," on page 7 for the architected IPL ROM starting address.

■ One and only one processor shall be executing instructions. This processor shall be the one in control of instruction execution (at IPL ROM address

0x100) after a POR sequence is complete. Other processors present must be disabled (effectively in a reset state) after the POR has completed.

Note

Although the architecture for the Available Processor Mask (APM) is defined to allow "Live Insertion," that is, installing and using in a new processor after power is applied, the complete support for this function is not defined in this book. For additional information regarding the APM, refer to Section 9.1 on page 157 and to Section 9.2.8 on page 171.

■ IPL ROM must be able to uniquely identify each processor so it can associate instruction execution with a processor.

■ IPL ROM must have the capability to start up each of the processors from its reset state.

■ IPL ROM must have the capability to selectively put each of the processors into its reset state.

■ IPL ROM must be able to determine the number of processors that are configured in a given system. This algorithm (if not a simple read of data from a system register) must be able to determine the presence of a processor that may not be able to execute instructions (a "broken" processor) and a processor that is not present (unplugged).

12.2 IPL Control Block (IPLCB) Interface

This document does not detail all of the structures within the control block. However, sufficient information is given to allow understanding, locating, and using any of the structures that may be present. The latest level of the iplcb.h header file should always be used when detailed information in the IPLCB is required.

12.2.1 Purpose of the IPLCB

The two main purposes for the existence of the IPLCB are:

■ IPL ROM Power-On Self-Tests (POSTs) and Device Interface Routines (DIR) use "scratch pad" areas defined within the IPLCB to keep track of machine state information.

■ IPL ROM passes configuration information, VPD information, and the like to the Operating System via the IPLCB. IPLCB is the preferred source for system configuration information required by AIX.

12.2.1.1 General Notes and Graphical Presentation of the IPLCB Definition

1. The address of the IPLCB is on a page boundary.

2. All offset values are referenced to the address of the IPLCB.

3. The gpr_save_area[32] is a fixed length (128 bytes) and is always the first structure in the IPLCB.

4. The ipl_directory is the second structure in the IPLCB and starts at the 129th byte.

5. The memory_bit_map is the last structure.

6. The ipl_directory structure contains the offset and size (in bytes) of all IPLCB structures except the first two. The size of the ipl_directory is the value of ipl_info_offset minus   sizeof(gpr_save_area). The size is used to determine the number of offset/size pairs that are present.

7. Except as noted above, the order of the structures within the control block are determined by the offset values that are maintained within the ipl_directory.

IPLCB Front End Structure :

```
typedef struct ipl_cb {

  unsigned int gpr_save_area[32];
   struct ipl_directory    s0;

} IPL_CB, *IPL_CB_PTR;
```

The front end structure is the only structure that should be referenced by name:

```
EX:
     my_var = IPL_CB.s0.ipl_info_offset;
```

All other references should be a pointer reference in order to be able to maintain
binary compatability with the operating system:

```
EX:
     my_var =

          (struct iocc_post *)((uint)IPL_CB_PTR + IPL_CB_PTR->s0.iocc_offset)->iocc_data;
```

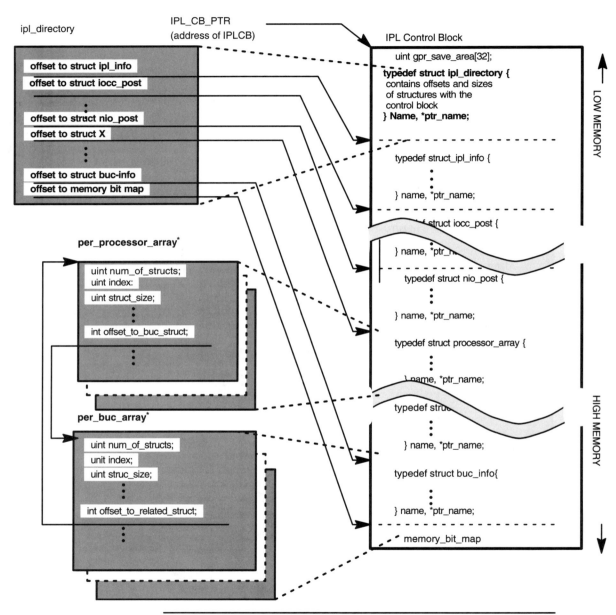

Figure 39. **Graphical representation of the IPLCB**

Vital Product Data (VPD) 13

Vital Product Data is the electronically sensed data which uniquely describes each hardware, software, and microcode configurable element of the system. Configuration is the information that identifies the physical and logical location of each element of the system. One of the requirements for VPD is in support of Reliability, Availability, and Serviceability (RAS), failure analysis, and administrative support systems which rely on this mechanism to describe a machine's installed configuration. The target of most VPD resources are field replaceable or customer replaceable devices.

In current AIX implementations, the VPD data is gathered by a software device driver and stored in a repository (the ODM). The defined VPD format is described below. If the data format for a device deviates from the defined standard, then the individual device driver must convert that data into the correct format before storing in the repository provided by the Operating System. It should be noted here that if any data values are stored in binary on a device, it is the responsibility of the individual device driver to convert the data to ASCII or a hexadecimal representation of the binary value in ASCII before storing data in the repository.

13.1 VPD Format

The keyword header on the device is composed of 4 bytes of information. The first character is "*" in ASCII. The next two characters are an abbreviated mnemonic associated with a specific descriptor. The last byte is in binary and represents the total length (in words) of the keyword descriptor including its header. The length byte is represented in Section 13.1.1, "Keyword Definitions," on page 192 by "$\mathcal{L}$". The value of $\mathcal{L}$ is the total byte count divided by two (2) (to convert from words to bytes). Hence, descriptor data is always an even number of bytes. Padding of fields to achieve an even byte count is required for each keyword.

The format for the data as it appears on the hardware differs from the format used by the Product Topology Service Aid interface. The data on the device and in the ODM contains the $\mathcal{L}$ (length) byte as part of the data. The Product Topology Service Aid interface strips the length ($\mathcal{L}$) out and retains the "*", the two character mnemonic, and the actual data. An example is shown below:

VPD data on the part:	"*PN" || 06 || "099F9999"
VPD data on a PT diskette:	"*PN" || "099F9999"

Note that the length field has been dropped in the service aid interface but the actual data, "099F9999" is replicated exactly as it appears on the part.

Binary data must be described as the ASCII representation of its hexadecimal value.

13.1.1 Keyword Definitions

The following list identifies the descriptor keywords currently defined for electronically sensed VPD data.

13.1.1.1   Addressing Field: "*AD" \|\| $\mathcal{L}$

The addressing field format is unique to each component described. It must include the Bus Unit Id, and slot designation if appropriate. In addition, it specifies sufficient addressing information in order to program the adapter. The format of the addressing field is specified by software. This descriptor is not present within the machine-readable VPD field contained within an adapter or channel. It is added by software to the Configuration/VPD file or NVRAM area for VPD.

13.1.1.2   Card Id (Adapter Card Id) = "*CD" \|\| $\mathcal{L}$

Note

Refer to the *IBM Personal System/2 Hardware Interface Technical Reference–Architectures* (S84F-9808) manual for information on the POS registers.

The Card ID field is supplied by software after reading the Card ID from POS 0 and POS 1. This descriptor only applies to Micro Channel adapters. This descriptor is not present within the machine-readable VPD field contained within an adapter or channel. It is added by software to the Configuration/VPD file or NVRAM area for VPD.

13.1.1.3 Device Driver Level (Minimum Required) = "*DD" || $\mathcal{L}$

The data portion of this descriptor is in ASCII. It represents the minimum device driver level required. The first release is level zero. Levels are incremented by one for each successive level, independent of Operating System version/modification level. This field is required for all adapters and channels. If not present, level zero is implied. The minimum value for $\mathcal{L}$ is 3, which is two bytes or two ASCII character numbers of descriptor data plus header.

This represents a "generic" interface level to software. If the interface between software and hardware changes such that a new interface is required by hardware, then the value of this level is incremented. This level is independent of the Operating System being used.

13.1.1.4 Diagnostic Level (Minimum Required) = "*DG" || $\mathcal{L}$

The data portion of this descriptor is in ASCII. It represents the minimum diagnostic level required. The first release is level zero. Levels are incremented by one for each successive level independently of Operating System version/modification level. This field is required, however, if not present, level zero is implied. The minimum value for $\mathcal{L}$ is 3, which is two bytes or two ASCII character numbers of descriptor data plus header.

This represents a "generic" interface level to diagnostics. If the interface between diagnostics and hardware changes such that a new interface is required by hardware, then the value of this level is incremented. This level is independent of the Operating System being used.

13.1.1.5 Drawer Level = "*DL" || $\mathcal{L}$

The data portion of this descriptor is in ASCII and is two numeric characters in size. It represents the drawer location within a rack for an Enclosure. Levels are specified beginning with the number "01" in increments of one. The bottom drawer is designated as level "01" and each level higher is incremented by one. A "filler" cover or "dummy" location used as a cover to provide spacing in the rack is assigned its corresponding number. These levels are unrelated to EIA unit values. These values are originally entered by manufacturing when a rack is in final manufacturing test. In the field, configuration changes which alter drawer information must be supplied by the trained customer, or customer engineer installing the change.

13.1.1.6 Displayable Message (ASCII) = "*DS" || $\mathcal{L}$

This is an optional field which may include a message to be printed or displayed for this record type. The ASCII character "*" should be avoided within the data content of this message.

13.1.1.7 Engineering Change Level = "*EC" || $\mathcal{L}$

The data portion of this descriptor is in ASCII. The characters are alphanumeric and represent the Engineering Change level for this element. The values of $\mathcal{L}$ may range from 6 to 8, which represents descriptor data counts of 8 to 12 alphanumeric characters. This descriptor number is left-justified. For IBM released parts this field must contain the IBM EC number.

13.1.1.8 FRU Number for Replacement Parts = "FN" || $\mathcal{L}$

The data portion of this descriptor is in ASCII. The characters are alphanumeric and represents the IBM FRU (Field Replaceable Unit) for this element for the RISC System/6000 product. The values of $\mathcal{L}$ may range from 6 to 8, which represents descriptor data counts of 8 to 12 alphanumeric characters. The data is right-justified and padded with higher order zeros. For IBM released parts this field contains the IBM FRU Number.

13.1.1.9 Pointer to Loadable Microcode on the Adapter = "*LA" || $\mathcal{L}$

If an adapter chooses to implement Loadable Microcode using the POS registers for writing/reading microcode, then this field is used.

13.1.1.10 Load ID = "*LI" || $\mathcal{L}$

The Load Identification is a part of the name of the base "down load" which may be required by adapters during the IPL process. Data in the field may be encoded in binary on the device but is externalized in ASCII or a hexadecimal representation of a binary value in ASCII.

13.1.1.11 Loadable Microcode Level (Minimum Required) = "*LL" || $\mathcal{L}$

The data portion of this descriptor is in ASCII. It represents the minimum loadable microcode level required. The first release is level zero. Levels are incremented by one for each successive level. Loadable microcode is associated with a given Card ID rather than Part Number/EC level. Therefore, as changes are made to a particular adapter, a corresponding microcode level may be required for correct operation. This field is required if loadable microcode is required for functional operation of the adapter. Its presence notifies the initialization code of this additional requirement. The minimum value for $\mathcal{L}$ is 3, which is two ASCII characters of descriptor data plus header.

This is a "generic" level equivalent in use to device driver or diagnostic level. It indicates that a significant change has been implemented on the adapter that a new minimum level of loadable microcode is required.

13.1.1.12 Location (Internal or External) = "*LO" ‖ $\mathcal{L}$

This descriptor is optional. The data portion of the descriptor contains the ASCII characters "IN" for internal devices or "EX" for external devices or other components. The default value for this descriptor is "IN" and is implied if this field is not specified. This field is generated dynamically by software for hard files attached to a SCSI adapter which provides "internal" reset capability. For other devices, it may be entered by the user in the Configuration/VPD utility. Its use is required for power domain and security domain requirements. The value of $\mathcal{L}$ is 3.

13.1.1.13 Manufacturer and Location = "*MF" ‖ $\mathcal{L}$

The manufacturer descriptor field is typically six characters of ASCII data. For IBM built components the first three characters are "IBM". The next three characters are the alphanumeric code assigned to each IBM location.

13.1.1.14 Network Address = "*NA" ‖ $\mathcal{L}$

This field is an optional field use by those adapters which require a unique network address for a local area network. Adapters such as Token Ring or Baseband use this field. Data in the field may be encoded in binary on the device but is externalized in ASCII or a hexadecimal representation of a binary value in ASCII.

When specified, this field must be implemented as the first descriptor keyword and therefore "*NA" ‖ $\mathcal{L}$ is located at address 00 08. The first data byte is, therefore, located at byte 12 within the extended storage area located by POS registers 6 and 7.

13.1.1.15 Address of VPD Data for Next Adapter in Multi-adapter Cases = "*NX" ‖ $\mathcal{L}$

This is used by multi-card adapters including those which occupy more than one card slot. The primary card must provide POS registers. Additional (secondary) cards must be plugged in slots adjacent to the primary card. This field specifies the VPD address to be specified in POS registers 7, and 6 respectively, in order to address VPD data on the adjacent (secondary) adapters. Data in the field may be encoded in binary on the device but is externalized in ASCII or a hexadecimal representation of a binary value in ASCII.

13.1.1.16 Operating System Level = "*OS" || $\mathcal{L}$

The data portion of this descriptor contains the name of the Operating System (such as "AIX") followed by Version, Modification, and PTF level. All characters are specified in ASCII. Additional data can be included to specify specific options being used (such as cluster). This descriptor is required in the Enclosure Record store in NVRAM and the Configuration/VPD file.

13.1.1.17 Processor Component Definition = "*PC" || $\mathcal{L}$

The processor component description list identifies each chip within the processor complex including IOCC and SLA components. The first two bytes of data represent the cycle time of the processor, and the model of the processor, respectively. Each module (or chip) is then defined with four bytes of information in binary format sequentially. The first byte for each module specifies a position on the planar. The second byte specifies a compressed Part Number. Bytes three and four specify a change level. A group of four bytes is specified for each chip or module within the processor complex.

13.1.1.18 Processor ID = "*PI" || $\mathcal{L}$

The data portion of this descriptor is an ASCII alphanumeric field which represents the Processor ID for a Processor Enclosure. This data is normally extracted from IPL ROM associated with the System Planar.

13.1.1.19 Part Number = "*PN" || $\mathcal{L}$

The data potion of this descriptor is in ASCII. The characters are alphanumeric and represent the IBM Part Number for this element. The values of $\mathcal{L}$ may range from 6 to 8, which represents descriptor data counts of 8 to 12 alphanumeric characters. This descriptor number is right-justified and may be padded with high-order zeros.

13.1.1.20 Pointer to ROM Code on Adapter = "*RA" || $\mathcal{L}$

If an adapter chooses to access on-board ROM using the POS registers for reading microcode, then this field is used. Data in the field may be encoded on the device in binary, but is externalized in ASCII or a hexadecimal representation of a binary value in ASCII. The first data byte represents a POS register to use as a Port to read/write data to the adapter for purposes of reading microcode on the adapter. Any POS register (0–5) may be specified. The second byte specifies the number of low-order bit positions of POS register 5 to use for expanding the address range of POS registers 6 and 7. The address so formed is specified as:

POS 5 (n low order bits), POS 6, POS 7

The second byte may be specified from 0 to 6 bits of additional addressability. Data bytes 3, 4, 5, and 6 specify the initial address for reading microcode. This is an optional descriptor type available for use.

13.1.1.21 ROM Level / ID = "*RL" || $\mathcal{L}$

This descriptor is used to identify the part number of any non-alterable ROM code on the adapter. The data field of the keyword is defined as follows:

■ Bytes 0 – 11   Part number of the ROM code (alphanumeric ASCII).

■ Bytes 12 – 23   EC level of ROM code (alphanumeric ASCII), this is optional if the ROM code PN is not changed when updated.

Previous definitions of the data field for the "*RL" keyword should be phased out over time.

13.1.1.22 Alterable ROM ID = "*RM" || $\mathcal{L}$

This descriptor is used to identify the part number of any alterable ROM code on the adapter. The data field of the keyword is defined as follows:

■ Byte 0   An optional "field patch level." A value of "0" indicates "no field patch applied" (ASCII).

■ Bytes 1 – 12   Part number of ROM code (alphanumeric ASCII).

■ Bytes 13 – 24   EC level of ROM code (alphanumeric ASCII), this is optional if the ROM code PN is not changed when updated.

13.1.1.23 Pointer to Read / Write Adapter Registers = "*RW" || $\mathcal{L}$

This is an optional descriptor type available for use. If an adapter chooses to implement read/write registers using the POS registers, then this field is used. Adapters may use the POS extended addressing facility or any other method of their choice to implement access to read/write registers/storage.

The data portion of this descriptor is in BINARY. The first data byte represents a POS register to use as a Port to read/write data to the adapter for specific adapter purposes. Any POS register (0–5) may be specified. The second byte specifies the number of low-order bit positions of POS register 5 to use for expanding the address range of POS registers 6 and 7. The address so formed is specified as:

POS 5 (n low order bits), POS 6, POS 7

The second byte may be specified from 0 to 6 bits of additional addressability. Data bytes 3, 4, 5, and 6 specify the initial address for accessing read/write registers or storage. The size and use of this Read/Write area is adapter specific. The minimum value for L is 5, which represents 6 bytes descriptor data plus keyword.

13.1.1.24 Serial Number = "*SN" || L

The data portion of this descriptor is in ASCII. The characters are alphanumeric and represent the serial number of the device. The value of L is 6 representing a descriptor data count of 8. The descriptor data is left justified and may be padded with low order blanks.

13.1.1.25 Size = "*SZ" || L

Memory board adapters use this description to specify the size in megabytes. The data portion contains 1 to 8 digits, left justified, with no leading zero's and padded on the right with blanks as required.

13.1.1.26 Machine Type / Model = "*TM" || L

The data portion of this descriptor specifies the machine type in ASCII for a length of four characters followed by a "–" and a machine model of three characters for a total data length of eight characters. Therefore, L is specified as 6 representing 8 characters of data plus header.

13.1.1.27 User Data = "*US" || L

The data portion of this field is an ASCII character string which is specified by the user utilizing the Configuration/VPD utility. It could be used to specify owner, location, or similar information. It must contain an even number of bytes.

13.1.1.28 Pointer to VPD Extended Data = "*VE" || L

This optional descriptor is used as an address pointer in the sub-address space of VPD for a Micro Channel adapter. It points to a storage location that contains additional keyword descriptors in order to support an implementation of non-contiguous keyword descriptor data.

The data portion of this descriptor is an address pointer in the POS sub-address space. Byte 0 is the most significant address byte, and Byte 1 is the least significant address byte in binary-form.

13.1.1.29 Available for Specific Use = ("*Z0"–"*Z9" | "*ZA"–"*ZZ") || ℒ

These fields are available for device specific data for which no unique keyword has been defined.

13.1.2 Device Specific VPD Data Requirements

The following tables indicate the VPD data expected for each class of part. An "R" indicates REQUIRED data, a "CR" indicates CONDITIONALLY REQUIRED, and an "O" indicates the data is OPTIONAL but desired. "Conditionally Required" means that if the data type is relevant for the part it should be supplied.

Bus Attached Adapters and Attached devices include currently implemented architectures such as Micro Channel, PCMCIA and other local defined I/O busses.

Keyword Header – Description	Use	Required
*PN – Part Number	VPD	R
*EC – Engineering Change Level	VPD	R
*SN – Serial Number	VPD	R
*FN – FRU (Field Replaceable Unit) Number	VPD	R
*MF – Manufacturer	VPD	R
*TM – Part Type/Model	VPD	R
*RN – Rack Name	VPD	CR

Table 64. **Rack VPD**

Keyword Header – Description	Use	Required
*PN – Part Number	VPD	R
*EC – Engineering Change Level	VPD	R
*SN – Serial Number	VPD	R
*FN – FRU (Field Replaceable Unit) Number	VPD	R
*MF – Manufacturer	VPD	R
*PL – Part Location	AIX	R
*AX – AIX Device name	AIX	R

Table 65. **I/O Planar VPD**

Keyword Header – Description	Use	Required
*PN – Part Number	VPD	R
*EC – Engineering Change Level	VPD	R
*SN – Serial Number	VPD	R
*FN – FRU (Field Replaceable Unit) Number	VPD	R
*MF – Manufacturer	VPD	R
*TM – Part Type/Model	VPD	R
*DL – Drawer Level	VPD	CR
*DU – Drawer Unit	VPD	CR

Table 66. **Enclosures VPD**

Keyword Header – Description	Use	Required
*PN – Part Number	VPD	R
*EC – Engineering Change level	VPD	R
*FN – FRU (Field Replaceable Unit) Number	VPD	R
*MF – Manufacturer	VPD	R
*PI – Processor ID	VPD	R
*PC – Processor Component Definition	VPD	CR
*RL – ROM Level/ID	VPD	R
*ZN – Part Specific Data	VPD	R
*PL – Part Location	AIX	CR
*AX – AIX Device name	AIX	CR

Table 67. **System Planar/Processor Card VPD**

Keyword Header – Description	Use	Required
*PN – Part Number	VPD	R
*EC – Engineering Change level	VPD	R
*SN – Serial Number	VPD	R
*FN – FRU (Field Replaceable Unit) Number	VPD	R
*MF – Manufacturer	VPD	R
*ZN – Part Specific Data	VPD	R
*DS – Displayable Message	VPD	R
*SZ – Size	AIX	CR
*PL – Part Location	AIX	CR
*AX – AIX Device name	AIX	CR

Table 68. **Memory VPD**

Keyword Header – Description	Use	Required
*PN – Part Number	VPD	R
*EC – Engineering Change Level	VPD	R
*SN – Serial Number	VPD	R
*FN – FRU (Field Replaceable Unit) Number	VPD	R
*MF – Manufacturer	VPD	R
*TM – Part Type/Model	VPD	CR
*LL – Loadable Microcode Level	VPD	CR
*RL – ROM Level/ID	VPD	CR
*ZN – Part Specific Data	VPD	CR
*SZ – Size	AIX	R
*PL – Part Location	AIX	R
*AX – AIX Device name	AIX	R

Table 69. **SCSI and Direct Attached I/O Devices VPD**

Keyword Header – Description	Use	Required
*PN – Part Number	VPD	R
*EC – Engineering Change Level	VPD	R
*SN – Serial Number	VPD	R
*CD – Card ID (Micro Channel POS Register)	POS	R
*FN – FRU (Field Replaceable Unit) Number	VPD	R
*MF – Manufacturer	VPD	R
*DD – Device Driver Level	VPD	CR
*DG – Diagnostics Level	VPD	CR
*DS – Displayable Message	VPD	CR
*RM – Alterable ROM level	VPD	CR
*RL – ROM Level/ID	VPD	CR
*LL – Loadable Microcode Level	VPD	CR
*NA – Network Address	VPD	CR
*LI – Load ID	VPD	CR
*RA – Pointer to ROM Code	VPD	0
*RW – Pointer to Read/Write Registers	VPD	0
*LA – Pointer to Loadable Microcode	VPD	0
*ZN – Part Specific Data	VPD	0
*PL – Part Location	AIX	R
*AX – AIX Device name	AIX	R

Table 70. **Bus Attached Adapters and Attached Devices**

AIX Based Diagnostics Requirements

14

The information in this chapter provides an overview of the hardware support required by AIX maintenance package developers. For more detailed information and future updates regarding AIX diagnostics, refer to *POWERstation and POWERserver Common Diagnostics and Service Guide (SA23–2687)*. For additional explanations of the three-digit display numbers, refer to the *Problem Solving Guide (SC23–2204)*.

14.1 AIX Based Diagnostics Dependencies

For the AIX Diagnostics maintained with current RISC System/6000 products, diagnostics has dependencies on the following areas:

- Hardware

- IPL ROM

- VPD

14.1.1 Hardware Dependencies

All hardware shall provide the following items or equivalent facilities:

Engineering Note

Hardware testing is often done by IPL ROM, OCS, or a Service Processor.

The Mode Selection Facility is often implemented via 3 position mode switch (keylock) that supports Normal, Secure, and Service positions.

■ Operator Panel with:

  – Power Control

  – Power-On Indicator

  – Mode Selection Facility

    ○ A means to indicate and select three (3) different modes, refer to Table 56 on page 155 for example names and icons for this facility.

  – Display (or LEDs) with scroll capability or a large enough multi-digit display that scrolling is not necessary.

  – Reset Function.

■ Ability to test the Central Electronic Complex (CEC) by Built-In Self-Tests (BISTs), see Section 14.1.5 on page 220 or Power-On Self–Tests (POSTs), see Section 14.1.6 on page 222.

  – The current AIX Diagnostics do not provide any tests for the CEC. The BISTs and POSTs shall report progress and problems via the Operator Panel Display.

■ Ability to identify the type of Field Replaceable Units (FRUs), for example, system planar, adapter, daughter card, device, etc., in the system.

■ Ability to identify the location of any adapter and device that plugs into a slot.

■ Ability to physically identify any device that attaches to a bus, such as a SCSI bus.

■ Ability to detect changes in the configuration.

■ Ability to read VPD at anytime.

See Sections 14.1.4, 14.1.5, and 14.1.6 for additional information about the operator panel, BISTs, and POSTs, respectively.

14.1.2 Hardware Testing Dependencies

Hardware shall provide tests for areas that cannot be or is not easily tested using the AIX Diagnostics, that is, once the OS is loaded. This includes any function that, if tested, could cause the OS to crash or could cause data integrity problems. An example of a function that is more easily tested before the OS is loaded is the memory testing. The current AIX Diagnostics do not provide any tests for memory. Other examples of areas normally tested before the OS is loaded include functions on the I/O Planar and buses.

Hardware shall provide the following information to the Operating System:

■ Time that the IPL (boot) occurred.

■ Results of all tests.

■ Any VPD that can only be obtained by hardware.

■ Results of memory test and initialization:

  − Bit Map that shows which pages of memory are available and which pages have errors and are not available for Operating System usage.

    ○ Memory size (total size, extent sizes, card sizes, etc.)

    ○ Memory types and locations

    ○ If a problem is detected, then the location of the broken FRU, for example, which Single In-line Memory Module (SIMM) needs replacement

Hardware should record the result of all adapter self-test and make the results available to the Operating System.

14.1.3 VPD Requirements from AIX Based Diagnostics

Diagnostics requirements for VPD information are:

■ Each system shall be able to uniquely identify its type and model.

■ Each FRU (system planar, adapter, daughter card, device, etc.) shall be able to uniquely identify itself.

■ Each FRU (system planar, adapter, daughter card, device, etc.) shall support VPD.

  − The VPD that shall be supported is

    ○ Model Type

    ○ Hardware EC level

    ○ Microcode level

- The VPD that should be supported is

  ○ Part number

  ○ Serial number

■ Items such as ROM and BISTs shall provide a readable EC level.

14.1.4 Maintenance Package Operator Panel Requirements

The RISC System/6000 maintenance package assumes a specific Operator Panel user interface which consists of power control, power-on indicator, mode selection facility, Reset function, and a display (3 digits or more). The requirements for the Operator Panel are provided in the following sections. Any deviations from these requirements requires the approval of the System Diagnostics Department or a new maintenance package.

14.1.4.1   Power Control Facility

The power control controls the system power.

14.1.4.2   Power-On Indicator

The power-on indicator indicates that all voltages in the power supply are present and within limits and that a sufficient number of fans are running. The power-on indicator is used to help analyze power and cooling problems.

14.1.4.3   Mode Selection Facility

The mode selection facility has three states (refer to 8.1.2 on page 154 for naming convention):

■ Mode 1 or "the secure" state prevents the system from performing an initial program load (IPL). If an IPL is attempted with the mode selection facility in the secure state, the number 200 is displayed in the operator display. If the system is already IPLed, this state does not lock the keyboard or block system network communication. When the mode selection facility is in the secure state, then:

- The reset facility is disabled to prevent resetting the system unit.

■ Mode 3 or "the normal state" allows IPL from the Normal Bootlist. This state is used to prevent IPLing from non-secure devices such as the diskette drives. Normally, it is used to load AIX. The Reset button is enabled in this state.

■ Mode 2 or "the service state" allows IPL from the Service Bootlist. This state is used to allow IPLing from non-secure devices such as the diskette drives. Normally, it is used to load diagnostics and install AIX. The Reset and Power-Off functions are enabled in this state.

The mode selection facility is also used for the following:

■ To indicate to the diagnostic programs that there is no console available. This is done by switching the mode selection facility from service to normal and then back to service when a c31 is displayed in the operator panel display.

■ With the reset function to start a dump. If the system is IPLed in Normal mode, a manual dump is started by placing the mode selection facility in Service and activating the Reset function. If the system is IPLed in Service mode, a dump is started by placing the mode selection facility in Normal and activating the Reset function. If the Reset function is pressed twice, the system is IPLed.

■ With the reset function to enter the Built-In Diagnostics. If the system is IPLed in Secure mode, the Built-In Diagnostics are entered by placing the mode selection facility in Service and activating the Reset function.

The state of the mode selection facility should always be visible. The state of the selection facility shall not be lost due to a power failure, etc. This can be accomplished by using a mechanical selection facility or by storing the state in NVRAM.

14.1.4.4 Reset Function

The Reset function is used to:

■ Reset the system unit and cause an IPL when the mode selection facility is set to Normal or Service.

■ Read out messages (scroll) after a flashing 888 is displayed.

■ Start the dump program when a manual dump is needed.

■ Enter the Built-In Diagnostics.

■ Used in conjunction with the mode selection facility to bring up IPL ROM network boot menus.

Engineering Note

On and off push–buttons are used to control the power on racks while on/off switches are used on the other systems. The on/off switch allows the system to automatically power itself back on when there is a power failure. The on/off button does not provide this capability. Unattended applications require an on/off switch or an on/off button scheme that can remember the state of the system if a power failure occurs such as storing the state in NVRAM.

On IBM RISC System/6000 model 7015 type systems (racks), the power-off push button is disabled to prevent powering off the system unit.

A three position keylock is used on all systems except the RISC System/6000 model 220. The RISC System/6000 model 220 uses a three state selection facility with the same labels used on the keylock. On a model RISC System/6000 model 220, if the system is IPLed in secure mode and the mode selection facility is turned to normal or service mode, then activating the reset function, causes the IPL ROM to put up a network boot menu.

14.1.4.5   Operator Panel Display

The Operator Panel Display shall have three or more digits. The display is used for:

■ Event indications and problem reporting during Built-In Self Tests (BISTs), Power-On Self-Tests (POSTs), and Configuration Methods.

■ Progress and command indications when loading diagnostics from diskette.

■ Event indications while the Diagnostic Programs are running when a Console-Display is not available or has not been tested.

■ Problem reporting by the Diagnostic Programs when a Console-Display is not available, has a problem, or has not been tested. Problems are reported by a Diagnostic Message.

■ Checkstop indications when the machine can not recover from a checkstop. This indication is displayed by BISTs.

■ Crash reporting when the machine can not recover from a Crash. Crashes are reported by a Crash Message.

■ Dump progress and command indications during dump.

■ Problem reporting when there is a power problem. This feature is only supported on newer racks and deskside systems.

A blank display is used to indicated that the configuration methods have completed and AIX, diagnostics, etc., have started.

14.1.4.6   3-Digit Display Message Format and Examples

The rules for displaying information on the 3-digit display are:

■ Event, progress, and command indication are displayed in the 3-Digit Display.

■ All messages that begin with an 888 on the 3-Digit Display shall begin with a flashing 888 in the 3-Digit Display. The flashing 888 indicates that there is additional information and assures the user that all segments of the 3-Digit Display are working. The first number displayed after the blinking 888 is the message type. The following values are defined:

  – 102 – a system crash message is being displayed.

  – 103 – a diagnostic message is being displayed. This is the number that should be used when reporting a problem.

- 104 – a manufacturing message is being displayed.

- 105 – an encoded diagnostic message is being displayed.

- The numbers following the message type are dependent on the message type.

■ The Reset function is used to scroll through the message 3 digits at a time.

■ After all the message has been displayed, a flashing 888 is displayed. The message can be displayed again.

■ Blanks should not be used.

■ A ccc is displayed between concatenated diagnostic messages.

■ A coX is used to identify the beginning of a location code in a diagnostic message. X indicates which location code, i.e., first, second, etc.

■ Location codes and some SRNs contain alpha characters that cannot be displayed in 3-digit display. These codes are encoded as follows:

If the character is a digit, then it is displayed as "X0Y" where X indicates the sequence and Y is the digit.

If the character is an alpha character, then it is displayed as "XYY" where X indicates the sequence and YY is the alpha character where the alpha characters are translated as follows:
a = 11, b = 12, ... j = 20, ... t = 30 ... z = 36.

14.1.4.7 Message Concatenation

A Diagnostic Message can be concatenated with a Crash Code or with another Diagnostic Message. If a Diagnostic Message is concatenated with a Crash Message, the Diagnostic Message immediately follows the Dump Status in the Crash Message. An example of a Diagnostic Message concatenated with a Crash Message is shown below:

888 102 XXX YYY 103 SSS RRR
1 AB–CD–EF–GH

XXX = Crash Code
YYY = Dump Status
SSS & RRR = Service Request Number
1 AB–CD–EF–GH indicates FRU 1 location

The 103 following the YYY Dump Status indicates the beginning of a Diagnostic Message.

The following is an example of a Diagnostic Message concatenated with a Diagnostic Message:

```
888 103 SSS RRR
1 AB–CD–EF–GH
ccc
103 SSS RRR
1 AB–CD–EF–GH
```

SSS & RRR = Service Request Number

The ccc indicates the ending of one Diagnostic Message and the beginning of another Diagnostic Message.

14.1.4.8 Location Identification

RISC System/6000 is a family of systems that consists of racks, a desksides, and desktops. Expansion boxes, rack drawers, portable files, etc., can be attached to the system. FRUs can be located in any of these units. To locate a FRU the repair technician needs to know the following information:

- For rack the following are needed:

    - rack

    - drawer

    - slot if adapter, memory card, or serial link adapter

    - I/O Planar

    - physical location if a device such as a disk or diskette

    - location on card for memory SIMM

- For desksides and desktops the following are needed:

    - slot if adapter, memory card, or serial link adapter

    - physical location if a device such as a disk or diskette

    - location on card for memory SIMM

- For expansion boxes and devices the following are needed:

    - expansion box or device

    - slot if adapter

    - physical Location if a device such as a hardfile or diskette

The rules for labeling is that items should be labeled going from left to right, top to bottom, and front to back. The first label should begin with the smallest label.

Software can identify the following location information:

■ the system type

■ adapter slot

■ I/O Planar

■ memory slot

■ SCSI Address

■ The adapter an external device or expansion box is attached to.

Software can NOT identify the following location information:

■ rack

■ drawer

■ SCSI device's physical location

■ Diskette Drive physical location

The location code is defined as follows:

     AB–CD–EF–GH

For planars, cards, and non–SCSI devices the location code is defined in Figure 40.

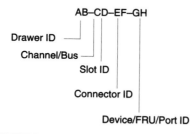

Figure 40.   **Location code for Planars, Cards, and Non-SCSI Devices**

where:

■ AB is the Drawer ID

     –   It is used to identify CPU and Async Drawers.

- For CPU Drawers and non-rack systems AB is 00.

- For Async Drawers, A identifies the Channel/Bus (I/O Planar) and B identifies the Slot ID of the Async Adapter that attaches to the drawer. This corresponds to the CD value of the Async Adapter location code.

■ CD is the Channel/Bus and Slot ID.

- It is used to identify the location of an adapter, memory card, or Serial Link Adapter.

  ○ For CPU Cards that attach to the system bus, C shall be equal to 0. D shall identify the Slot ID. D shall be equal to the slot letter. Slots shall be numbered starting with the letter P.

  ○ For microchannel adapters, C identifies the Channel/Bus (I/O Planar) and D identifies the Slot ID. For systems with 2 I/O Planars, C is equal to 0 for the first I/O Planar and 1 for the second I/O Planar.

  ○ For GIO and SIO adapters that attach to the system bus, C identifies the Channel/Bus and D identifies the Slot ID. C shall be equal to A for the first GIO bus, B for the second GIO bus, etc. D shall be equal to the slot number. Slots should be numbered starting with number 1.

  ○ For integrated adapters, C identifies the planar and D is 0.

  ○ For memory, C (Channel/Bus) is equal to 0 and D is equal to the slot number (A to H) for cards on non-RISC System/6000 220 systems and SIMMs on System/6000 220 systems.

  ○ For devices, CD is equal to the CD value of the adapter which the device attaches to.

  ○ For a Serial Link Adapter, C identifies the Channel/Bus (1) and D identifies the slot (A or B).

■ EF is the Connector ID.

- It is used to identify the adapter connector that a resource is attached to.

- If the external connectors are not labeled, then they should be numbered from 1 to n starting at the top of the card. The top of the card is defined as the side opposite the connector that plugs into the bus.

- Some examples of connectors are:

  ○ The 64 port connectors should be 01 to 04.

  ○ The GIO connectors should be 01 and 02.

- ○ The 8 port and 16 port connector should be 01.

- ○ S1 and S2 should be used for the Standard I/O Planar Serial connectors.

- ○ 0P should be used for the Standard I/O Planar parallel connector.

- ○ 0K should be used for the Standard I/O Planar keyboard connector.

- ○ 0M should be used for the Standard I/O Planar mouse connector.

- ○ 0T should be used for the Standard I/O Planar tablet connector.

- ○ 0D should be used for the Standard I/O Planar diskette connector.

- ○ The Serial Link Adapter connectors should be 01 and 02.

■ GH is the Port/Device/FRU ID

- – It is used to identify a port, device, or a FRU. GH has several meanings depending upon the resource type. They are:

  - ○ For memory cards GH defines a memory SIMM. Values for GH are 1, 2, or 16.

  - ○ For caches GH defines the cache. Values for GH are 1, 2, or 16.

  - ○ For PCMIAs GH defines the PCMIA. Values for GH are 1, 2, or 16.

  - ○ For async devices GH defines the port on the fanout box. Values are 00 to 15.

  - ○ For a diskette drive H defines which diskette drive 1 or 2. G is always 0.

  - ○ For all other devices GH is equal to 00.

The Location Code for SCSI and Serial Disk Devices is defined in Figure 41.

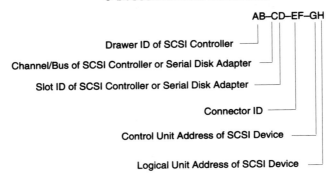

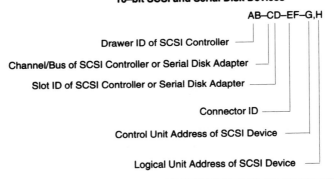

Figure 41. **Location code for SCSI and Serial Disk Devices**

where:

■ AB is the Drawer ID that contains the adapter.

  – AB is always equal to 00 at release 1 and 2.

■ C is the Channel/Bus (I/O Planar) for the adapter and D is the Slot ID for the adapter. If the SCSI Controller is integrated, then CD is 00.

■ EF is the Connector ID that the Device is attached to.

■ CD–EF can be used as the Drawer ID.

■ G (0–15) defines the control unit address of the device.

■ H (0–255) defines the logical unit address of the device.

SCSI device drawers should be labeled with the CD–EF value of the device location code.

14.1.4.8.1 Location Code Examples

Some examples of Location Codes are as follows:

■ A CPU drawer is

  – 00

■ An async drawer attached to the async adapter in slot 1 of the first I/O Planar is

  – 01

  – The drawer should be labeled 01.

■ An async drawer attached to the async adapter in slot 4 of the second I/O Planar is

  – 14

  – The drawer should be labeled 14.

■ A TTY device attached to port 13 of a fanout box attached to the second connector of a 64 port card in slot 5 of an async drawer attached to the async adapter in slot 3 of the second I/O Planar is

  – 13–05–02–13

  – The TTY device should be labeled.

  – 13–05–02–13

■ A TTY device attached to port 5 of a fanout box attached to an 8–port card in slot 6 of a deskside system is

  – 00–06–01–05

■ A fanout box attached to second connector of a 64 port card in slot 8 of an async drawer attached to the async adapter in slot 3 of the first I/O Planar is

  – 03–08–02

  – The fanout box should be labeled.

  – 03–08–02

- A 64 port card in slot 5 of an async drawer attached to the async adapter in slot 7 of the second I/O Planar is

  - 17–05

- An internal SCSI device attached to SCSI adapter in slot 2 of a desktop system with a control unit address of 3 and a logical unit address of 1 is

  - 00–02–00–31

  - The device should be labeled.

  - 00–02–00–31

- An external SCSI device in a drawer attached to SCSI adapter in slot 2 of the second I/O Planar with a control unit address of 3 and a logical unit address of 1 is

  - 00–12–00–31

  - The drawer should be labeled.

  - 00–12–00–31

- An external SCSI device in a drawer attached to SCSI adapter in slot 2 of the second I/O Planar with a address of 3 and a logical unit address of 1 is

  - 00–12–00–31

  - The drawer should be labeled.

  - 00–12–00–31

- An external device in a drawer attached to the third port of a Serial Disk Adapter in slot 6 of the second I/O Planar with a control unit address of 3 and a logical unit address of 1 is

  - 00–16–02–31

  - The drawer should be labeled.

  - 16–02

- The first diskette drive attached to the Standard I/O Planar is

  - 00–00–0D–01

- The second diskette drive attached to the Standard I/O Planar is

  - 00–00–0D–02

■ The keyboard attached to the Standard I/O Planar is

- 00–00–0K–00

■ A display attached to the display adapter in slot 2 of the CPU drawer is

- 00–02–01

■ The fourth memory SIMM on the memory card in slot D of the CPU is

- 00–0D–00–04

14.1.4.9 System Crash Messages

System Crash Messages are displayed whenever a crash occurs. They are formatted as follows:

888 102 XXX YYY

XXX = Crash Code
YYY = Dump Status

14.1.4.9.1 System Crash Message Example

An example of a single Crash Message being displayed is shown below:

Crash Code = 503
Dump Status = 0c4

3–Digit Display format:

 888 102 503 0c4

2X16 LCD format:

■ Line 1   888 102 503 0c4
  Line 2   888 102 XXX YYY

14.1.4.10 Diagnostic Messages

Diagnostic Messages are displayed to report a problem. Diagnostic Messages shall be displayed on the control panel display when:

■ A problem is detected that prevents the completion of the IPL.

■ A Console-Display problem is detected.

■ No Console-Display is available.

■ A crash occurs when running diagnostics.

14.1.4.10.1 Diagnostic Message Format and Examples

Diagnostic Messages are formatted as follows:

888 103 SSS RRR c01 1DD 2DD 3DD 4DD 5DD 6DD 7DD 8DD
           c02 1DD 2DD 3DD 4DD 5DD 6DD 7DD 8DD
           c03 1DD 2DD 3DD 4DD 5DD 6DD 7DD 8DD
           c04 1DD 2DD 3DD 4DD 5DD 6DD 7DD 8DD

SSS & RRR = Service Request Number (SRN)
c01 indicates FRU 1 location
c02 indicates FRU 2 location
c03 indicates FRU 3 location
c04 indicates FRU 4 location
DD = location
Eight location characters are read out.
If the location is a digit, then it is displayed as "X0Y"
where X indicates the sequence and Y is the digit.
If the location is an alpha character, then it is displayed as "XYY"
where X indicates the sequence and YY is the alpha character
where the alpha characters are translated as follows:
a = 11, b = 12, ... j = 20, ... t = 30 ... z = 36.

SSS and RRR are decoded to a FRU bucket with confidences
applied to each FRU.

An example of a memory SIMM on a card at location 00–0H–00–04 called out
during POSTs is

888 103 104 101 c01 100 200 300 418 500 600 700 804

The 104 101 identifies which FRUs to bring while the c01 100 200 300 418 500
600 700 804 identifies the location of the FRU.

An example of a memory SIMM on a 7011 at location 00–0D called out during
POSTs is

888 103 105 396 c01 100 200 300 414

The 105 396 (SRN) identifies the FRUs while the c01 100 200 300 414
identifies the location of the FRU.

14.1.4.11 Encoded Diagnostic Messages

Encoded Diagnostic Messages are displayed to report problems on resources
that use a four digit Service Request Number (SRN). They are formatted as
follows:

888 105 WXYZ
1 AB–CD–EF–GH

WXYZ = the Encoded SRN
1 AB–CD–EF–GH indicates FRU 1 location

14.1.4.11.1 Encoded Diagnostic Message Example

The only difference between an Encoded Diagnostic Message and a Diagnostic Message is the way the SRN is displayed. The Encoded Diagnostic Message (105) contains SRN(s) in encoded form because the SRN contains characters that cannot be displayed in the 3–Digit Display. This type of message is required to support displaying of SRNs that are reported by attached devices that report problems via a 4 character SRN. The location code are the same for both messages.

Encoded Diagnostic Messages are formatted as follows:

888 105 1xx 2xx 3xx 4xx c01 1DD 2DD 3DD 4DD 5DD 6DD 7DD 8DD

1xx 2xx 3xx 4xx = the Encoded SRN
c01 indicates FRU 1 location
DD = location

If the Encoded SRN is a digit, then it is displayed as "X0Y"
where X indicates the sequence and Y is the digit.
If the Encoded SRN is an alpha character, then it is displayed as "XYY"
where X indicates the sequence and YY is the alpha character
where the alpha characters are translated as follows:
a = 11, b = 12, ... j = 20, ... t = 30 ... z = 36.

An example of a four digit SRN equal to C3F2 with a location code of 00–08–00–30 being displayed is as follows:

888 105 113 203 316 402 c01 100 200 300 408 500 600 703 800

The 113 203 316 402 (Encoded SRN) identifies which FRUs to bring while the c01 100 200 300 408 500 600 703 800 identifies the location of the FRU.

14.1.4.12 2X16 LCD Message Format and Examples

Some systems have two lines of 16 chararacters, that is, a 2X16 LCD in place of the 3-Digit Display. The same types of messages that are displayed in the 3-Digit Display shall be displayed in the 2X16 LCD.

These messages are:

■ Event, progress, and command indicators

■ Crash Messages

■ Diagnostic Message and Encoded Diagnostic Message

- A single Crash Message concatenated with a Diagnostic Message

- Several Diagnostic Messages concatenated with each other

Whenever there is more information than can be displayed at a time in the 2X16 LCD, the reset function is used to scroll through the information.

The rules for displaying information on the 2X16 LCD are:

- Event, progress, and command indication are displayed in the first three digits of the 2X16 LCD. These codes are the same codes as displayed in the 3-Digit Display.

- All messages that begin with a flashing 888 on the 3-Digit Display shall begin with a flashing 888 on the 2X16 LCD.

- Whenever a SRN and a location code is displayed, the SRN is displayed on line 1 and the location code is displayed on line 2. Position 1 of line 2 identifies the location code. The location code begins in position 3. If there are more than one location code, then the scroll key (Reset function) is used to scroll the information. Each time the scroll key is pressed the data is scrolled one line i.e., line 1 is replaced with line 2 and new information is displayed on line 2. When all the information has been displayed, the SRN shall again be displayed along with the first location code.

- Crash Messages are displayed on line 1 beginning in position 1.

- Whenever a Crash Message is concatenated with a Diagnostic Message, the Crash Message is displayed on line 1 and the first part of the Diagnostic Message is displayed on line 2. If the SRN contains location codes, the messages are scrolled as follows. When the scroll function is pressed, the Crash Message is removed, the SRN is moved to line 1, and the location code is displayed on line 2. If additional information is to be displayed, it is scrolled as defined above. When all the information has been displayed, the Crash Message and the first line of the SRN shall again be displayed.

- Whenever a Diagnostic Message is concatenated with another Diagnostic Message, the first Diagnostic Message is displayed (as defined above) with the next message following it. After all the messages have been displayed, the first SRN shall again be displayed. To signal the beginning of a concatenated message, only the first 888 is flashed.

14.1.5 Built-In Self-Tests (BISTs)

BISTs test the processor complex. BISTs are run whenever the power is turned on and whenever a checkstop occurs. FRUs that are tested by the BISTs include the System Planar and the I/O Card. Failures are shown via the 3-Digit Display.

Numbers 100 to 199 are reserved for BISTs. Service Request Numbers (SRN) source numbers 120 to 129 are reserved for used by BISTs. These numbers should be used whenever BISTs needs to uniquely identify a FRU. Note that Non-OCS systems run POSTs.

There are two ways that failures can be shown by the 3-Digit Display: single 3-Digit Event Indicator and Diagnostic Messages consisting of a sequence of numbers.

Event Indicators show which test or function is being performed. They are used to diagnose problems that cause the system to hang. BISTs issues Diagnostic Messages as indicated in Section 14.1.4.10.1 on page 218.

14.1.5.1 BISTs Requirements

The information required by the maintenance and diagnostic package developers is as follows:

■ A 3-Digit Display Code List that contains the following:

– All 3-Digit Display codes that are displayed by BISTs. Numbers 100 to 199 are reserved for BISTs.

– A description of what is being done or tested when each code is displayed.

– Names FRUs that can cause the system to fail with each code. If more than one FRU can cause the failure, then the probability of each FRU being the broken FRU shall be provided.

■ SRN List containing the following:

– The SRNs that are reported by BISTs.

– The FRUs that are identified by each SRN along with the probability of each FRU being the broken FRU.

– A description of which tests or events caused the SRN to be displayed.

■ The following SRN Source Numbers are assigned to BISTs:

– 120 to 129 are reserved for use by BISTs. These numbers should be used to identify problems caused by the System Planar and I/O Planar. If the SRN is defined as 12x–xyy, then x–x provides 100 (00 to 99) numbers to uniquely identify the planar type and yy provides 100 (00 to 99) numbers to uniquely identify the test that failed.

■ A list of OCS model IDs.

14.1.6 Power-On Self-Tests (POSTs)

The purpose of the POSTs are to test the system memory, the functions required to IPL the system, and the functions that can not be tested after the AIX kernel is loaded. POSTs shall also determine the presence of IPL devices. POSTs are resident in the hardware and run whenever power is turned on and whenever a checkstop occurs. FRUs that are checked by POSTs include the System Planar, Memory, I/O Planar, Standard I/O Planar, and the adapters and devices used to IPL. The POSTs for IPL adapters and devices are used to determine presence of and the ability of a device to IPL. Other functions are not tested by POSTs. Fatal failures shall be shown via the 3-Digit Display. Non-fatal failures shall be logged in the IPL Control Block.

There are two ways that failures can be shown by the 3-Digit Display: single 3-Digit Event Indicator and Diagnostic Messages consisting of a sequence of numbers.   POSTs issues Diagnostic Messages as indicated in Section 14.1.4.10.1 on page 218.

Event Indicators show which test or function is being performed. They are used to diagnose problems that cause the system to hang.

14.1.6.1   POSTs Requirements

The information required by the maintenance and diagnostic package developers is as follows:

■ A 3-Digit Event Indicators List that contain the following:

  – All 3-Digit Event Indicator codes that are displayed by POSTs. Numbers 200 to 299 are reserved for POSTs.

  – A description of what is being done or tested when each code is displayed.

  – Names of FRUs that can cause the system to fail with each code. If more than one FRU can cause the failure, then the probability of each FRU being the broken FRU shall be provided.

■ SRN List that contain the following:

  – The SRNs that are reported by POSTs.

  – The FRUs that relate to each SRN along with the probability of each FRU being the broken FRU.

  – A description of which tests or events caused the SRN to be displayed.

■ The following SRN Source Numbers are assigned to POSTs:

- 104 is generated by POSTs for S1 and U1 memory problems when more than 1 3-Digit Display code is required to report a problem.

- 105 is generated by POSTs for 7011 memory problems when more than 1 3-Digit Display code is required to report a problem.

- 106 and 107 is generated by POSTs memory problems other than S1 and U1 when more than 1 3-Digit Display code is required to report a problem. 106 shall be used to report SIMM problems while 107 shall be used to report card problems.

- 108 is generated by POSTs for problems other than memory.

- 140 to 149 are reserved for use by POSTs. These numbers should be used to identify problems caused by the System Planar and I/O Planar. If the SRN is defined as 14x–xyy, then x–x provides 100 numbers (00 to 99) to uniquely identify the planar type and yy provides 100 numbers (00 to 99) to uniquely identify the test that failed.

- 201 to 210 is generated by POSTs when a check condition occurs.

■ The following SRN Reason Codes are assigned to POSTs:

- For Source Number 104, the "Reason Code" (message: 888 104 Nnn) is equal to Nnn, where N specifics a broken SIMM or card. Values for N are:

    ○ N = 1 broken SIMM.

    ○ N = 2 broken card.

    ○ nn defines the size of the SIMM and card. nn is encoded 10 to 13 as 64K to 256MB. Valid values for nn include:

        - nn = 08 as a 1 MB SIMM or an 8 MB card.
        - nn = 09 as a 2 MB SIMM or a 16 MB card.

- For Source Number 105 the Reason Code shall identify the SIMM size and type. These values are to-be-defined by the POSTs Developers.

- For Source Numbers 106 and 107 the Reason Code is equal to Nnn. N is the EC level of the memory card. nn is defined as follows:

    ○ nn = 00 identifies an incompatibility on the card (SIMM defective or missing).

    ○ nn = 01 to 62 is the PD code describing the smallest SIMM on the card.

    ○ nn = 63 is invalid PD code (SIMM defective or missing).

- For Source Number 108 the Reason Code are To-Be-Defined by the POSTs Developers.

   – For Source Numbers 201 to 210 the Reason Code is equal to the 3-Digit Display code that was displayed when the exception occurred.

■ IPL Control Block Error Entries List

   – The IPL Control Block Error Entries List shall define all possible error entries that can be stored in the IPL Control Block during POSTs. The list shall include which FRUs are related to each entry and the probability of each FRU being the broken FRU.

Since all POSTs shall fit into IPL ROM, the size of POSTs becomes an important factor. Since POSTs are run each time the machine is hard IPLed, the time to run them should be kept to a minimum. To handle POSTs that take a long time to run, some POSTs may only be run when the mode selection facility is in the service state. Some POSTs may be placed on the IPL device instead of being resident in IPL ROM. These POSTs are called Extended-Power-On Self-Tests (EPOSTs). This approach allows POSTs to be easily corrected for detection and isolation of problems.

No tools or user intervention can be used when POSTs or EPOSTs are run.

14.1.7 Service Processor (SP) Diagnostics

Service Processor (SP) Diagnostics can be resident in IPL ROM or EPROM, stored on removable media, stored on hardfile, etc. They are used to test the SP and portions of the system that cannot be tested with the systems BISTs, POSTs, or Diagnostic Programs (AIX Diagnostics). Note that a SP is optional and is not required for all implementations. The guidelines for the SP Diagnostics are:

■ An SP Console shall not be required to install the SP microcode or AIX.

   – The SP microcode shall be installable and upgradable via:

      ○ AIX when AIX is up.

      ○ From removable media at power-on.

   – When the system is powered on and the keylock is in the service mode, the SP shall check the removable media to determine if SP microcode media is inserted. If these conditions are true, then SP shall install the microcode.

   – AIX shall be installable and the Diagnostics Programs shall be loadable from supported loadable media at power-on. When the system is powered on, the system needs to check the loadable media to determine if the AIX Install/Maintenance or Diagnostics Programs media is inserted. If the one of these are inserted, then they shall be loaded and control transferred to the loaded code without any interaction with the SP. This is only done when the keylock is in service mode.

■ At power-on the SP shall run diagnostics on itself. Items that shall be checked include the processor, memory, non-removable media, etc. Problems that prevent IPL shall be report via the control panel. Problems that are detected that do not prevent IPL are logged. AIX shall have access to this log. No user interaction is allowed while running these diagnostics.

■ The SP Diagnostics that are run at power-on shall also be invokable from AIX. When invoked by AIX, the results shall be reported back to AIX.

■ The SP should only call the Remote Support Center if AIX cannot come up. If AIX is up, then AIX should be the only one that calls the Remote Support Center.

■ The SP interface for reporting problems should be defined in a consistent manner for all systems.

■ The SP shall report problems using the AIX diagnostic format for reporting problems. This includes the use of 3-Digit Event Indicators, Service Request Numbers (SRNs), Failing Function Codes, Location Codes, etc.

■ AIX shall have the capability to run diagnostics on any of the SP adapters and devices. This includes the SCSI devices, diskette, the serial port adapters, and the parallel port adapter.

■ AIX shall have the capability to instruct the SP to run diagnostics on any processor. Results shall be reported to AIX.

■ If AIX is running, there should be no need for the user to interface to the SP.

   – All flags, parameter, phone numbers, etc., required by the SP shall be controllable from AIX.

■ The user should not have to enter any command to the SP to diagnose any problem.

■ Common diagnostic and service functions should use the same terms for all RISC System/6000 PowerPC machines. All menus should look the same, etc.

14.1.7.1 SP Requirements

The information required by the maintenance and diagnostic package developers is as follows:

■ A 3-Digit Event Indicators List that contains the following:

   – Numbers 050 to 099 are reserved for SP.

- A description of what is being done or tested when each code is displayed.

- Names of FRUs which can cause the system to fail with each code. If more than one FRU can cause the failure, then the probability of each FRU being the broken FRU shall be provided.

■ SRN List which contain the following:

- The SRNs that are reported.

- The FRUs that relate to each SRN with the probability of each FRU being the broken FRU.

- A description of which tests or events caused the SRN to be displayed.

■ The SRN Source Numbers 420 to 429 are assigned to the SP Diagnostics.

■ SP-IPL Error Entries List

- The SP-IPL Error Entries List shall define all possible error entries that can be stored by the SP during IPL. The list shall include which FRUs are related to each entry along with the probability of each FRU being the broken FRU.

14.1.8 Built-In Diagnostics and Off-Line Diagnostics

Engineering Note

Built-In Diagnostics are available on the IBM RISC System/6000 model 7011.

The Off-Line Diagnostics are entered in service mode whenever a Bring-Up Micro Processor (BUMP) Console is enabled.

Built-In Diagnostics and Off-Line Diagnostics are resident in IPL ROM or EPROM. They differ from POSTs and BISTs by having their own user interface.

Non-interactive Built-In Diagnostics are run whenever the system is IPLed in service mode. The Interactive Built-In Diagnostics are accessible whenever the system is IPLed in service mode and the AIX Diagnostics cannot be loaded. They should be used when there is no IPL device or LAN available.

14.1.8.1 Built-In Diagnostics Requirements

The information required required by the maintenance and diagnostic package developers is as follows:

■ SRN List that contain the following:

- The SRNs that are reported.

- The FRUs that relate to each SRN along with the probability of each FRU being the broken FRU.

- A description of which tests or events caused the SRN to be displayed.

■ The SRN Source Numbers 700 to 799 and 811 to 999 with Reason Codes of 002 to 100 are assigned to Built-In Diagnostics.

14.1.8.2 Off-Line Diagnostics Requirements

The information required required by the maintenance and diagnostic package developers is as follows:

■ SRN List containing the following:

- The SRNs that are reported.

- The FRUs that relate to each SRN along with the probability of each FRU being the broken FRU.

- A description of which tests or events caused the SRN to be displayed.

■ The SRN Source Numbers 400 to 410 are assigned to the Off-Line Diagnostics.

14.1.8.3 Event, Progress, and Command Indicators

An "Event Indicator" is an indication of an intended action. It is put into the display before the event is started. This allows the user to determine where the system is if the system hangs during the event. Event Indicators are three solid (non-blinking) digits. Only digits (0 to 9) should be used for Event Indicators.

Progress and Command Indicators are three solid (non-blinking) digits. Only digits (0 to 9) and the lower case c should be used for Progress and Command Indicators.

Hardware Event Indicators are displayed by the BISTs and POSTs. They are independent of which Operating System is running. They are defined as follows:

Reserved – 000 to 049

Service Processor – 050 to 099

BISTs – 100 to 199

An example set of BISTs indicators are defined in Table 71 on page 228. For more detailed information regarding the BIST indicators and future updates regarding the BIST indicators, refer to *POWERstation and POWERserver Common Diagnostics and Service Guide (SA23–2687)*.

14.1.8.3.1 Hardware Event Indicators

POSTs – 200 to 325

The 3-digit-display codes as indicated in Table 72 starting on page 229 are displayed as progress indicators by IPL ROM during Initial Program Load (IPL). For more detailed information regarding the POST indicators and future updates regarding the POST indicators, refer to *POWERstation and POWERserver Common Diagnostics and Service Guide (SA23–2687)*. Normally these codes are displayed for only a few seconds (less than 10 seconds in most cases). If a problem is encountered which prevents IPL from completing, the system shall halt with either a single value displayed or with two or more values displayed repeatedly.

When two or more codes are used, the range from 222 thru 295 are displayed repeatedly, it indicates that IPL ROM is in a loop attempting to load the boot program. The devices that it is attempting to IPL from are indicated by the values in the operator panel display.

14.1.8.3.2   AIX Command and Event Indicators

An example listing of the AIX Command and Event Indicators is provided in the appendix starting on page 277.

Event Code	Event
100	BISTs completed successfully, control was passed to IPL ROM.
101	Initial BISTs started following reset.
102	BISTs started following Power-On Reset.
103	BISTs could not determine the system model number.
104	BISTs could not find the CBA.
105	BISTs could not read from the EPROM.
106	BISTs detected a module failure.
111	BISTs detected a module failure.
112	Checkstop occurred during BISTs and checkstop results could be not logged out.
113	The BISTs checkstop count was greater than 1.
120	BISTs started CRC check on EPROM
121	BISTs detected an invalid CRC on the EPROM.
122	BISTs started CRC check on the EPROM.
123	BISTs detected an invalid CRC on the NVRAM.
124	BISTs started CRC check on the NVRAM.

Table 71. **BISTs Event Indicators**

Event Code	Event
125	BISTs detected an invalid CRC on the time of day NVRAM.
126	BISTs started CRC check on the time of day NVRAM.
127	BISTs detected an invalid CRC on the EPROM
130	BISTs presence test started.
140	BISTs Failed.
142	BISTs Failed.
144	BISTs Failed.
151	BISTs started AIPGM test code.
152	BISTs started DCLST test code.
153	BISTs started ACLST test code.
154	BISTs started AST test code.
180	BISTs logout failed.
185	Checkstop occurred during BISTs.
195	BISTs logout completed.

Table 71. **Continued**

Event Code	Event
200	IPL attempted with keylock in the secure state.
201	Checkstop occurred during IPL. Fatal.
211	IPL ROM CRC miscompare during IPL. Fatal.
212	Processor Planar Bad. Fatal.
213	Memory Card failure or Processor Planar Bad. Fatal.
214	Memory buses test failure. Fatal.
215	Memory refresh test failure. Fatal.
216	IPL ROM code being uncompressed into memory.
217	End of boot list encountered.
218	RAM POSTs testing for 1 MB of good memory
219	RAM POSTs bit map being generated.

Table 72. **POSTs Event Indicators**

Event Code	Event
220	IPL Control Block being initialized.
221	Normal mode NVRAM CRC check not valid.
222	Attempting normal mode IPL from NIO attached devices specified in NVRAM IPL Device List.
223	Attempting normal mode IPL from SCSI attached devices specified in NVRAM IPL Device List.
224	Attempting a normal mode restart from 9333 subsystem device specified in NVRAM IPL device list.
225	Attempting normal mode IPL from bus Attached internal hard file specified in NVRAM IPL Device List.
226	Attempting a normal mode restart from Ethernet specified in NVRAM IPL device list.
227	Attempting a normal mode restart from Token Ring specified in NVRAM IPL device list.
228	Attempting normal mode IPL using expansion code in NVRAM.
229	Normal mode device list empty, or fails IPL.
22C	FDDI selected for IPL from normal device list.
230	Attempting a normal mode restart from adapter feature ROM specified in IPL ROM device list.
231	Attempting a normal mode restart from Ethernet specified in IPL ROM device list.
232	Diskette selected for IPL from normal mode default device list.
233	Attempting normal mode IPL from SCSI attached devices specified in IPL ROM default device list.
234	Attempting a normal mode restart from 9333 subsystem device specified in IPL ROM device list.
235	Attempting normal mode IPL from bus Attached internal hard file specified IPL ROM default device list.
236	Attempting a normal mode restart from Ethernet Specified in IPL ROM default device list.
237	Attempting a normal mode restart from Token Ring specified in IPL ROM default device list.
238	Attempting a normal mode restart from Token Ring specified by the user.
239	System failed to restart from the device specified by the user.
23C	FDDI selected for IPL from normal mode default device list.
240	Attempting a service mode restart from adapter feature ROM.

Table 72. **Continued**

Event Code	Event
242	Attempting service mode IPL from NIO attached devices specified in NVRAM IPL Device List.
243	Attempting service mode IPL from SCSI attached devices specified in NVRAM IPL Device List.
244	Attempting a service mode restart from 9333 subsystem device specified in NVRAM device list.
245	Attempting service mode IPL from bus Attached internal hard file specified in NVRAM IPL Device List.
246	Attempting a service mode restart from Ethernet specified in NVRAM device list.
247	Attempting a normal mode restart from Token Ring specified in NVRAM device list.
248	Attempting service mode IPL using expansion code in NVRAM.
249	Service mode NVRAM device list empty, or fails IPL.
24C	FDDI selected for IPL from service mode NVRAM device list.
250	Attempting a service mode restart from adapter feature ROM specified in IPL ROM device list.
251	Attempting a service mode restart from Ethernet specified in IPL ROM default device list.
252	Attempting service mode IPL from NIO attached devices specified in IPL ROM default device list.
253	Attempting service mode IPL from SCSI attached devices specified in IPL ROM default device list.
254	Attempting a service mode restart from 9333 subsystem device specified in IPL ROM device list.
255	Attempting service mode IPL from bus Attached internal hard file specified IPL ROM default device list.
256	Attempting a service mode restart from Ethernet specified in IPL ROM default device list.
257	Attempting a service mode restart from Token Ring specified in IPL ROM device list.
258	Attempting a service mode restart from Token Ring specified by the user.
259	FDDI selected for IPL from service mode specified by the user.
25C	FDDI selected for IPL from service mode IPL ROM default device list.
260	IPL ROM attempting to display information on the native console.
261	IPL ROM did not find a native display adapter. Information shall be displayed on the TTY console.

Table 72. **Continued**

Event Code	Event
262	IPL ROM did not detect a keyboard while attempting to display information.
263	Attempting a normal mode restart from adapter feature ROM specified in NVRAM device list.
271	Mouse and mouse port POSTs executing.
272	Tablet port POSTs executing.
278	Video ROM scan POSTs executing.
279	FDDI POSTs executing.
281	Keyboard POSTs executing.
282	Parallel port POSTs executing.
283	Serial port POSTs executing.
284	POWER Gt1 graphics adapter POSTs executing.
285	POWER Gt3 graphics adapter POSTs executing.
286	Token Ring adapter POSTs executing.
287	Ethernet adapter POSTs executing.
288	Adapter card slots being queried.
290	IO Planar Bad.
291	NIO Power-On Self-Test being executed.
292	SCSI Power-On Self-Test being executed.
293	Bus Attached Internal Hard File Power-On Self-Test being executed.
296	ROM scan POSTs executing.
297	System model number could not be determined.
298	Attempting warm IPL.
299	IPL ROM passed control to loaded code.

Table 72. **Continued**

Processor Dependencies

This appendix describes requirements of the RISC System/6000 PowerPC System Architecture on PowerPC Processor Implementations.

A.1 Segment Register (SR) or Segment Table Entry (STE) Bits

Certain bits of the SR or STE are required by the current IOCC Architecture, for the T=1 case, and some other bits are reserved for future expansion of the IOCC Architecture, and for other BUC architectures, see Table 73. The bits which are required by a BUC Architecture place the requirement on processor implementations to bring those bits out of the processor (externalize them) during a Load or Store instructions for use by the BUC during the Load or Store instruction. Failure to bring out bits which are required by a BUC implementation may prevent the use of that processor in a particular system which uses that BUC, or may prevent use of (or require redesign of) the BUC in a system with that processor design. On a Load instruction, SR bits 3 to 31 or STE Dword 1 bits 0 to 63 shall be returned by the hardware as the same value that software previously stored into them with a Store instruction.

SR bit	STE bit (Dword 0) (Dword 1)	BUC Architecture Req'd, Not Req'd, Optional	Description
–	0–35	–	Not Req'd	Effective Segment ID
–	36–55	–	Not Req'd	Reserved by the Processor Architecture
–	56	–	Not Req'd	Valid bit
0	57	–	Required	Used by all BUCs (T bit). Although this bit does not have to be sent to the BUCs directly, there at least must be a control signal (or combination of control signals) which will let the BUCs know that an access is a T=0 versus a T=1 access.
1–2	58–59	–	Required	Used by IOCC implementations and potentially by other BUCs (K_s and K_p bits). Only one of these bits is sent to the BUC depending on the state that the processor is in at the time of the T=1 Load or Store instruction: the supervisory or the problem state.
3–4	60–61	–	Required	Used by all T=1 BUCs (BUID)
–	62–63	–	Not Required	Reserved by the Processor Architecture
–	–	0–24	Not Required	Reserved by the Processor Architecture
5–11	–	25–31	Required	Used by all T=1 BUCs (BUID)
12–13	–	32–33	Optional; Not Req'd for current IOCC Arch, possible future BUC use	Potentially could be used by future BUC Architectures (previously defined by the POWER IOCC Architecture)
14–16	–	34–36	Optional; Not Req'd for current IOCC Arch, but would like to have for possible future BUC use	Potentially could be used by future BUC Architectures (not previously defined by the POWER IOCC Architecture). If there is a choice between bringing out these bits or bits which were previously defined by the POWER IOCC Architecture, choose these bits.
17–23	–	37–43	Required	Used by the IOCC Architecture (Authority Mask)
24	–	44	Required	Used by the IOCC Architecture (alternate IOCC address space bit)

Table 73.   **SR or STE Bit Usage by the BUC Architecture**

SR bit	STE bit (Dword 0) (Dword 1)		BUC Architecture Req'd, Not Req'd, Optional	Description
25–26	–	45–46	Optional; Not Req'd for current IOCC Arch, possible future BUC use	Potentially could be used by future BUC Architectures (previously defined by the POWER IOCC Architecture)
27	–	47	Optional; Not Req'd for current IOCC Arch, possible future BUC use	Potentially could be used by future BUC Architectures (not previously defined by the POWER IOCC Architecture). If there is a choice between bringing out this bit or a bit which was previously defined by the POWER IOCC Architecture, choose this bit.
28–31	–	48–51	Required	Address extent field. These bits are appended to the low order 28 bits of the processor effective address to form the 32-bit I/O address. They are appended as the most significant bits of the 32-bit address. In other words, these bits *replace* bits 0 to 3 of the Effective Address
–	–	52–63	Not Req'd	Reserved for the Processor Architecture

Table 73. **Continued**

A.2 EXternal Interrupt Request Register (XIRR) Latency

In order for the Interrupt routing layer to guarantee that the Interrupt Request to the processor is handled in an appropriate manner (no phantom interrupt as defined in the programming note in the CPPR Section, 9.2.2, on page 167), each PowerPC Processor User's Manual must define the latency between the time interrupt pin, IRQ_ reaches the processor to the time that an interrupt is activated, that is, to the AND gate of the EE and the IRQ_.

A.3 T=1 Direct-Store Segments

T=1 (direct-store segments) are required

Data Storage Interrupts (T=1) errors must be ordered and precise.

All Data Storage Interrupt (T=1) errors must be reported before taking any interrupt (hardware must provide "implied" sync's, if necessary).

A.4 Alignment Interrupts

From a performance standpoint, there should be no alignment interrupt when
4K page boundaries are crossed.

Standard I/O Interface

Standard I/O devices are defined as those intrinsic to a basic work-station and, as such, are included as part of the base machine. Not being optional features, these devices do not necessarily occupy feature slots. The list of items which fall into this category is implementation specific. For example, if there is an integrated (native) keyboard on the machine, it may be accessed via the Standard I/O Interface.

B.1 Recommended Mapping

The Standard I/O Interface addresses are mapped into I/O space (T=1) on to the Microchannel address space from 0x00000000 to 0x000000ff, as shown in Table 74. All other addresses are reserved. This mapping is defined to be a compatible superset of the Standard I/O mapping on the Risc System/6000 POWERstation Model 320.

Consult the system workbook for implementation differences with Table 74.

Hex Address Range		Standard I/O Device
0030	0037	Serial Port 1
0038	003f	Serial Port 2
0040	0041	Serial DMA Registers
0048	004f	Mouse
0050	0059	Keyboard/Sound
0060	0068	Diskette
0070	0077	Tablet
0078	007e	Parallel Port
007f	00df	SCSI
00f0	00fb	LAN

Table 74. **Standard I/O Map**

Target Market Categories

The classes of "Target Market Categories" defined here is intended to assist in understanding the applicability of the system exception architecture to a particular implementation.

C.1 Exception Handling by Target Market Categories

Class-1

- It provides low end, personal user functionality and price, as a stand-alone or networked system. It is a single user system without being the sole source of data stored locally. The data is backed-up or can be recreated without significant financial loss, and has no implications to other users. On error, the system hangs or the user notices anomalies in operation, and reboots the system with only localized impact. Therefore, as specified, no exception processing support is required of these systems.

Class-2

- As more processing is distributed to the system, memory errors which are propagated from the system may corrupt centralized data, and mechanism to prevent this corruption must be implemented. At a minimum, parity protection of memory is required and error propagation is not allowed. The registers and the JTAG interface are needed to assist in the fault isolation, as it may not be cost effective to discard system components.

Class-3

- As the system becomes more expensive, and more memory is added to a system, the protection and increased availability afforded by ECC on the system memory is warranted. The parity protection of system buses and caches is common practice in the industry and should be included. The JTAG interface, along with the exception registers, will assist in error detection and isolation.

Class-4

- This category encompasses the first of the multi-user systems, including small to medium commercial On-Line Transaction Processing (OLTP). In addition to the elements of the Class-3 category, it must have time-out detection and recovery to reduce system outage since multiple users are being impacted.

Class-5

- Class-5 systems include multi-user, multi-processor systems with, possibly, hundreds of users attached, which rely on the system for compute and file service or commercial OLTP. The extended hardware recovery provided by ECC on the buses, and the off-site access to the system through the service processor is, again, warranted by the user impact and financial cost of system outages.

Class-6

- The high availability features, provided by hardware redundancy and software, of these configurations demand that hardware and software recovery be of utmost priority within each of the systems. Within this category, additional ECC protection is defined, as well as, I/O retry capability.

System Function	Class-1	Class-2	Class-3	Class-4	Class-5	Class-6
Hardware Error Checking						
– ECC Memory		(X)	X	X	X	X
– ECC Buses					-	
– ECC Caches						X
– Parity Memory	X	X				
– Parity Buses	(X)	(X)	X	X	X	X
– Parity Caches			X	X		
– Time-outs		(X)	X	X	X	X
– None	X					
Error Handling						
– D / NP / L / R				(X)	X	X
– D / NP / L / NR		(X)	X	X		
– D / NP / NL / NR	X	X				
– D / P / NL / NR						
– None						
Service Facilities						
– Service Processor					X	X
– JTAG	(X)	(X)	(X)	(X)	(X)	(X)
– None						
Exception Registers						
– SESR / SEAR			X	X	X	X
– MCSR / MEAR		(X)	X	X	X	X
– None	X					
Retry						
– I/O					(X)	X

D = Detect; P = Propogate; L = Log; R = Recovery; NR = No Recovery
Blank = not required; (X) = Recommend only; X = Required

Table 75. **System Implementation Product Classes**

Memory Controller Example

The following is an example of the memory controller on the RISC System/6000 model 250, a uniprocessor, 32-bit machine using the 60X bus as a system bus.

The memory controller in this example is not a Field Replaceable Unit (FRU) and, as such, is not required to have VPD. There is no VPD in this example.

At power on, the machine tries to configure memory by placing the memory controller in configuration mode and reading its Device Characteristics Register (DCR). According to the definition of the DCR contained in the Section 4.2.3.1 on page 24, bits 8 through 11 and bits 12 through 15, tell the system whether memory allocation is required or not. All devices that resides in memory space need to allocate space in memory. For memory controllers two spaces are needed, data and control.

Bit	Description
8–11	Memory Allocation Indicator for control space
12–15	Memory Allocation Indicator for data space
16–31	See Table 13 on page 25

Table 76. **Memory Controller's Device Characteristics Register (DCR)**

A non zero value in the fields of the DCR, must go with the presence of the Device Base Real Address 1 (DBRA1) and Device Base Real Address 2 (DBRA2) registers defined in Section 4.2.3.4. These two registers must be loaded with the base address for memory control space and executable memory as defined in Table 17 on page 28.

D.1 Device ID Register for Memory Controller

Bits 8 through 31 of the Device ID register are set as required by configuration software for a memory controller as per Table 77.

Bit	Description
0–7	See Table 14 in Section 4.2.3.2 on page 27
8–23	0x1000 unique device ID type. See Table 15 on page 27
24–31	See Table 14 in Section 4.2.3.2 on page 27

Table 77. **Memory Controller's Device ID Register**

D.2 Device Specific Configuration Registers

During configuration cycles the value of MCCR(0) is 0b0, after configuring the memory subsystem MCCR(0) must be set to 0b1. The register is set to 0x0000 0000 after reset.

Bit	Description
0	Enable Memory Controller 0 – Memory Controller only responds to configuration cycles 1 – Memory Controller enabled for addresses in its Control and Data Spaces
1	Diagnostic Mode: 0 – Normal Mode, multi-bit ECC errors generate Machine Check 1 – Diagnostic Mode, multi-bit ECC errors generate external interrupt
2	Disable ECC checking: 0 – ECC checking Enabled 1 – ECC checking Disabled
3–4	Diagnostic ECC error: 00 – Normal generation of ECC codes 01 – Used to generate ECC errors in the data field 10 – Used to generate ECC errors in the ECC check code field 11 – Reserved
5–31(63)	Reserved

Table 78. **Memory Controller's Control Register (MCCR)**

D.3 Error Correction Codes (ECC)

The architecture does not require ECC to be implemented. See Table 81 on page 251 for system ECC recommendations. If employed, however, its implementation should explore being compatible with previous implementations as described in Chapter "System Exception Processing" starting on page 173. The way an ECC error is processed and presented depends on the state of the machine and on the error that was detected. This information may be retrieved from the two registers: the Memory Controller Status Register (MCSR) described in Table 79 on page 248 and the Memory Error Address Register (MEAR) described in Section E.4.3, "Memory Error Address Register," on page 249. Both the MCSR and the MEAR are defined in the Device Specific Configuration register space.

The status of the machine is contained in the MCCR register defined in Table 78 on page 244.

There are two ECC errors that are detectable by the memory controller, multi-bit ECC error and single-bit ECC error. These errors are presented by the Memory Controller Status Register (MCSR). The MCSR is located in the control space at address [Base Control Address + 0x0004] and holds the status information.

System Exception Implementation Examples

This appendix contains a brief description of implementations that follow the System Exception Architecture.

The RISC System/6000 model 250 was under development during the definition of the RISC System/6000 PowerPC System Architecture and consideration was given to its design. In addition, the architecture is designed to support an SMP system.

E.1 RISC/System 6000 Model 250

The RISC System/6000 model 250 implements only the MCSR and MEAR exception registers, and these are located through the Device Base Real Address in System Architected space. The SESR and SEAR are not implemented by the RISC System/6000 model 250.

The system specific area of the MCSR is used by the RISC System/6000 model 250 to record syndrome data to assist in isolating memory failures.

E.2 Typical SMP System

The system exception registers in a typical SMP system may be distributed across multiple internal components and may not be directly addressable by the system. If this is case and the system has a Service Processor (SP), then the SP may scan them into NVRAM, where the system software, through its machine Device Driver (DD) can examine their contents.

A typical SMP system may define a General Status Register (GSR) in each of its components whose fields map to the SESR register defined in the architecture.

The system specific areas of the SESR are used in a typical SMP system to record unique error conditions and parity or ECC syndrome data.

E.3 AIX

The AIX components that interface to the exception facilities, such as the interrupt handlers, diagnostics, error logging, and machine device drivers will still require machine dependent processing to be supported. Differences in accessing facilities, interpreting exception pointers and system-specific exception registers will exist in different system implementations. The architected register set will result in a common method to log and report most system error conditions.

E.4 System Exception Registers

The registers identified in this section are used to contain hardware error related information.

E.4.1 Memory Controller Status Register (MCSR)

The MCSR is a 32-bit register used to log errors associated with the memory subsystem.

The system specific area of the MCSR could be used to record syndrome data associated with the error. The RISC System/6000 model 250 implementation uses bits 24–31 for this purpose.

Bit	Description
0	Hardware Uncorrectable Error 0 = No error 1 = Uncorrectable error
1	Hardware Correctable Error 0 = No error 1 = Correctable error
2	Address Range Error 0 = No error 1 = Address Range error
3 – 31	System specific

Table 79. **Memory Controller Status Register (MCSR)**

E.4.2 System Exception Status Register (SESR)

Each BUC in the system defines an SESR register to hold the status information as defined in Table 80.

Bit	Description
0	Hardware uncorrectable error 0 = No error 1 = Uncorrectable error
1	Hardware correctable error 0 = No error 1 = Single-bit error
2	Checkstop 0 = No error 1 = Checkstop error
3 – 7	System specific
8	Bus Error indicator 0 0 = No error 1 = Parity error
9	Bus Error indicator 1 0 = No error 1 = Parity error
10 – 12	System Specific
13	Address Bus Error 0 = No error 1 = Address bus error
14	Data Bus Error 0 = No error 1 = Data bus error
15	Time-out Error 0 = No error 1 = Time-out error
16–31	System Specific

Table 80. **System Exception Status Register (SESR)**

E.4.3 Memory Error Address Register (MEAR)

The MEAR is a 32-bit register or 64-bit register containing the address of the highest priority memory error which occurred since the MCSR register was last read. There shall be one MEAR/MCSR pair per memory subsystem. The memory error priority in order from most to least urgent, is hardware uncorrectable memory or addressing range error, and, then, hardware correctable memory errors.

The first occurrence of the highest priority error shall be kept in the MEAR/MCSR pair. When software reads the MEAR, a new MCSR/MEAR pair may be written by hardware.

The bus error indicator bits fields, bits 8 and 9, are used to further identify the error on the bus. For example in one implementation they signify whether the high or low portion of the bus contained a parity error, in another case, whether the data or control portion of the bus was in error. Other examples, include the use of bit 13 and 14 to specify a generic bus error or more specifically, to identify parity errors on the buses. In another implementation, the system specific bits are used to identify which bus (processor or I/O) in the system the error was detected on.

E.4.4 System Exception Address Register (SEAR)

The SEAR is a 32-bit or 64-bit register, containing either the address or data value associated with the system exception.

E.4.5 Time-Out Registers

The specification of these registers is implementation dependent.

E.5 Processing Examples

Table 81 contains the system processing approach to a variety of error conditions with some qualifications as to the class of implementation.

Different busses may have different characteristics. The "System Time-Out Processing" table, Table 82, is intended to represent the least disruptive action which can be supported, if the condition is able to occur. The 60X column indicates the ability for the condition to occur on the 60X bus.

Operation	Error	Detected	Preferred Actions
Load or Mem-to-BUC (DMA)	Hardware Correctable Memory Error	System	Interrupt may not be signalled Error into MCSR Address in MEAR
Load or Mem-to-BUC (DMA)	Hardware Uncorrectable Memory Error	System	Signal Machine Check (TEA) or BusChk Error into MCSR Address in MEAR
Load or Mem-to-BUC (DMA)	Address Parity	All	Signal Machine Check Error into SESR Addr in SEAR Signal Checkstop for $\leq$ Class-2
Load or Mem-to-BUC (DMA)	Data Parity	Master BUC (not processor)	Signal Machine Check Error into SESR Addr in SEAR Signal Checkstop for $\leq$ Class-2
Load	BUC Error	Master BUC	Signal Machine Check/Buscheck or External Error into SESR Address into SEAR
Store or BUC-to-Mem (DMA)	Address Parity	All	Signal Machine check Error in SESR Address in SEAR Signal checkstop for $\leq$ Class-2
Store	Data Parity	Slave BUC (not memory controller)	Signal Machine Check Error into SESR Addr in SEAR Signal Checkstop for $\leq$ Class-2
Store or BUC-to-Mem (DMA)	BUC error	Master BUC	Signal Machine Check / BusChk Error in SESR Address in SEAR Signal checkstop for $\leq$ Class-2
Load / Store or memory map I/O	Address Range	System	Signal Machine Check / BusChk Error in SESR Address in SEAR Signal checkstop or no detect for $\leq$ Class-2
DSS (Load / Store) last	Address Range	System	Set error bit or signal Derr Send reply packet. Init Direct Store Interrupt Error into DSIER
DSS Load / Store	Address Parity	All	Signal Machine Check / BusChk Error in SESR Address in SEAR Signal checkstop for $\leq$ Class-2

Table 81. **System Exception Processing**

Operation	Error	Detected	Preferred Actions
DSS Load	Data Parity	Processor	Machine Check Error into SESR Address into SEAR Signal Checkstop for $\leq$ Class-2
DSS load	BUC error	Slave BUC	Set Error bit or signal Derr Send reply packet. Error into DSIER Signal Checkstop for $\leq$ Class-2
DSS Store	Data Parity	Slave BUC	Set error bit or Signal Derr Send error reply packet Error into DSIER Signal Checkstop for $\leq$ Class-2
DSS Store	BUC error	Slave BUC	Set error bit or signal Derr Send error reply packet Error into DSIER Signal Checkstop for $\leq$ Class-2
BUC-to-Mem (DMA)	Data Parity	Mem. Ctl.	Write ECC error code indicating bad parity on write, causing latent machine check on read or generate high priority external interrupt to avoid the machine check.
Processor/BUC Internal	Parity	Processor/ BUC	Signal Checkstop and propagate to system.

Table 81. **Continued**

Operation	Time-out	Detected By	Preferred Actions	60X
Internal	No instruction dispatch	Processor	Signal CheckStop	Yes
Processor reads Memory Processor writes Memory Processor reads BUC Processor writes BUC		Processor/ System Logic	Signal Machine Check Error into SESR Address into SEAR	Yes
Processor reads BUC (DSS)	"last" reply not received	Processor	Signal Machine Check Error into SESR Address into SEAR	Yes
Processor writes BUC (DSS)	"last" reply not received	Slave BUC	Signal External Interrupt Error into SESR Address into SEAR	Yes
BUC read Memory (DMA) BUC to BUC Arb request but no grant		Master BUC	Signal External Interrupt Error into SESR Address into SEAR	Yes
Arb request but no grant		Processor	Signal Machine Check Error into SESR Address into SEAR	Yes
BUC writes Memory (DMA)		Master BUC	Signal External Error into SESR Address into SEAR	Yes
BUC receives addr but no data		Slave BUC	Signal BusChk	No
Continuous ARB/Artry/Rerun		System Logic	Signal Machine Check Error into SESR Address into SEAR	Yes
DBSY with no address cycle		System Logic	Signal External Interrupt or TEA Error into SESR Address into SEAR	No
No Ack		Master BUC	Signal Machine Check Error into SESR Address into SEAR	No

Table 82. **System Time-Out Processing**

IPLCB Example

Refer to Section 12.2 on page 188 for the description of the IPLCB.

F.1 IPLCB Structure Definition

The number of structures within (hence the size of) the IPLCB in any given environment is dynamically determined and depends on the number of supported adapters that reside in the environment. Also, the amount of information that AIX will want to retrieve is a very small subset of the total IPLCB size. Therefore, a front end structure containing a directory of offsets and sizes was created. Accesses to IPLCB data outside the front end structure must be through an indirect access to that data by obtaining the offset of the data structure from the IPL_DIRECTORY that is part of the front end structure. With this approach it is not necessary to require that the header file for each of the internal structures be available to AIX. AIX only needs the header file for the front end structure and those structures from which it needs to retrieve data (a very small subset of the total). This technique also allows the IPL ROM development team to make changes to the IPLCB without affecting compatibility with existing (i.e. released) versions of the IPLCB and AIX (see Appendix "AIX Dependencies on the IPLCB" starting on page 271). The following is an example of the header/directory portion of the ipl_cb structure.

```
typedef struct ipl_cb{      /* IPL Control Block front   */
    unsigned int gpr_save_area[32];  /* end GPR save area, ROS */
                                      /* interrupts    */
    IPL_DIRECTORY SD;    /* Offsets/sizes directory       */
}IPL_CB, *IPL_CB_PTR;
```

NOTE: IPL_CB_PTR (in GPR3) shall be the real address of the first byte of the gpr_save_area[]
array.

```
typedef struct ipl_directory {  /* IPL ROS DIRECTORY */
    char ipl_control_block_id[8]; /* IPL ROS ASCII string ID */
    unsigned int  ipl_cb_and_bit_map_offset; /* offset to */
                                      /* gpr_save_area */
    unsigned int  ipl_cb_and_bit_map_size;   /* IPL CB and bit */
                                      /* map size */
    unsigned int  bit_map_offset;     /* offset to RAM bit map */
    unsigned int  bit_map_size;       /* size of the RAM bit map */
    unsigned int        ipl_info_offset;
    unsigned int        ipl_info_size;
    unsigned int        iocc_post_results_offset;
    unsigned int        iocc_post_results_size;
    unsigned int        nio_dskt_post_results_offset;
    unsigned int        nio_dskt_post_results_size;
    unsigned int        ent_post_results_offset;
    unsigned int        ent_post_results_size
    unsigned int        vrs40 offset;
    unsigned int        vrs40 size;
    unsigned int  gpr_save_area1[64];  /* GPR save area, ROS */
                                      /* interrupts */
    unisigned int        system_info_offset;
    unsigned int        system_info_size;
    unsigned int        buc_info_offset;
    unsigned int        buc_info_size;
    unsigned int        processor_info_offset;
    unsigned int        processor_info_size;
    unsigned int        fm2_io_info_offset;
    unsigned int        fm2_io_info_size;
    } IPL_DIRECTORY, *IPL_DIRECTORY_PTR;
```

F.2 Notes on IPLCB Front End and IPL Directory Structures

1. In 32-bit implementations, gpr_save_area[32] is sufficient to save all of the General Purpose Registers (GPRs) during interrupts. In a 64-bit environment this is not possible; therefore, in 64-bit environments, the gpr_save_area1[64] is added to the ipl_directory structure.

2. IPL ROM shall guarantee that the size of the ipl_directory (in bytes) is always equal to: IPL_CB.s0.ipl_info_offset – sizeof(gpr_save_area). In other words, IPL ROM code shall always place the ipl_info structure immediately following the directory structure. The size of ipl_directory is required by AIX in order to be able to determine if a given component is available in a particular environment.

3. An offset/size pair in which either value is 0 implies that the corresponding component structure is not present.

4. IPL ROM shall guarantee that the control block is in contiguous memory space and that its total size, including the memory bit map, is "ipl_cb_and_bit_map_size" bytes. The implication is that the bit map is at the end (the last structure) of the control block.

F.2.1 Memory Allocation and Access Rules for IPLCB

Once the IPLCB has been created, IPL ROM code shall guarantee that a pointer (IPL_CB_PTR) to the real memory address of the beginning of the IPLCB shall always be available to any called routine or to the Operating System, as though it were the first parameter of a "C" function call. In assembler parlance, IPL_CB_PTR shall be present in GPR3 at the time of the "call."

IPL ROM shall place the IPLCB in a contiguous area (with no holes) in high memory. In other words, the control block shall not contain any unusable memory (memory that tested bad) or any memory not assigned to a control block structure. Refer to Appendix F.2, "Notes on IPLCB Front End and IPL Directory Structures" for additional information about control block memory.

On a WARM IPL, before passing control to IPL ROM, AIX must guarantee that the IPL_CB_PTR is valid and resident in GPR3 and that the IPLCB is resident at the same real memory locations in which it was originally passed to AIX.

AIX must access the individual components of the IPLCB via the offsets contained in the ipl_directory in order to maintain compatibility between various levels of AIX and the IPLCB.

The sections starting with Section F.2.3, "Per-Processor Scratch Pad Array Structure" provide examples of scratch pad implementations.

F.2.2 IPL ROM Arrays

The example below and the notes which accompany it explain the IPL ROM implementation techniques and usage rules for arrays of structures. If one follows the rules, it will appear as though the following "array of structures" definition exists:

```
struct struct_name array_name[num_of_structs];


typedef struct struct_name {
    uint num_of_structs:/* contains the runtime value    */
                        /* corresponding to the number of */
               /* these structures contained in this array */
    uint  index;        /* 0 <= index <= num_of_structs - 1, */
                        /* assume index = n, then this    */
                        /* is the n+1th array element     */
    uint struct_size;   /* size of this structure (in bytes) */


    /* additional structure variables go from here on down */
} STRUCT_NAME, * STRUCT_NAME_PTR;
```

F.2.2.1 Notes on IPL ROM Arrays

1. The three variables, "num_of_structs," "index," and "struct_size," shall exist in all IPL ROM IPL structures that are to be used as arrays.

2. The structure address shall either be given or it shall have to be determined by getting its offset from the IPL directory in the usual way.

3. To guarantee compatibility between different levels of IPL ROM and AIX, one must traverse the array structure using pointers and offset values such as illustrated in the following code excerpt.

```
STRUCT_NAME_PTR   my_struct_ptr;
/* my_struct_ptr may have to be determined from the IPL     */
/* directory or it may be a "given." If from the directory, */

/* to get to the beginning of the array: */
my_struct_ptr =  (STRUCT_NAME_PTR)
((uint)IPL_CB_PTR + IPL_CB_PTR->s0.struct_name_offset);
```

To determine which array element your addressing:

```
if (my_struct_ptr->index = = 0)   then "at first element of array"
if (my_struct_ptr->index = = n)   then "at (n–1)th element of array"
(0 < n < = (my_struct_ptr->num_of_structs - 1))
                              then "at n+1th  element of array"

if (my_struct_ptr->index = = (my_struct_ptr->num_of structs-1))
                      then "at last element of array"
```

Rules for traversing the array:

Postfix and prefix incrementing or decrementing e.g., (my_struct_ptr+ + or —my_struct_ptr) SHOULD NEVER BE USED since the structures' size is dynamically determined at run time. Always use the type of arithmetic as shown above and below.

To get to the next array element:

```
my_struct_ptr = (STRUCT_NAME_PTR) ((uint)my_struct_ptr +
my_struct_ptr->struct_size);
```

To get to the previous array element:

```
my_struct_ptr  =  (STRUCT_NAME_PTR)  ((uint)my_struct_ptr  -
my_struct_ptr->struct_size);
```

To find the total size of the array:

```
total_array_size     =       (my_struct_ptr->struct_size)      *
(my_struct_ptr->num_of_structs)
```

or you may read it directly from the ipl_directory, if present.

4. All arrays of the same type structure should be merged together, even ones that are associated with different BUCs. For example, if a system contains two Ionian chips, each chip would result in an array of fm2_io_info structures (refer to F.2.5, "Per-Adapter Family 2 Scratch Pad Array Structure"). In the IPL ROM environment, these "two" arrays shall be grouped together to form one array which shall be twice the size of either one of the original arrays and the "num_of_structs" and "index" variables in each individual structure shall reflect the size and element, respectively, of the merged array.

F.2.3 Per-Processor Scratch Pad Array Structure

The following example of the "per-processor data area array" IPLCB extension for an MP environment illustrates a number of details for implementing a IPLCB scratch pad:

```
typedef struct processor_info {
    uint num_of_structs;       /* contains the runtime value    */
                               /* corresponding to the number of */
                               /*processors supported           */
    uint  index;          /* 1 <= index <= num_of_structs - 1   */
                               /* assume index = n, then this   */
                               /* is the n+1th array element    */
    uint struct_size;    /* size of this structure (in bytes)  */
    int per_buc_info_offset; /* the iplcb offset to the        */
                               /* "buc_info" structure related  */
                               ?* to this device                */
    void *proc_int_area:/* Base Address (BA) of the processors */
                               /* interrupt presentation layer  */
                               /* registers BA+ (CPPR||XISR without */
                               /* side effects)                 */
                               /* BA+4 (CPPR||XISR with side effects)*/
                               /* BA+8   (DSIER)                */
                               /* BA+12  (MFRR)                 */
                               /* BA+xx  (Additional Optional MFRRs) */
    uint proc_int_area_size: /* proc_int_area_size 4 is the   */
                               /* number of interrupt           */
                               /* presentation registers        */
    int processor_present;    /* 0 implies not present, !=0 is */
                               /* present                       */
                         /* -1 implies not operational (failed */
                               /* test)                         */
                    /* 1 implies processor is "running" AIX    */
                    /* 2 implies processor is "looping"        */
                    /*   with link = 0 (see NOTE 1 below)      */
                    /* 3 implies this processor is available   */
                    /*   in the reset state                    */
                    /* additional values to be defined         */
    uint test_run: /* this is a bit significant variable       */
                    /* indicating which tests were run on      */
                    /* this processor. bits are or'ed for      */
                    /* each test.                              */
                    /* the corresponding bit values are        */
                    /* herein defined:                         */
                    /* bit 0 is the least significant bit      */
                    /* test was run if and only if bit == 1    */
                    /* bit: state definition:                  */
                    /* 0 : local address bus test              */
```

```
                        /* 1 : shared address bus test          */
                        /* 2 : local data bus test              */
                        /* 3 : shared data bus test             */
                        /* 4 : local memory data test           */
                        /* 5 : shared memory data test          */
                        /* 6 : fixed point unit test            */
                        /* 7 : floating point unit test         */
                        /* undefined bits are reserved          */
      uint test_stat: /* this status is valid whenever         */
                        /* test_run contains a non-zero value.  */
                        /* value of 1 signifies the test        */
                        /* corresponding to the                 */
                        /* test_run bit has failed, a value of 0 */
                        /* signifies the test passed.  The test */
                        /* results DO NOT necessarily imply the */
                        /* processor present value = = -1       */
                        /* if = 0, loop until non-zero          */
                        /* if !=0, branch to link address       */
                        /* (see NOTE 1 below)                   */
      void *link_address;/* this is branch address when link !=0 */
                        /* (see NOTE 1 below)                   */
      uint phys_id;   /* unique processor identifier           */
                        /* from system register                 */
      int architecture: /* POWER_RS   processor architecture   */
                        /* POWER_PC   etc                       */
      int implementation /* POWER_RS1  processor implementation */
                        /* POWER_RS2                            */
                        /* POWER_RSC                            */
                        /* POWER_601 etc                        */
      int version     /* processor version number              */
                        /* PPC_601 etc.                         */
      int width;      /* max processor data word size          */
                        /* (32 or 64)    NOT the current execution */
                        /* mode                                 */
      int cache_attrib:   /* cache attribute bit field         */
                        /* bit 0 is the least significant bit   */
                        /* bit: state definition:               */
                        /* 0  cache-not-present/cache-present    */
                        /* 1 separate-cache/combined-inst-data   */
                        /* undefined bits are reserved          */
      int coherency_size; /* size of coherence block           */
      int resrv_size;    /* size of reservation granule        */
```

```
        int icache block;     /* L1 instruction cache block size    */
        int dcache block;     /* L1 data cache block size           */
        int icache_size;      /* L1 instruction cache size          */
        int dcache-size;      /* L1 data cache size                 */
        int icache_line;      /* L1 instruction cache line size     */
        int dcache_line;      /* L1 data cache line size            */
        int icache_asc;       /* L1 instruction cache associativity */
        int dcache_asc;       /* l1 data cache associativity        */
        int L2_cache_size;    /* L2 cache size (0=> no L2 cache)    */
        int L2_cache_asc;     /* L2 cache associativity             */
        int tlb_attrib;       /* tlb attribute bit field            */
                              /* bit 0 is the least significant bit */
                              /* bit: state definition:             */
                              /* 0 tlb-not-present/tlb-present       */
                       /* 1 separate-tlb/combined-inst-data-tlb */
                              /* undefined bits are reserved        */
        int itlb_size;        /* entries in instruction tlb         */
        int dtlb_size;        /* entries in data tlb                */
        int itlb_asc;         /* instruction tlb associativity      */
        int dtlb asc;         /* data tlb associativity             */
        int slb_attrib;       /* slb attribute bit field            */
                              /* bit 0 is the least significant bit */
                              /* bit: state definition              */
                              /* 0 slb-not-present/slb-present       */
                       /* 1 separate-slb/combined-inst-data-slb */
                              /* undefined bits are reserved        */
        inst_islb_size;       /* entries in instruction slb         */
        int dslb_size;        /* entries in data slb                */
        int islb_asc;         /* instruction slb associativity      */
        int dslb_asc;         /* data slb associativity             */
        int priv_lck_cnt;     /* supervisor state spin lock count   */
        int prob_lck_cnt      /* problem state spin lock count      */
        int rtc_type; /* processor's time base type         */
        int rtcXint;  /* nano-seconds per time base tick    */
                      /* integer multiplier (see NOTE 4 below)   */
        int rtcXfrac; /* nano-seconds per time base tick    */
                      /* fraction multiplier                */
                      /*              (see NOTE 4 below)     */
} PROCESSOR_DATA, * PROCESSOR_DATA_PTR;
```

The array appears to be like:
```
    struct processor_info per_processor_info[num_of_structs];
```

F.2.3.1   Notes on Per-Processor Pad Array Structure

1. Each processor_info structure is a template for a processor that may exist in
    a given "slot" (Location). Any processor "slots" that are empty shall
    contain a value of 0 in their processor_present variable.

    Any processors that are present but unavailable (due to test failure) shall be
    in a reset state and shall contain a value of −1 in their corresponding
    processor_present variable.

    When IPL ROM transfers control to AIX, one and only one processor shall
    be running the AIX code and its processor_present variable shall contain a
    value of "1". This processor shall be referred to as the "master" processor.
    When AIX gets control, R3 shall contain the IPL_CB_PTR and R4 shall
    contain the address of the "processor_info" structure of the running
    processor.

    Any remaining processors in an MP environment may be running a
    protected, memory resident program provided by IPL ROM (a value of "2"
    in the processor_present variable), or shall be "available" (test passed) but
    in the reset state (a value of "3" in the processor_present variable). In the
    former case, the code continually interrogates the value of the "link"
    variable within its own processor_info structure as follows: If this value is
    0, the processor continues to interrogate it; if the value is non-zero, the
    link_address variable is interpreted as a branch address and a branch to the
    address is affected by IPL ROM for the corresponding processor. When the
    branch is affected, R3 shall contain the IPL_CB_PTR and R4 shall contain
    the address of the "processor_info" structure of the processor. The link and
    link_address variables of the master processor shall be set, by IPL ROM, to
    indicate the starting address of the loaded code.

2. num_of_structs is a value that is dynamically determined by IPL ROM. Its
    value shall be placed in each processor_info structure contained within the
    array. This value shall specify the number of processors that is supported
    (but not necessarily present) in the processor complex that is controlled by
    the IPL ROM.

3. To guarantee compatibility between different levels of IPL ROM and AIX,
    one must traverse through the array structure using pointers and offset
    values as defined in F.2.2, "IPL ROM Arrays."

    *To get to the beginning of the processor_info array, define your pointer variable and assign
    to it as follows:*

```
PROCESSOR_DATA_PTR  per_proc_info_ptr =
(struct processor_info *)  ((uint)IPL_CB_PTR +
IPL_CB_PTR->s0.processor_info_Offset);
```

per_proc_info_ptr may now be used for accessing and traversing the array .

To find the size of the array, read it directly from the ip_directory.

4. These values shall allow for conversion between time base counter ticks and time-of-day.

5. This array is pointed to by IPL directory entry "processor_info_offset."

F.2.4 Per-BUC Scratch Pad Array Structure

```
typedef struct buc_info {
    uint  num_of_structs:     /* contains the runtime value    */
                              /* corresponding to the number of */
                              /* BUCs present                  */
    uint    index;            /* 0 <= index <= num_of_structs - 1 */
                              /* assume index = n, then this   */
                              /* is the n+1th array element     */
    uint struct_size;         /* size of this structure (in bytes) */
    inst bsrr_offset;         /* bus slot reset register offset */
                              /* (see NOTE 2 below )            */
    uint bsrr_mask;           /* bus slot reset register mask   */
                              /* a one bit only mask which      */
                              /* identifies the bit that controls */
                              /* the reset of                   */
                              /* this BUC (see NOTE 2 below)    */
    int bscr_value;           /* configuration register value to */
                              /* enable configuration of this BUC */
    int cfg_status;           /*  0 => this BUC is not configured */
                              /*  1 => this BUC is configured    */
                              /* -1 => configuration failed      */
    int device_type;          /* 1 => this BUC is executable memry */
                              /* 2 +> this BUC is a processor   */
                              /* 3 => this BUC is an io type     */
    int num_of_buids:         /* num of BUIDs requred by this BUC */
                              /* (<=4)                          */
    struct buid_data {
      int buid1_value;        /* assign BUID value              */
                              /* these values have meaning if and */
                              /* only if the num_of_buids !=0,   */
                              /* they are assigned in order      */
                              /* until the num_of_buids is       */
                              /* satisfied.                      /*
```

```
                                  /* Unused BUIDs shall = -1              /*
          void *buid_Sptr;  /* pointer to BUID's own post            /*
                                  /* structure                            */
     } buid_data[4];
     int mem_alloc1;          /* 1st memory allocation required       */
                                  /* (in MB)                              */
     voic *mem_addr1;         /* real address of mem_alloc1 area      */
                                  /* if mem_alloc1 !=0, otherwise N/A     */
     int mem_alloc2;          /* 2nd memory allocation required       */
                                  /* (in MB)                              */
     void *mem_addr2;         /* real address of mem_alloc2 area      */
                                  /* if mem_alloc2 !=0, otherwise N/A     */
     int vpd_rom_width;       /* width of vpd interface in bytes      */
                                  /* -1 => not applicable, no VPD ROM     */
                                  /* present                              */
     int cfg_addr_inc;        /* configuration address increment      */
                                  /* in bytes                             */
                                  /* Refer to NOTE 4 below                */
     int device_id_reg;       /* standard configuration register      */
                                  /* contents                             */
     void *aux_info_offset;    /* the IPLCB offset to the             */
                                  /* "device specific"                    */
                                  /* array defined for this BUC. e.g.,    */
                                  /* if this is a processor BUC, the      */
                                  /* auxilary struct is the               */
                                  /* processor_info array struct          */
                                  /* if the device type is I/O type,      */
                                  /* the aux struct is an io_Info         */
                                  /* array struct, etc.                   */
                                  /* Refer to NOTE 1 below                */

} BUC_DATA, *BUC_DATA_PTR;
```

The array appears to be like:

```
    struct buc_info  per_buc_info[num_of_structs];
```

F.2.4.1   Note on Per-BUC Scratch Pad Array Structure

1. An auxiliary pointer shall always point to the array element that describes
    the device that is related to the BUC. For example, if the BUC is a
    processor, the aux ptr shall point to the appropriate array element, within
    the per-processor array, that is associated with this BUC. If there is more

than one aux array element related to the BUC (such as an IOCC BUC, which can support an IO bus that can contain up to sixteen adapters), the aux ptr shall point to the first array element in the array. The array can be traversed as explained in F.2.2, "IPL ROM Arrays." Also, each array element contains a "pointer" back to its related BUC structure.

2. This value, bsrr_offset, added to the bsrr_address contained in struct system_info, provides the address for the appropriate bus slot reset register for this BUC. The value bsrr_mask, when effectively or'ed into the bus slot reset register, shall enable the appropriate BUC. The bit inversion of bsrr_mask, when effectively ANDed into the bus slot register, shall represent the appropriate BUC.

3. This array is pointed to by IPL directory entry "buc_info_offset."

4. This value, cfg_addr_inc, added to the scr_addr contained in struct system_info, provides the addressing for the standard configuration registers.

F.2.5 Per-Adapter Family 2 Scratch Pad Array Structure

```
typedef struct fm2_io_info {
                          /* family 2 adapter support ie.    */
                          /* devices that support Programmable */
                          /* Option Select feature (POS)       */
                          /* registers                         */
    uint  num_of_structs;    /* contains the run time value  */
                          /* corresponding to the number of io */
                          /* adapters defined in             */
                          /* this array                      */
    uint   index;         /* 0 <= index <= num_of_structs - 1, */
                          /* assume index = n, then this     */
                          /* is the n+1th array element      */
    uint struct_size;     /* size of this structure (in bytes) */
    ROS_TEST_TYPE_test_mode; /* the post test mode           */
    int detected_error;   /* 0 implies no error detected     */
                          /* !=0 implies device specific error */
    int adapter present:/* 0 implies not present, !=0 is      */
                          /* present                         */
    int adapter_bad;      /* only valid if adapter present !=0 */
                          /* 0 implies good, !=0 implies bad   */
    uint pos0_id;         /* 0xff IN BOTH pos0id and pos1_id   */
                          /* fields                          */
    uint pos1_id;         /* indicate that there is no adapter */
```

```
                        /* present in the corresponding   */
                        /* BUID/slot. any other values are */
                        /* the values obtained from the    */
                        /* pos registers of the BUID/slot   */
    uint buid_value;    /* BUID to which this data applies  */
    uint slot_value;    /* the slot number within the given */
                        /* BUID                            */
    uint scan_code_present; /* romscan post controls this flag */
                        /* ==0, no test performed for      */
                        /* romscan code                    */
                        /* ==1, implies romscan code device */
                        /* bootcode detected on this card  */
                        /* ==2, implies video romscan code  */
                        /* detected on this card.          */
                        /* ==3, implies both video and     */
                        /* device boot code are present on  */
                        /* this crd                        */
                        /* ==4->7, Reserved                */
                        /* ==8 & slot <=7, no romscan code  */
                        /* found                           */
                        /* ==8 & slot > 7, no romscan code  */
                        /* allowed                         */
                        /* ==9, A PS/2 ROM failed Checksum  */
                        /* ==10, RISC/6000 ROM CRC failure  */
                        /* ==11, Address of RISC/6000 ROM   */
                        /* Invalid                         */
    uint supports_ipl;  /* ==0 => no, != 0 => adapter      */
                        /* supports ipl                    */
#define HW_ADDR_BYTE_LEN 16   /* Usually six bytes, allow for */
                        /* expansion                       */
                        /* The actual length is dictated by */
                        /* the adapter type. i.e., token,  */
                        /* ethernet, etc.                  */
    unchar hw_net_addr[HW_ADDR_BYTE_LEN];/* The network address*/
                        /* array, beginning in byte 0      */
    void *hmb_ptr;
    uint user_defined3;
    uint adapter_flag;  /* to identify bluebonnet or lace  */
                        /* adapter                         */
    uint user_defined1;
    uint user_defined0;
    int per_buc_info_offset; /* the iplcb offset to the    */
```

```
                                    /* "buc_info" structure related to   */
                                    /* this device                       */
} FM2_TO_DATA, *FM2_IO_DATA_PTR;
```

The array appears to be like:

```
    struct  fm2_io_info   per_fm2_io_info[num_of_structs];
```

This array is pointed to by IPL directory entry
"fm2_io_info_Offset"

F.2.6 System Info Scratch Pad

```
typedef struct system_info {
    int num_of_procs;     /* number of processors supported   */
                          /* in this system                   */
                          /* num_of_procs == 1 => Uniprocessor */
                          /* num_of_procs > 1   =>  n-way MP   */
                          /* This value refers to the number   */
                          /* that this platform is              */
                          /* designed to handle. One must look */
                          /* at processor_info structure to    */
                          /* determine the number of           */
                          /* processors actually               */
                          /* present in the system.            */
    int coherency_size;   /* size of the coherence block       */
    int resv_size;        /* size of the reservation granule   */
    void *arb_cr_addr:    /* real address of arbiter control   */
                          /* reg                                */
    void *phys_id_reg_addr; /* real address of physical id reg */
    int num_of_bsrr;      /* number of 4 byte bus slot reset   */
                          /* regs                              */
    void *bsrr_addr;      /* real address of bus slot reset    */
                          /* reg                                */

    int tod_type;         /* type of time of day structure     */
    void *todr_addr;      /* real address of time of day regs  */
    void *rsr_addr;       /* real address of reset status reg  */
    void *pksr_addr;      /* real address of power/keylock      */
                          /* status reg                         */
    void *prcr_addr;      /* real address of power reset        */
                          /* control reg                        */
```

```
        void *sssr_addr;      /* real address of system specific    */
                              /* regs                               */
        void *sir_addr;       /* real address of system interrupt   */
                              /* regs                               */
        void *scr_addr;       /* real address of standard config    */
                              /* reg                                */
        void *dscr_addr;      /* real address of device specific    */
                              /* cfg reg                            */
        int NVRAM_size;       /* byte size of NVRAM                 */
        void *NVRAM_addr;     /* real address of NVRAM              */
        void *vpd_rom_addr;   /* real address of VPD ROM Space      */
        int ipl_rom_size;     /* byte size IPL ROM space           */
        void *ipl_rom_addr;   /* real address of IPLROM space       */
        void g_mfrr_addr;     /* real address of global MFRR reg    */
                              /* if !=0                             */
        void g-tb_addr;       /* real address of global time base   */
                              /* if !=0                             */
        int g_tb_type;        /* global time base type              */
        int g_tb_mult; /* global time base multiplier              */
} SYSTEM_INFO, *SYSTEM_INFO_PTR;
```

This structure is pointed to by IPL directory entry
`"system_info_offset"`

AIX Dependencies on the IPLCB

The IPLCB is a continually changing structure. It must be designed as such to enable the addition of new function, especially in the form of new adapters. In order to maintain compatibility between various levels of AIX and IPLCBs, the following must be adhered to:

■ Once a component structure has been defined, the definition may only be changed by adding new variables to the end of the existing structure. Existing variables must never be deleted and must always be supported (i.e. be kept up to date). This is required by IPL ROM to enable a newer level of IPL ROM to be released in an environment that supports an older level of AIX.

■ IPL ROM shall maintain one and only one current version of the IPLCB. Each new version that supersedes a previous version shall contain all of the information that was supported in the superseded version.

G.1 IPLCB/Implementation Dependent Placements

The access_id is a communication mechanism between IPL ROM and AIX software to allow for the placement of architected facilities in NVRAM. The access_id is a four byte field used within individual IPLCB structures. A value of zero for the access_id indicates normal memory map (T=0) access and a value of one (1) indicates that the machine DD is to be used to access the facility. The access_id refers to a four byte real address of the facility which is always in the upper four (4) gigabytes, because on a 64-bit word machine, software shall assume that the upper 32-bits are all ones.

Note

If the facility is such that no data integrity or security exposure exists and the facility is initialized at IPL time, then an access_id value of zero may be appropriate, in which case, a normal memory access is used by the software. If any of these conditions are not true, then additional error checking, such as, a CRC is required and a non-zero value for the access_id field is required. A value of 1 for the access_id requires that the AIX software use the machine DD for access to the facility. The machine DD uses the address to determine if a CRC update is required on a write, see Section on page 35 for more details.

G.2 Dependencies for PowerPC System Platforms

Programming Note

Refer to Section 12.2 on page 188 for ways to find the actual iplcb.h.

The following descriptions are concise, as intended. Refer to the iplcb.h header file for a more complete definition of each variable.

G.2.1 Struct ipl_directory

```
unsigned int      bit_map_offset;
unsigned int      bit_map_size;
unsigned int      ipl_info_offset;
unsigned int      iocc_post_results_offset;
unsigned int      ram_post_results_offset;
unsigned int      sga_post_results_offset;
unsigned int      net_boot_results_offset;
unsigned int      global_offset;
```

G.2.2 Struct ipl_info

```
int nvram_section_1_valid
   /* The low order 3 bits of this field are used by IPL ROS.    */
   /* The low order 2 bits of this field are used to signify     */
   /* the condition of area of NVRAM known as AREA1 from NVRAM   */
   /* offset 0x0 through 0x2ff.  The other bit is used to        */
   /* signify a "low" battery condition.                         */
   /* b01xx => a bad battery condition                           */
   /* b0x00 => IPL ROS found AREA1 CRC bad and could not         */
   /*          correct it                                        */
   /* b0x01 => IPL ROS found AREA1 CRC good                      */
   /* b0x11 => IPL ROS found AREA1 CRC bad and corrected it      */
   /* This value is used by the machine device driver           */

unsigned char *BIOS_code_ptr
   /* Contains pointer to the compressed BIOS code in IPL ROM.   */
   /* This value is used by the machine device driver when      */
   /*  reading the PC BIOS code                                  */

unsigned int BIOS_code_size
   /* Contains the size in bytes of BIOS code contained in ROM.  */
   /* This value is used by the machine device driver when      */
   /* reading the PC BIOS code                                   */

int cache_line_size
   /* Contains the cache line size.  This is used in several     */
   /* places in analyzing RS1 memory extents                     */

int IO_planar_level_reg
int IO_planar_ldev_reg21
int IO_planar_ldev_reg22
```

```
int IO_planar_ldev_reg23
   /* Contains information about the IO planar.  This field is   */
   /* used by AIX to determine machine configurations            */

unsigned int Power_Status_and_keylock_reg
   /* Contains the the PSR value at IPL time.  This value is      */
   /* accessed in the system reset interrupt handler to          */
   /* determine if a dump needs to be initiated.                 */
   /* If the IPL was normal key position and the key at          */
   /* reset push button time was service key position, a dump    */
   /* is initiated        */

int model
   /* Contains model code field.  This value is used by AIX      */
   /* to make machine dependent code decisions and when          */
   /*  initializing the uname structure                          */

char vpd_processor_serial_number[8]
   /* Contains copy of serial number for VPD area of ROM.        */
   /* This is used by AIX in initializing uname structure        */


unsigned int bit_map_bytes_per_bit
   /* Contains number of bytes per bit in the RAM bit map.       */
   /* This is used during VMM initialization and by memory       */
   /*  scrubbing code                                            */

unsigned char previpl_device[36]
   /* Contains last normal mode IPL device.  This is used by     */
   /* boot code to determine the IPL device                      */

unsigned int cre[16]
   /* Contains the values assigned to CRE registers at power     */
   /* up.  This is used by AIX config to determine memory        */
   /* configuration on RS1 machines   */

union SIMM_INFO
   /* This union contains information about SIMMs on RS1 memory   */
   /* cards.  This is used by AIX config to determining memory    */
   /* configuration                                              */

int soft_ipl_flag
   /* Contains the number of soft IPLs since power on.           */
   /* This is use by AIX config                                  */

int dcache_size
int icache_size
   /* Size of I and D cache.  These fields are used by AIX config */

char ipl_ros_timestamp[10]
   /* Contains ROS timestamp saved from ROM VPD data.  This value */
   /* is saved by AIX config                                      */
```

G.2.3 Struct iocc_post_results

```
int length
 /* Contains the number of IOCCs tested by ROS.        */
 /* This is used in determining if a second IOCC is    */
 /* present                                            */

int results[N]
  /* Contains 0 if IOCC tested good.  This is used in  */
  /* determining if a second IOCC is present           */
```

G.2.4 Struct ram_data

```
uint cfg_tbl_array[8][2]
  /* This is valid only on RSC based machines.         */
  /* The array contains the starting address and size  */
  /* of memory.  It is used by AIX to determine        */
  /* memory extents after faults                       */

uint simm_size[8]
  /* Contains size of simms (Megs) in physical order.  */
  /*  This is used by AIX config in determining RSC    */
  /*  memory configuration                             */

uint bad_simm_report[8]
  /* Contains information on bad simms.  This is used by */
  /* AIX config in determining RSC memory configuration  */
```

G.2.5 Struct net_data

```
unsigned int slot_number
  /* Contains slot number of communication adapter after */
  /* net boot. This is used by AIX network boot code.    */
  /*                                                     */

unsigned int network_type
  /* Contains the type of network ROS booted over       */
  /* (ethernet/tokenring).  This is used by the AIX     */
  /* network boot code                                  */

unsigned int is_802_3
  /* Flag for 803.3 Ethernet protocol flag.  This is    */
  /* used by the AIX network boot code                  */

t_bootp bootpr
  /* Contains the BOOTP reply packet after a network boot.  */
  /* This structure is examined by the AIX network boot code */
```

G.2.6 Struct global_spad

```
struct adapt_info fm2_adpat_info[]
   /* Contains information on micro channel adapters.      */
   /*  Fields of this structure are examined by AIX boot code */
```

G.2.7 Struct sga_data

```
int adapter_present
   /* Flags for SGA presence.  For SGA configuration on      */
   /* RSC based machines                                     */
uint mem_size
   /* Number of SIMMS on a SGA adapter.  Used in SGA         */
   /* configuration on RSC based machines                    */
```

G.2.8 Additional Dependencies for PowerPC System Platforms

All of the dependencies described in the above sections must be maintained (primarily for AIX binary compatibility). The following list describes additional AIX dependencies on the control block contents.

Note: In the following itemized list, there exists a reference to "most of the data". This means that the actual AIX dependencies for this data are not known at the present but the general importance of the data in these new (or extended) control block structures is such that they can generally be assumed to be AIX dependencies, and as such should be supported by all PowerPC platforms. However, "a few" of the items may not actually be depended upon by AIX:

■ Most of the data contained in "struct system_info" and "System Info Scratch Pad" sections.

■ Most of the data contained in "struct buc_info" and "Per-buc Scratch Pad Array Structure" sections.

■ Most of the data contained in "struct processor_info" and "Per-processor Scratch PAd Array Structure" sections.

■ The "struct fm2_io_info" is a duplicate of "struct adapt_info" which exists in the original IPL Control Block. The same fields shall be supported in both the new and the old structure. The reason for the duplication is that the old format does not allow the degree of expansion that will be required in the PowerPC system platforms and eventually (after AIX supports the new structure) the old structure shall be eliminated.
Note that this structure is part of an IPL ROM array (described in "IPL ROM Arrays" section). Hence, the number of these structures that are present will be dependent on the number of devices present that the structure represents.

AIX Command and Event Indicators

This appendix contains indicators for a variety of conditions.

H.1 Encoded Messages

The AIX command and event indicators are encoded message indicators which are typically displayed on LEDs when the normal AIX Operating System is not operational. Refer to the 3 Digit Display Message Format and Examples in Section 14.1.4.6 on page 208 for the general rules which are followed. Also refer to the System Crash Message Section 14.1.4.9 on page 217 as well as the Message Concatenation Section 14.1.4.7 on 209 for more usages of these command and event indicators.

H.2 Event Indicators

For more detailed information regarding the AIX command and event indicators and future updates regarding the AIX command and event indicators, refer to *POWERstation and POWERserver Common Diagnostics and Service Guide (SA23–2687)*. For additional explanations of the three-digit display numbers, refer to the *Problem Solving Guide (SC23–2204)*.

H.2.1 Dump Indicators

The following dump indicators are defined:

0c0 – Dump completed successfully
0c2 – User Requested Dump started

0c3 – Dump inhibited
0c4 – Dump completed unsuccessfully
0c5 – The system is attempting to open the dump device.
0c6 – Secondary dump device is not ready. Make it ready
　　　by pressing Ctrl-Alt-Numpad2 again.
0c7 – Network dump in progress.
0c8 – Dump Disabled
0c9 – Auto Dump in progress

These indicators should be used when dumping to any device.

H.2.2 Debugger Indicator

The following debugger indicators are defined:

c20 – Debugger started due to unexpected system halt.

H.2.3 Boot and Install Indicators

The following boot and install indicators are defined:

c21 – ifconfig failed to configure network for client network boot.
c22 – tftp failed to read client's client.info file from network boot.
c23 – nfs qfsinstall failed for client network boot.
c25 – Client failed to mount remote miniroot during network install.
c26 – Client failed to mount remote /usr file system during network boot.
c27 – Attempting to boot from a device other than tok(0–3) or ent(0–3)
c28 – The system is unable to set the attributes of the network device.
c29 – The system is unable to configure the network device.

H.2.4 Diskette Command and Progress Indicators

The following diskette command and progress indicators are defined:

c00 – Operation completed
c01 – Insert first diskette
c02 – Wrong diskette sequence used Reboot.
c03 – Wrong diskette
c04 – Crash
c05 – Diskette error
c06 – Fatal error – rc.boot unable to determine type of boot.
c07 – Insert next diskette
c06 – Fatal error – RAM file system started incorrectly.
c09 – Writing or reading diskette

These indicators should be used when loading diagnostics from diskette, etc.

H.2.5 Console Indicators

The following indicators are for console is configuration:

c31 – Select your console. The system will time-out after 30
     seconds when loading in service mode if no console is
     selected.
c32 – A HFT Console is defined.
c33 – A TTY Console is defined.
c34 – A File Console is defined.

H.2.6 Diagnostic Controller Event Indicators

Diagnostic Controller Event Indicators are defined as follows:

c99 – Diagnostics have completed.

This code is only used when there is no console.

H.2.7 AIX Event Indicators

AIX Event Indicators are displayed by AIX. The product being configured is
dependent on the system implementation. For more specific information, refer
to the product specific documentation. The following have been implemented
by AIX.

Reserved – 300 to 499

Configuration Method Event Indicators – 500 to 550

The following 3-digit-display codes are displayed as progress indicators during
bus configuration. They are normally displayed for only a few seconds.

500 Querying SIO
501 Querying card in slot 1.
502 Querying card in slot 2.
503 Querying card in slot 3.
504 Querying card in slot 4.
505 Querying card in slot 5.
506 Querying card in slot 6.
507 Querying card in slot 7.
508 Querying card in slot 8.

510 to 519 are for boot and install process.

510 – Starting device configuration.
511 – Device configuration complete.
512 – Restoring device configuration files from media.
513 – Restoring BOS installation files from media.

516 – Contacting server during network boot.

517 – Mounting client remote file systems during network boot.

518 – Remote mount of root and /usr file system during network boot did not complete successfully.

520 bus configuration running.

The following numbers are used for error reporting during configuration:

521 – /etc/init invoked cfgmgr with invalid options, /etc/init has been corrupted or incorrectly modified. Fatal.

522 – The configuration manager has been invoked with conflicting options. Fatal.

523 – The configuration manager is unable to access the ODM data base. Fatal.

524 – The configuration manager is unable to access the config rules object in the ODM data base. Fatal.

525 – The configuration manager is unable to get data from customized device object in the ODM data base. Fatal.

526 – The configuration manager is unable to get data from customized device driver object in the ODM data base. Fatal.

527 – The configuration manager was invoked with the phase 1 flag, however, running phase 1 at this point is illegal. Fatal.

528 – The configuration manager can't find sequence rule or no program name was specified in the ODM data base. Fatal.

529 – The configuration manager is unable to update ODM data.

530 – The program "savebase" returned an error.

531 – The configuration manager is unable to access the PdAt object class. Fatal.

532 – There is not enough memory to continue (malloc failure). Fatal.

533 – The configuration manager could not find a configure method for a device.

534 – The configuration manager is unable to acquire data base lock. Fatal.

535 – HIPPI diagnostic interface driver being configured.

536 – The configuration manager encountered more than one sequence rule specified in the same phase. Fatal.

537 – The configuration manager encountered an error when invoking the program in the sequence rule.

538 – The configuration manager is going to invoke a configuration method.

539 – The configuration method has terminated and control has returned to the configuration manager.

Reserved – 540 to 550

551 – IPL Varyon is running.

552 – IPL Varyon failed.

553 – IPL Phase 1 is complete.

554 – The IPL device could not be opened or a read failed.

555 – ODM error when trying to varyon the rootvg.

556 – LVM subroutine error from ipl_varyon.
557 – The root filesystem will not fsck or mount.

The following indicators are for IPL problems with memory and the RAM-disk.

558 – There is not enough memory available to continue the IPL.
559 – There is less than 2 MB of good memory to load the AIX
     kernel into. Fatal.

Reserved – 560 to 569

570 to 599 will be used when configuring software applications.

570 is for configuration of virtual SCSI devices.
571 is for configuration of hippi common functions driver.
572 is for configuration of IPI-3 master transport driver for use with HIPPI.
573 is for configuration of IPI-3 slave transport driver for use with HIPPI.
574 is for configuration of IPI-3 transport services user interface driver.
575 is for configuration of IBM 9570 (FC9300) RAID 3 Disk array driver.
576 is for a vendor Async device driver configuration.
577 is for a vendor SCSI device driver configuration.
578 is for a vendor Commo device driver configuration.
579 is for a generic vendor device driver configuration.
580 is for HIPPI TCPIP network interface driver configuration
581 is for PD TCPIP.
582 is for configuring a token ring data link control.
583 is for configuring a ethernet data link control.
584 is for configuring a IEEE ethernet data link control.
585 is for configuring a SDLC MPQP data link control.
586 is for configuring a QLLC X.25 data link control.
587 is for configuring a NETBIOS.
588 is for configuring a BSCRW.
591 is for configuring LVM Device Driver.
592 is for configuring HFT Device Driver.
593 is for configuring SNA Device Drivers.
595 is for X.31 pseudo device (X.25 over ISDN).
596 is for SNA DLC/LAPE device.
597 is for Outboard Communications Server.
598 is for Outboard Communications Server hosts being
     configured during system reboot.
599 is for FDDI data link control configuration.

Reserved – 600 to 711

Configuration Method and diagnostics – 711 to 999

A code should be displayed when:

■ an adapter is being configured at IPL.

- devices attached to an adapter are being identified at IPL.

- a device is being configured at IPL.

- diagnostics are being run on a resource and no console is available.

These numbers are called LED Values.

570	Virtual SCSI devices being configured.
571	HIPPI common function device driver being configured.
572	HIPPI IPI-3 master transport driver being configured.
573	HIPPI IPI-3 slave transport driver being configured.
574	HIPPI IPI-3 transport services user interface dev. driver being configured.
575	IBM 9570 RAID 3 disk array device driver being configured.
576	Vendor Async device driver being configured.
577	Vendor SCSI device driver being configured.
578	Vendor Commo device driver being configured.
579	Vendor generic device driver being configured.
580	HIPPI TCPIP network interface driver being configured.
581	TCP/IP being configured.
582	Token Ring DLC (Data Link Control) being configured.
583	Ethernet DLC (Data Link Control) being configured.
584	IEEE Ethernet (802.3) DLC (Data Link Control) being configured.
585	SDLC (MPQP) DLC (Data Link Control) being configured.
586	QLLC (X25) DLC (Data Link Control) being configured.
587	NETBIOS being configured.
588	BSCRW being configured.
589	SCSI Target Mode Device.
590	Diskless Remote Paging Device being configured.
594	Asychronous I/O being defined/configured.
595	X.31 Pseudo device being configured (X.25 over ISDN).
596	SNA DLC/LAPE pseudo device being configured.
597	Outboard Communications Server software being configured.
711	Unknown Adapter being identified/configured.
712	Special graphics slot being configured (SGA graphics slot).
720	Unknown Read/Write optical drive being identified/configured.
721	Unknown Disk being identified/configured.
721	Unknown SCSI device being identified/configured.
722	Unknown Disk being identified/configured.
723	Unknown CDROM being identified/configured.
724	Unknown Tape being identified/configured.
725	Unknown Display being identified/configured.
726	Unknown Input device being identified/configured.
727	Unknown Async device being identified/configured.
728	Parallel Printer being identified/configured.
729	Unknown Parallel device being identified/configured.

730   Unknown Diskette being identified/configured.
731   PTY being identified/configured.
732   Unknown SCSI Initiator.
811   Processor Complex being identified/configured.
812   Common Standard Adapter Logic being identified/configured.
812   Memory being identified/configured.
813   Battery for Time-of-Day, NVRAM, etc., being identified/configured.
813   System I/O Control Logic being identified/configured.
814   NVRAM being identified/configured.
815   Floating Point Processor being identified/configured.
816   Operator Panel Logic being identified/configured.
818   Used by DA to report checkstop/machine checks.
817   Time of Day Logic being identified/configured.
819   Graphics Input Device Adapterbeing identified/configured.
821   Standard Keyboard adapter being identified/configured.
823   Standard Mouse adapter being identified/configured.
824   Standard Tablet adapter being identified/configured.
825   Standard Speaker adapter being identified/configured.
826   Serial Port 1 adapter being identified/configured.
827   Parallel port adapter being identified/configured.
828   Standard Diskette Adapter being identified/configured.
831   3151 Adapter being identified/configured.
831   Serial Port 2 being identified/configured.
834   64-Port Async Controller being identified/configured.
835   16-Port Async Concentrator being identified/configured.
836   128-Port Asynchronous Controller being identified/configured.
837   128-Port Remote Asynchronous Node being identified/configured.
838   Ethernet Adapter being identified/configured.
839   Connection Station being identified/configured.
841   8-Port Async Adapter (EIA-232) being identified/configured.
842   8-Port Async Adapter (EIA-422A) being identified/configured.
843   8-Port Async Adapter (MIL-STD 188) being identified/configured.
844   RAID array controller being identified/configured.
845   RAID array being identified/configured.
847   16-Port Serial Adapter (EIA-232) being identified/configured.
848   16-Port Serial Adapter (EIA-422) being identified/configured.
849   X.25 Communications Adapter being identified/configured.
850   Token-Ring Network adapter being identified/configured.
851   4 Port MP Adapter being identified/configured.
852   Ethernet adapter being identified/configured.
853   SCSI D I/O controller being identified/configured.
854   3270 Connection being identified/configured.
855   4-Port Multiprotocol Controller being identified/configured.
857   FSLA adapter being identified/configured.
858   5085/86/88 adapter being identified/configured.
859   FDDI adapter being identified/configured.
860   Twin Tail adapter being identified/configured.

861	Optical adapter being identified/configured.
862	370 Parallel Channel adapter being identified/configured.
863	Reserved.
864	Serial Channel adapter being identified/configured.
865	370 Serial Channel adapter being identified/configured.
866	SCSI Adapter being identified/configured.
867	Async Expansion adapter being identified/configured.
868	Integrated SCSI Adapter being identified/configured.
869	SCSI Adapter being identified/configured.
870	SCSI Adapter being identified/configured.
871	Graphics Subsystem Adapter being identified/configured.
872	Grayscale Graphics adapter being identified/configured.
873	Display adapter being identified/configured.
874	Color Graphics adapter being identified/configured.
875	Color Graphics display adapter being identified/configured.
876	8-Bit Color Graphics Processor being identified/configured.
877	Graphics Display Adapter being identified/configured.
878	GT4 Graphics adapter being identified/configured.
879	24-Bit Color Graphics Processor being identified/configured.
880	SGA Display Adapter being identified/configured.
881	Channel Attached Printer Adapter being identified/configured.
882	Serial Attached Printer Adapter being identified/configured.
883	Reserved.
884	3117 Scanner Adapter being identified/configured.
885	3118 Scanner Adapter being identified/configured.
886	3119 Scanner Adapter being identified/configured.
887	Integrate Ethernet Adapter being identified/configured.
889	SCSI-2 High Performance External I/O Controller being identified/configured.
890	SCSI-2 Differential adapter being identified/configured.
891	Vendor SCSI adapter being identified/configured.
892	Vendor Display adapter being identified/configured.
893	Vendor LAN adapter being identified/configured.
894	Vendor Async/Communications adapter being identified/configured.
895	Vendor IEEE 488 adapter being identified/configured.
896	Vendor VME Bus adapter being identified/configured.
897	370 Block Multiplexer channel adapter being identified/configured.
898	Graphics Adapter Power 6T1X being identified/configured.
899	Attachment adapter being identified/configured.
901	Vendor SCSI device being identified/configured.
902	Vendor Display being identified/configured.
903	Vendor Async device being identified/configured.
904	Vendor Parallel device being identified/configured.
905	Vendor other being identified/configured.
906	IBM Premier Speech Recognition Adapter I being identified/configured.
907	IBM Premier Speech Recognition Adapter II being identified/configured.
908	Graphics Adapter being identified/configured.

909   LSA (LAN SCSI/ADAPTER) being identified/configured.
910   FCS 1/4 Speed Adapter being identified/configured.
911   FCS Full Speed Adapter being identified/configured.
912   2E DE Drive being identified/configured.
913   5 GB 8 mm DE Drive being identified/configured.
914   5 GB 8 mm DE Tape Drive being identified/configured.
915   Tape drive being configured.
920   Bridge Box being identified/configured.
921   Keyboard 101 being identified/configured.
922   Keyboard 102 being identified/configured.
923   Keyboard Kanji being identified/configured.
924   Two-Button Mouse being identified/configured.
925   Three-Button Mouse being identified/configured.
926   Tablet 5083 Model 21 being identified/configured.
927   Tablet 5083 Model 22 being identified/configured.
928   Standard Speaker being identified/configured.
929   Dials being identified/configured.
930   Lighted Program Function Keys (LPF) keyboard being identified/configured.
931   5086 Keyboard being identified/configured.
932   IP Router being identified/configured.
933   Async Planar being identified/configured.
934   Async Expansion Drawer being identified/configured.
935   2 MB 3.5-Inch Diskette Drive being identified/configured.
936   5.25-Inch Diskette drive being identified/configured.
937   HIPPI adapter being identified/configured.
938   122 Keyboard being identified/configured.
939   Tablet for 6 button cursor being identified/configured.
940   Used by memory DA.
941   6180 Plotter being identified/configured.
942   Power GTX Graphics adapter being identified/configured.
948   Portable Disk Drive being identified/configured.
949   Unknown Bus Attached Disk Drive being identified/configured.
950   Missing SCSI Options being identified/configured.
951   670 MB SCSI Disk Drive being identified/configured.
952   355 MB SCSI Disk Drive being identified/configured.
953   320 MB SCSI Disk Drive being identified/configured.
954   400 MB SCSI Disk Drive being identified/configured.
955   857 MB SCSI Disk Drive being identified/configured.
956   670 MB SCSI Disk Drive being identified/configured.
957   120 Bus Attached Disk Drive being identified/configured.
958   160 Bus Attached Disk Drive being identified/configured.
959   160 SCSI Disk Drive being identified/configured.
960   1.37 GB SCSI Disk Drive being identified/configured.
961   2 Port Serial adapter being identified/configured.
962   Ethernet Adapter being identified/configured.
963   SCSI Scanner (2456) being identified/configured.
965   Token Ring Adapter being identified/configured.

968   1.2 GB SCSI Disk Drive being identified/configured.
970   .5-Inch 9-Track Tape drive being identified/configured.
971   150 MB .25-Inch Tape drive being identified/configured.
972   8mm SCSI Tape drive being identified/configured.
973   Other SCSI Tape drive being identified/configured.
974   CDROM drive being identified/configured.
975   R/W Optical Drive being identified/configured.
976   RISC System/6000 SCSI I/O Controller Initiator being identified/configured.
977   M-Audio Capture Playback adapter being identified/configured.
978   IEEE 4888 Adapter being identified/configured.
979   7246 SBS Frame Buffer Adapter being identified/configured.
980   IBM Switching Network interface adapter being identified/configured.
981   SCSI Disk Drive 540 MB being identified/configured.
982   Graphics Visualization Server Adapter being identified/configured.
983   XGA graphics adapter being identified/configured.
984   SCSI Disk Drive 1 GB being identified/configured.
985   VCA adapter being identified/configured.
986   2.4 GB SCSI Disk Drive being identified/configured.
987   CD-ROM XA being identified/configured.
988   FDDI Adapter being identified/configured.
989   200 MB SCSI Disk Drive being identified/configured.
990   2.0 GB SCSI Disk Drive being identified/configured.
991   525 MB 14 inch SCSI Tape being identified/configured.
992   4755 Crytographic adapter being identified/configured.
993   File Server Product being identified/configured.
994   5 GB 8mm Tape Drive being identified/configured.
995   1.2 GB 1/4 inch Tape Drive being identified/configured.
996   MP/A adapter being identified or configured.
997   Twisted pair FDDI adapter being identified/configured.
998   Suite 4 mm tape being identified/configured.
999   Compression card being identified/configured.

EEE   Reserved for FAA to do a reset to control panel.
        This displays as a big E with the top missing.

Power IOCC Architecture versus PowerPC IOCC Architecture

This appendix identifies the changes made to the POWER IOCC Architecture (as documented in the *RISC System/6000 POWERstation and POWERserver Hardware Technical Information General Architectures* manual) in order to get to the RISC System/6000 PowerPC IOCC Architecture.

I.1 Changes from Power IOCC Architecture

The following are the changes made to the POWER IOCC Architecture:

- Remove support for inconsistent I/O; support only unbuffered mode

- Expand TCW to 2 words for 64-bit systems with larger RPNs:

    - Rename TCW to TCE (Translation Control Entry) because it can be a double-word *instead of a word* in 64-bit systems

- Remove Load/Store error checking as previously defined:

    - Remove I/O low and high limit registers

    - Remove TCE key to CSR authority mask checking

    - Remove Bypass bit in Segment register

- Add Load/Store error checking support via SR or STE authority field to TCE protection key field checking

■ Remove the following Segment register bits:

  – Remove Address check bit (always check)

  – Remove Address increment bit (always increment)

  – Remove RT compatibility mode bit

  – Remove Bypass bit (no PIO to system memory)

■ Changed the following Segment register bit:

  – The IOCC bit was changed to the alternate IOCC address space bit (most IOCC facilities now mapped into Micro Channel address space). This bit allows for the decoding of the BCRs at the old POWER addresses.

■ Change the way that the SR (32-bit machines) or STE (64-bit machines) K bit(s) work:

  – Used to prevent access to the IOCC facilities only

  – Now prevents access to IOCC facilities and the Micro Channel address space

  – There are now 2 K bits in the SR or STE instead of one before (the applicable one is sent to the IOCC)

■ Remove the following TCE bits:

  – Remove Buffer number bits

  – Remove VPI bits

  – Remove RC bits

■ The **time delay** command was simplified with only 1 microsecond (–0, +1 tolerance) and 8 microsecond (–1, +1 tolerance) being specified

■ Remove support for non-system-memory resident TCEs

■ Remove DMA Slave Tag support (TCE support only)

■ Remove the following IOCC commands:

  – Remove Buffer Flush (bus master and DMA slave

  – Remove Buffer Invalidate

  – Remove Next Buffer Invalidate

■ IOCC Configuration register: remove the following fields because they are not used by software:

- Burst Control

- Disable

- Refresh control

- TCE Table size (move to the TCE Anchor Address register)

- Arbitration time

- Mapping register support bit (always support the Bus Mapping register)

■ Add an implementation dependent register, where the items deleted from the IOCC Configuration register might be put if the implementation determines that they need or want them.

■ Lump together errors for bus master and DMA slave operations that software treats the same into several classes:

- Micro Channel errors, which include: Data parity error, Address parity error, and Card Selected Feedback error

- System errors, which include: TCE extent errors, ECC errors, System Address errors, TCE reload errors, and IOCC errors

- Authority error (write to a read-only page)

- Page Fault

- I/O bus (protocol) error

- Machine check which would occur if an error is received on a delayed write

■ End Of Interrupt: keep the specific form only

■ Major change to external interrupt structure

■ Bus Mapping register support changed from four 1-word registers to one 1-word register; and, they were made mandatory instead of optional. Also, with the Bus Mapping register no longer being optional, the mapping bit in the CSRs were no longer needed and were removed. Also the mapping code point in the TCE which indicated mapped to bus was removed.

■ CSR 15 removed; system is required now to provide a register to accept Load or Store instruction exception status

■ Remove the following I/O load and store instruction errors:

- – Limit check
- – Page fault
- – ECC
- – I/O bus
- – System address

■ Remove the System I/O and Standard I/O

32-Bit/64-Bit BUC Architecture Differences and Considerations

This appendix summarizes the differences in the BUC Architecture between 32-bit implementations and 64-bit implementations.

J.1 32-Bit BUCs Versus 64-Bit BUCs

The following are the differences in the BUC Architectures:

- 32-bit machines have SRs, 64-bit machines have STEs

- 32-bit BUCs have 4-byte TCEs, 64-bit BUCs have 8-byte TCEs

    - 32-bit BUCs can only address 4 GB of system memory, and therefore cannot be used on machines which have a real memory address space of greater than 4 GB

- A 32-bit BUC has a 4-byte TCE Address register, a 64-bit BUCs has an 8-byte TCE Address register

- 32-bit BUCs can only run in 32-bit mode, 64-bit BUCs have the capability of running in 32-bit mode as well as 64-bit mode (thus using 4-byte TCEs and saving TCE table space); see the description of the 64-bit mode bit in the IOCC Configuration register description

Big-Endian and Little-Endian Tutorial

This appendix describes the big-endian and little-endian numbering conventions. For more processor-specific information, see the appendix of *PowerPC Architecture* (book I).

K.1 Endian Byte Ordering

If scalars (individual computational data items) were indivisible, then there would be no such concept as "byte ordering." It is meaningless to talk of the "order" of bits or groups of bits within the smallest addressable unit of memory, because nothing can be observed about such order. Only when scalars, which the programmer and processor regard as indivisible quantities, can be made up of more than one addressable unit of memory does the question of "order" arise.

For a machine in which the smallest addressable unit is the 64-bit doubleword, there is no question of the ordering of "bytes" within doublewords. All scalar transfers between registers and memory are for doublewords, and the address of the "byte" containing the high-order 8 bits of a scalar is no different from the address of a "byte" containing any other part of the scalar.

For PowerPC, as for most computers currently, the smallest addressable memory unit of memory is the 8-bit byte. Most computational scalars are made up of groups of bytes (halfwords, words, doublewords). When a 32-bit scalar is moved from a register to memory, the scalar occupies four consecutive byte addresses. It thus becomes meaningful to discuss the order of the byte addresses with respect to the value of the scalar: which byte contains the highest-order 8 bits of the scalar, which byte contains the next-highest-order 8 bits, and so on.

Given a scalar that spans multiple bytes, the choice of byte ordering is essentially arbitrary. There are 4! (factorial) = 24 ways to specify the ordering of four bytes within a word, but only two of these orderings are sensible:

■ The ordering that assigns the lowest address to the highest-order ("left-most") 8 bits of the scalar, the next sequential address to the next-highest-order 8 bits, and so on. This is called *big-endian* because the "big end" of the scalar, considered as a binary number, comes first in memory. IBM RISC System/6000, IBM System/370, and Motorola 680x0 are examples of computers using this byte ordering.

■ The ordering that assigns the lowest address to the lowest-order ("right-most") 8 bits of the scalar, the next sequential address to the next-lowest-order 8 bits, and so on. This is called *little-endian* because the "little end" of the scalar, considered as a binary number, comes first in memory. DEC VAX and Intel x86 are examples of computers using this byte ordering.

K.2 Structure Mapping Examples

Figure 42 on page 295 shows an example of a C language structure **s** containing an assortment of scalars and one character string, and the big-endian and little-endian mapping of that structure. The value presumed to be in each structure element is shown in hex in the C comments; these values are used to show how the bytes making up each structure element are mapped into memory.

Note that C structure mapping rules will introduce padding (skipped bytes) in the map in order to align the scalars on their proper boundaries: four bytes between A and B, one byte between D and E, and two bytes between E and F. The same amount of padding will be present for both big-endian and little-endian mappings.

For the big-endian mapping of structure **s** shown in Figure 42, addresses are shown in hex at the left of each doubleword, and in small figures below each byte. The content of each byte, as indicated in the C example in Figure 42, is shown in hex (as characters for the elements of the string).

Example of a C structure (s), showing values of the elements

```
struct {
    int    a;      /*  0x11121314                    word        */
    long   b;      /*  0x2122232425262728            doubleword  */
    int    c;      /*  0x31323334                    word        */
    char   d[7];   /*  'A', 'B', 'C', 'D', 'E', 'F', 'G'  array of bytes */
    short  e;      /*  0x5152                        halfword    */
    int    f;      /*  0x61626364                    word        */
} s;
```

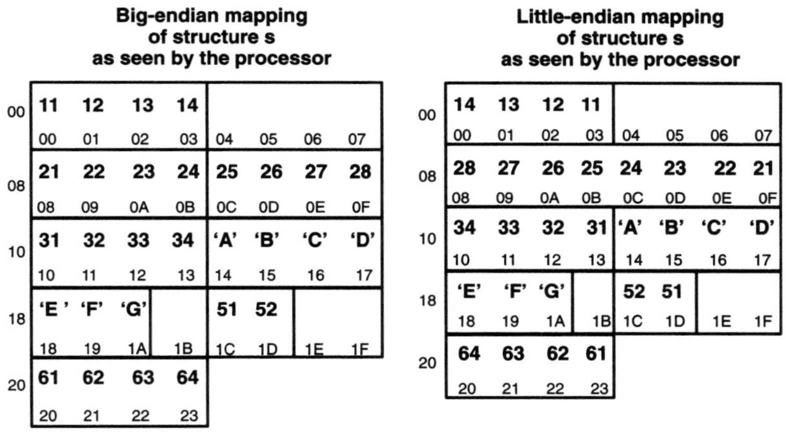

Big-endian mapping
of structure s
as seen by the processor

00	11	12	13	14				
	00	01	02	03	04	05	06	07
08	21	22	23	24	25	26	27	28
	08	09	0A	0B	0C	0D	0E	0F
10	31	32	33	34	'A'	'B'	'C'	'D'
	10	11	12	13	14	15	16	17
18	'E '	'F'	'G'		51	52		
	18	19	1A	1B	1C	1D	1E	1F
20	61	62	63	64				
	20	21	22	23				

Little-endian mapping
of structure s
as seen by the processor

00	14	13	12	11				
	00	01	02	03	04	05	06	07
08	28	27	26	25	24	23	22	21
	08	09	0A	0B	0C	0D	0E	0F
10	34	33	32	31	'A'	'B'	'C'	'D'
	10	11	12	13	14	15	16	17
18	'E'	'F'	'G'		52	51		
	18	19	1A	1B	1C	1D	1E	1F
20	64	63	62	61				
	20	21	22	23				

Figure 42. **Example of C structure, and the mapping of that structure**

Unfortunately, things are not always as clean as indicated by the above mappings. In a system we must talk about the mode of operation (big-endian versus little-endian) for the various components and subsystems in the system: the processor, external cache, memory, I/O, and, potentially, even the various buses. In a system which runs in either big-endian or little-endian mode all of the time, these mappings between the various components are at least fixed, and may very well be consistent (all big-endian or all little-endian). This may not be true in a system which can be operated in both big-endian and little-endian modes. The following sections will attempt to address some of the system related issues for systems which must run in both big-endian and little-endian modes.

K.2.1 PowerPC Processor Byte Ordering

By default, a PowerPC processor's byte ordering is big-endian. Unless an overt action (described below) is taken following Power-On Reset (POR), byte ordering in the PowerPC processors will be big-endian as shown in Figure 42.

However, it is possible to run a PowerPC processor in little-endian mode, such that the computational instruction set behaves as if the byte ordering were little-endian. To do this requires setting a bit in a Special Purpose Register that controls byte ordering. Which bit is used, and which SPR contains the bit, is implementation-dependent and is specified in *PowerPC 601 User's Manual* for each processor implementation. The symbolic name of the bit is LE, Little-endian Mapping. The LE bit is cleared to 0 (big-endian mode) on POR and may be set to 1 (little-endian mode) or reset to 0 by a privileged *Move To Special Purpose Register* (*mtspr*) instruction. An implementation may require that the *mtspr* be accompanied by certain synchronization instructions or that a specific sequence of instructions be used to modify LE; see the specific processor Book IV's.

The assumption for the remainder of this section is that the processor is talking to a big-endian system external to the processor. Figure 43 shows this configuration.

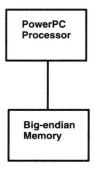

Figure 43. **PowerPC processor attached to a big-endian memory subsystem**

K.2.1.1 Two Processor Implementations of Little-Endian Mode

There are currently two defined implementations of the PowerPC Architecture for the processor relative to the little-endian mode. For convenience, they will be denoted as the True Little-endian (TLE) and the Little-Endian via Address Modification (LE/AM) processor implementations. The implications of the differences in these implementations will be discussed below.

K.2.1.2 PowerPC Processor Addressing of Data Memory with LE=1

One might expect from Figure 42 on page 295 that a PowerPC system operating with LE=1 would have to perform a 2-way, 4-way, or 8-way byte swap when transferring a halfword, word, or doubleword between the big-endian memory and a general or floating point register. However, that is not the case for LE/AM processors, which achieve the *effect* of little-endian byte ordering by manipulating the three low-order bits of the Effective Address (EA) as described below; no swapping of bytes is done, and individual multi-byte scalars actually appear in memory in big-endian byte order (that is, the highest-order 8 bits is at the lowest address). The primary effect of setting LE=1 for LE/AM processors is to adjust the way Effective Addresses (EAs) are computed, with the transfer of data between memory and registers unaffected and thus unencumbered by multiplexors for byte swapping. TLE processors, on the other hand, swap the bytes and do not modify the EA.

K.2.1.2.1 Aligned Scalars

This discussion applies to scalar data that are aligned on their natural boundaries. For unaligned data see Appendix K.2.1.2.2, "Unaligned Scalars" on page 298; for non-scalar data see Appendix K.2.1.2.3 "Non-Scalars" on page 298. For LE/AM processors, Load and Store instructions the EA is computed as specified in the instruction descriptions and is then modified as shown in Table 83.

Data Width (bytes)	EA Modified
8	(no change)
4	XOR with 0b100
2	XOR with 0b110
1	XOR with 0b111

Table 83. **Effective Address Modifications**

The modified EA is then passed to the data cache or to main memory and the specified width of data is transferred between a general or floating-point register and the (as modified) addressed memory locations(s). The EA modification makes it appear to the processor that data is stored little-endian, while in fact it is stored following big-endian byte order but not in the same bytes within doublewords as with LE=0.

To continue the example of structure **s**, Figure 44 on page 299 shows how the structure would be placed in memory from the point of view of the cache and memory subsystem and how for LE/AM processors, because of the modifications performed on EAs, the same structure **s** *appears* to the processor to be mapped into memory when LE=1.

Figure 44 shows that, as seen by the program executing in the processor, the mapping for structure **s** is identical to the *true* little-endian mapping. Figure 44 also shows that, from a point of view outside the LE/AM processor processor (in memory or cache), the addresses of the bytes making up structure **s** match neither the big-endian mapping nor the little-endian mapping. For this reason, allowance must be made for this when performing I/O in little-endian mode with LE/AM processor implementations (see Section 7.2, "Bit and Byte Numbering Conventions," on page 82 to see how Micro Channel I/O addresses this).

K.2.1.2.2   Unaligned Scalars

The "trick" of exclusive-oring the low order bits of the address of a scalar in LE/AM processors does not work unless the scalar is aligned on a boundary equal to a multiple of its length. Processors and system software may or may not implement unaligned scalar support. For more information, see the *PowerPC Architecture* (book I).

K.2.1.2.3   Non-scalars

PowerPC has two types of instructions that handle non-scalars, that is, multiple instances of scalars. These types are string and Load/Store Multiple. Neither type can deal with the modified EAs required in little-endian mode of LE/AM processors; both types cause Alignment Interrupts (see *PowerPC Architecture* (book III)). It is up to the system software as to what action is taken on the alignment interrupt; the software may decide to terminate the program.

K.2.1.3   PowerPC Instruction Memory Addressing with LE=1

Each PowerPC instruction occupies 32 bits (one word) of memory. PowerPC fetches and executes instructions as if the Current Instruction Address (CIA) had been advanced one word for each sequential instruction. For LE/AM processors, when operating with LE=1, the CIA is modified according to the LE/AM little-endian rule for fetching word-length scalars: it is exclusive-ored with 0b100. A program is thus an array of little-endian words with each word fetched and executed in order (discounting branches).

When LE=1, all references to the instruction stream must follow little-endian addressing, including addresses saved in system registers on interrupt, return addresses saved in the Link Register, and branch displacements and addresses. For more information, see the *PowerPC Architecture* (book I).

Example of a C structure (s), showing values of the elements

```
struct {
    int    a;    /*  0x11121314                    word          */
    long   b;    /*  0x2122232425262728            doubleword    */
    int    c;    /*  0x31323334                    word          */
    char   d[7]; /*  'A', 'B', 'C', 'D', 'E', 'F', 'G'   array of bytes */
    short  e;    /*  0x5152                         halfword      */
    int    f;    /*  0x61626364                    word          */
} s;
```

Big-endian mapping of structure s:
- **As seen by the processor**
- **As in Big-endian memory or cache with LE=0**

11	**12**	**13**	**14**				
00	01	02	03	04	05	06	07
21	**22**	**23**	**24**	**25**	**26**	**27**	**28**
08	09	0A	0B	0C	0D	0E	0F
31	**32**	**33**	**34**	**'A'**	**'B'**	**'C'**	**'D'**
10	11	12	13	14	15	16	17
'E'	**'F'**	**'G'**		**51**	**52**		
18	19	1A	1B	1C	1D	1E	1F
61	**62**	**63**	**64**				
20	21	22	23				

Little-endian mapping of structure s
- **As seen by all processors**
- **As in Big-endian memory or cache with TLE proc. and LE=1**

14	**13**	**12**	**11**				
00	01	02	03	04	05	06	07
28	**27**	**26**	**25**	**24**	**23**	**22**	**21**
08	09	0A	0B	0C	0D	0E	0F
34	**33**	**32**	**31**	**'A'**	**'B'**	**'C'**	**'D'**
10	11	12	13	14	15	16	17
'E'	**'F'**	**'G'**		**52**	**51**		
18	19	1A	1B	1C	1D	1E	1F
64	**63**	**62**	**61**				
20	21	22	23				

Reflection

Little-endian structure s in Big-endian memory or cache with LE/AM proc. and LE=1

				11	**12**	**13**	**14**
00	01	02	03	04	05	06	07
21	**22**	**23**	**24**	**25**	**26**	**27**	**28**
08	09	0A	0B	0C	0D	0E	0F
'D'	**'C'**	**'B'**	**'A'**	**31**	**32**	**33**	**34**
10	11	12	13	14	15	16	17
		51	**52**		**'G'**	**'F'**	**'E'**
18	19	1A	1B	1C	1D	1E	1F
				61	**62**	**63**	**64**
20	21	22	23	24	25	26	27

Figure 44. **Structures showing memory, cache, and processor views with LE=0 and 1**

Glossary

Acronym	Definition/Description
32-bit machine	A machine that implements the 32-bit subset architecture, see *PowerPC Architecture* (book I)
64-bit machine	A machine that implements the 64-bit architecture, see *PowerPC Architecture* (book I)
60x Bus	Processor bus used by the 601, 603, and 604 or a system bus
6xx Bus	Processor bus used by the 620 or a system bus
access_id	An IPLCB interface function used to determine if any special handling is required for a memory mapped, ordinary segment access
ACLST	A diagnostic hardware test run during IPL
addressing with T=0	Access to an ordinary segment that maps memory or I/O supported by the processor and system, see *PowerPC Architecture* (book III) and BUC Architecture
addressing with T=1	Access to a direct-store segment, supported by the processor and system, see *PowerPC Architecture* (book III) and Chapter 6, BUC Architecture
ADL	Micro Channel term
AIPGM	A diagnostic hardware test run during IPL
alternate IOCC Address Space	An alternative address supported by the IOCC during T=1 addressing, see Chapter 7, IOCC Architecture
APM	Available Processor Mask
applicable K bit	The K bit that applies to the state (privileged versus problem) of the processor running at the time, see Chapter 7, IOCC Architecture
arb bus lines	Micro Channel signal
arb Lvl	Micro Channel term

arb/gnt signal	Micro Channel signal
architected addresses	Specifc real memory address typically used to communicate between hardware and software
ASIC	Application Specific Integrated Circuit
AST	A diagnostic hardware test run during IPL
authority Mask	Storage mask supported by IOCCs, see Chapter 7, IOCC Architecture. These are bits in the segment descriptor that are passed from the processor to the system
Available Processor Mask	Communication Facility between hardware and software to identify which processors are available for interrupt handling
BA	Base Address, the address of a processor's interrupt management area
baseband	A type of local area network
Basic Transfer Cycle	Micro Channel term
BCR	Board Configuration Register
be0 be1 be2 be3	Micro Channel signals
big–endian	A memory addressing model, see Appendix K, Big-endian and Little-endian Tutorial and the *PowerPC Architecture* (book I)
BIST	Built-In Self-Test, diagnostic test run during IPL
BOOT	To prepare a computer system for operation by loading an operating system program, see IPL
bosboot diskettes	Diskettes that may be used to load AIX
bring–up	To prepare a computer system for operation by loading an operating system program, see IPL
BUC	Bus Unit Controller. e.g. and IOCC is the BUC for a Micro Channel
BUID	Bus Unit IDentifier
Built–In Self–Test (BIST)	A diagnostic test run during IPL
BUMP	Bring-Up MicroProcessor, a service processor, may be used to IPL the OS and to perform diagnostics

burst line	Micro Channel signal
burst signal	Micro Channel signal which allows several transfers before arbitrating for the bus again
bus Arb Lvl	Micro Channel term
Bus Mapping Register	Register used to map Micro Channel accesses to system memory
bus master	A Micro Channel device that contains its own direct memory access controller.
cache	A high speed buffer used to reduce the latency of memory accesses
card selected feedback (cd sfdbk)	Micro Channel signal
CBA	Common on-chip-processor Bus Address
CEC	Central Electronic Complex (computer less terminals, adapters, disks, ...)
cd chrdy signal	Card Channel Ready, a Micro Channel signal
cd sfdbk	Card Selected Feedback, a Micro Channel signal
chck	Channel Check, a Micro Channel signal
checkstop	Computer state after a failure which can be recovered only by rebooting the computer, see unrecoverable error
Central Electronic Complex (CEC)	Central Electronic Complex (computer less terminals, adapters, disks, ...)
Channel Status Register (CSR)	An IOCC register used in Bus Master operations
class–1 class–2 class–3 class–4 class–5 class–6	Target Market Categories
coherent	See memory coherence in the *PowerPC Architecture* (book II)
cold boot	An IPL as if the power had just been turned on
context synchronizing operation	See *PowerPC Architecture* (book III)

CPPR	Current Processor Priority Register
critical section of code	Code which tends to have timing restrictions
CSR	Channel Status Register, an IOCC register used in Bus Master operations
Dack	Device Acknowledge, an adapter arbitration signal
DASD	Direct Access Storage Device (disk)
DBRA1	Device Base Real Address 1
DBRA2	Device Base Real Address 2
d–cache	Data cache
DCLST	A diagnostic hardware test run during IPL
DCR	Device Characteristics Register
delta	The address displacement calculated from the device configuration word address increment field in the Device Characteristics Register
deskside	A computer that is normally kept beside a desk
desktop	A computer that is normally kept on a desk
Device Acknowledge (Dack)	An adapter arbitration signal
Device Request (Drq)	An adapter arbitration signal
DIR	Device Interface Routines, usually diagnostic hardware test run during IPL
Disable Command	An IOCC command used for DMA control
DMA	Direct Memory Access
DMA slave	A Micro Channel device that requires the system to provide the direct memory access control
Drq	Device Request, an adapter arbitration signal
DSI	Data Storage Interrupt, see *PowerPC Architecture* (book III)
DSIER	Data Storage Interrupt Error Register
DSS	Direct-Store Segment
Dynamic Bus Sizing	Micro Channel term

ECC	Error Correction Code
EE	External Interrupt Enable bit in the MSR, see *PowerPC Architecture* (book III)
EIA	Electronics Industries Association
eieio	Enforce In-order Execution of I/O, an instruction, see *PowerPC Architecture* (book II)
Enable Command	An IOCC command used for DMA control
endian	Memory addressing model, see Appendix K, Big-endian and Little-endian Tutorial and the *PowerPC Architecture* (book I)
EOI	End of Interrupt, an indication that processing of an interrupt has been completed, usually sent to a BUC
EPOST	Extended-Power–On Self-Test
EPOW	Early Power Off Warning
EPROM	Electronically Programmable Read Only Memory
ESP	Engineering Support Processor, often used for hardware debugging
Event Indicator	A code, typically displayed on LEDs indicating the occurrence of specific events, most often seen during IPL
exception	An error condition
External Interrupt	Interrupt from outside of the processor
fairness priority mode	Micro Channel arbitration mode
FCS	Fiber Channel Standard: a high speed fiber optic communications standard
FDDI	Fiber Distributed Data Interface (100 MBit/sec. fiber optic LAN)
firmware	The hardware portion of the computer, includes IPL ROM
FRS	Feature ROM Scan
FRU	Field Replaceable Unit
GB	GigaBytes
GIO	Graphics I/O
grant line	Micro Channel signal
G_MFRR	Global Most Favored Request Register
GQ_IRM	Global Queue Interrupt Routing Mask

G_QIRR	Global Queued Interrupt Request Register
GSR	General Status Register
hard initialization	An IPL, equivalent to starting the machine by turning on the power
hardwire	items that are part of the machine
i-cache	Instruction cache
ID	IDentification
IER	IOCC Interrupt Enable Register
initialization firmware	Hardware that supports initialization, including IPL ROM
IOCC	Input/Output Channel Controller
IP	InterProcessor
IPL	Initial Program Load
IPLCB	IPL Control Block
IPL ROM	Firmware that performs IPL
IRR	Interrupt Request Register
ISSR	Interrupt Source Specification Register
JTAG	Joint Test Action Group, a protocol for accessing devices, such as, processors
K or K bit	Key bit in a segment descriptor that controls the access privilege to the addressed memory location for both ordinary and direct-store segments. This is supported by both the processor and the system, see *PowerPC Architecture* (book III)
KB	KiloBytes
Key switch	See mode selection facility
LAN	Local Area Network
ldarx	Load Doubleword and Reserve Indexed, see *PowerPC Architecture* (book I)
LE	LE bit in the MSR that controls the little-endian versus big-endian mode, see *PowerPC Architecture* (book III)
LE/AM	Little-Endian via Address Modification, see *PowerPC Architecture* (book III)
LED	Light Emitting Diodes, especially the error/status LED on a RISC System/6000

level sensitive	Device reacts to a logic level, not the transition from one level to another
linear priority mode	Micro Channel arbitration mode
little–endian	A memory addressing model, see Appendix K, Big-endian and Little-endian Tutorial and the *PowerPC Architecture* (book I)
Live Insertion	Adding a processor after IPL
lwarx	Load Word and Reserve Indexed, see *PowerPC Architecture* (book I)
lwz	Load Word Zero, see *PowerPC Architecture* (book I)
M	M–bit or coherency bit, see *PowerPC Architecture* (book III) and memory coherence in *PowerPC Architecture* (book II)
machine check	A processor state after some error conditions
machine Device Driver (machine DD)	An AIX OS routine used to isolate machine differences
MB	MegaBytes
MCCR	Memory Controller Control Register
MCSR	Memory Control Status Register
MEAR	Memory Error Address Register
MEI	Cache line states: Modified/Exclusive/Invalid
MESI	Cache line states: Modified/Exclusive/Shared/Invalid
MFRR	Most Favored Request Register
Memory Controller	A BUC that accesses main memory
M/IO	Micro Channel signal
MIR	IOCC Miscellaneous Interrupts Register
mode selection facility	An operator interface, such as, a key switch used to select one of three modes (normal, secure, diagnostics)
Mode 1	"the secure" state
Mode 2	"the service state"
Mode 3	"the normal state"
MSR	Machine State Register, see *PowerPC Architecture* (book III)

mtmsr	Move to MSR, a processor instruction, see *PowerPC Architecture* (book III)
NIO	Native I/O devices
NUMA	Non–Uniform Memory Access time
NVRAM	Non–Volatile Random Access Memory
OCS	On-Card Sequencer, scans and initializes the processor
ODM	Object Data Manager – AIX's configuration database
OEM	Original Equipment Manufacturer
OLTP	On–Line Transaction Processing
OS	Operating System
ori	OR Immediate instruction, see *PowerPC Architecture* (book I)
park	Micro Channel term
Partial Transfer Cycles	Micro Channel term
PCI	Peripheral Component Interconnect (Intel bus standard)
PCMCIA	Personal Computer Memory Card International Association
PIDI	Physical Identifier Initialization register
pinning	preventing a portion of memory from being paged out
PIO	Programmed I/O, loads & stores mapped to a BUC
PIR	Processor ID Register
POR	Power-On Reset
POS	Programmable Option Select, Micro Channel registers
POST	Power–On Self-Test
preempt line	Micro Channel signal
PTF	Program Temporary Fix or Problem Tracking Form
QIRR	Queued Interrupt Request Register
RAS	Reliability, Availability, and Serviceability
ROS	Read-Only Storage
ROM	Read-Only Memory
RPN	Real Page Number
RSC	A processor chip used on the RISC System/6000 model 220

SBEC/DBED ECC	Single Bit Error Correction/Double bit Error Detection
sbhe/a0	Micro Channel signal
SCSI	Small Computer System Interface, industry standard protocol for attaching devices, such as, disks and tapes
sdr (0)	Micro Channel signal
sdr (1)	Micro Channel signal
SEAR	System Exception Address Register
SESR	System Exception Status Register
segment descriptor	A Segment Register or a Segment Table Entry
sfdbkrtn	Select Feedback Return, a Micro Channel signal
SIMM	Single In–Line Memory Module
SIO	Start I/O or Serial I/O or Standard I/O
SLA	Serial Link Adapter
SMP	Shared Memory Multiprocessor or a Symmetric Multi-Processor
soft boot	An IPL after the system has already been booted
soft initialization	An IPL after the system has already been booted
SP	Scanning or Service Processor
SPR	Special Purpose Register, see *PowerPC Architecture* (book I) and the individual processor implementation books.
SR	Segment Register, see *PowerPC Architecture* (book III)
SRN	Service Request Number
STE	Segment Table Entry, see *PowerPC Architecture* (book III)
Streaming Data	Micro Channel term
stwcx	Store Word Conditional Indexed, see *PowerPC Architecture* (book I)
stdcx	Store Doubleword Conditional Indexed, see *PowerPC Architecture* (book I)
sync	A synchronization instruction, see *PowerPC Architecture* (book I and book II)
System Memory	Traditional memory addressable by programs, see main storage in *PowerPC Architecture* (book II)
TBE_ pin	Time Base Enable pin

T bit	An addressibility flag supported by the processor and the system, see *PowerPC Architecture* (book III)
tc signal	Micro Channel signal
TCE	Translation Control Entry
TCW	Translation Control Word
TLE	True Little-Endian
TOD Clock	Time of day clock
UP	Uni–Processor
VPD	Vital Product Data
VLSI	Very Large Scale Integration
XIRR	External Interrupt Request Register
XISR	External Interrupt Source Register
XIVR	External Interrupt Vector Register

Index